KNIGHTS

KNIGHTS

ANDREA HOPKINS

ARTABRAS

NEW YORK · LONDON · PARIS

A QUARTO BOOK

First published in the United States of America in 1991 by
Artabras, a division of Abbeville Publishing Group, 488 Madison
Avenue, New York, NY 10022.

First published in Great Britain in 1990 by Quarto Publishing
plc, London, England.

Copyright © 1990 Quarto Publishing plc

ISBN 0-89660-013-0

First American edition, third printing

This book was designed and produced by
Quarto Publishing plc,
London, England

SENIOR EDITOR Susanne Clarke
DESIGNER William Mason
ARTISTS Jeffrey Burn, Jim Robins,
David Kemp
MAPS Euromap Ltd
PICTURE RESEARCHER Deidre O'Day
ART DIRECTOR Nick Buzzard
PUBLISHING DIRECTOR Janet Slingsby

CONTENTS

·I·NTRODUCTION

Shortly after the death of T. E. Lawrence (Lawrence of Arabia) in a motorcycle accident in 1935, the following obituary appeared in the *Montreal Daily Herald*:

> Lawrence belonged to the era of chain-mail and broadswords, when men broke their lances in impossible quests, and to the age of the troubadours when men boasted of their deeds under one moon and under the next covered their vanity with sackcloth ... One cannot dictate to posterity, but we hope that a few generations will remember him, if only as a baffling and arresting figure – a knight in shining armour in an age of colored shirts.

This response to the growing legend of Lawrence's exploits in the Arabian desert was typical. Visitors to St Martin's Church, Wareham, in Dorset, can see a splendid medieval-style tomb effigy of Lawrence as a crusader knight.

Forty years later, one of the most popular films of all time, *Star Wars*, though ostensibly a work of science fiction, told of a group of warrior heroes known as the Jedi Knights. These men fought with "light sabres" to protect the weak against unjust oppression, and their behaviour, in accordance with disciplines taught them by "masters", enabled them to perform superhuman feats with the aid of a mystical "Force". These examples alone suffice to demonstrate the extraordinary influence that the concept of knights continues to have, centuries after there had ceased to be any real knights left in Europe.

But what was a "real" knight? The modern conception of a medieval knight, or what he aspired to be, is familiar to everyone. He was a tall, strong, handsome man on a large white horse, clad in mid-fifteenth-century plate armour with a shield, banner and surcoat, while his horse's caparison displayed his coat of arms. He was characterized by such personal qualities as courage and prowess, and was jealous of his honour. Most important of all, he was dedicated to the service of an ideal, a code which dictated his behaviour in specific, predictable ways. We know, for example, that he would always come to the aid of a damsel in distress, and that he would never refuse a fight simply because the odds were greatly against him. In fact, he was more likely to engage in combat on that account, like Sir Lancelot who, in some medieval romances, refused to fight fewer than four men at once on the grounds that otherwise it would be unfair to his opponents. No consideration of personal advantage, in short, could sway him from adherence to his beliefs and loyalties. Excellence in combat and absolute integrity – these were the chief characteristics of that paragon, the knight in shining armour, who embodies the ideal of medieval chivalry in twentieth-century films, popular

LEFT *The tomb of T. E. Lawrence at St Martin's Church, Wareham, Dorset, is modelled directly on medieval "crusader" tomb effigies. These showed the dead warrior in arms and with his legs crossed, to signify that he had fought in the Holy Land.*

BELOW *The tomb of Robert Duke of Normandy in Gloucester Cathedral. He was the eldest son of William the Conqueror and one of the leaders of the First Crusade. It was this kind of medieval effigy which inspired the tomb of T. E. Lawrence.*

fiction, cartoons, and even advertisements.

This book seeks the reality behind that image. It is a reality which is difficult to identify, not least because in the Middle Ages the image of the noble knight was inspired almost from the first by the ideal of knighthood portrayed in the great medieval romances. These romances were extremely pervasive, so that even those sources where one would normally expect to find facts rather than fantasy (histories, chronicles, personal biographies and so on) are, in the Middle Ages, strongly flavoured with the exotic spices of romance.

In any case, the distinction between fact and fiction in literature was by

LEFT *The tomb of Hugh Despenser the Younger in Tewkesbury Abbey. The splendid Gothic tomb presents a noble and pious image of a singularly unpleasant reality. Originally a landless knight, Hugh used his influence as a favourite of King Edward II of England to amass vast wealth, and maintained a reign of terror until he was publicly executed in 1326.*

no means so clear cut in the Middle Ages as it is today. History and romance were inextricably intertwined, and both were seen as vessels of truth. In the Middle Ages, there was no such thing as "only a story". To discover the truth about medieval knights, we need to look closely at the ideal to which they aspired, as described in romances, as codified in treatises such as the *Ordene de Chevalerie*, and as celebrated in the biographies of great and famous knights, such as William the Marshal or Don Pero Nino.

A high standard was set, and history shows us that it was rarely attained in practice. Knights were primarily men who were trained to fight and they inhabited a violent world. But what distinguished a medieval knight from his predecessor, the mounted warrior of the early Middle Ages, was his consciousness of the ideal, including those aspects which were the hardest to live up to, and his desire for honour.

For a medieval knight, "honour" meant far more than mere courage and the skill of a warrior. The concept of chivalry developed, within a fairly brief period, from a simple warrior's code to a sophisticated system of values in which the principles of personal integrity, the duty to defend the weak from oppression, and the practice of knightly virtues, such as *largesse* (generosity), *pité* (compassion), *franchise* (a free and frank spirit) and *courtoisie* (courtliness, especially to women), combined with the more traditional virtues of loyalty and prowess. These qualities are repeatedly stressed in medieval accounts of knights, where the conduct of both real knights and fictional heroes is measured against this standard.

The chivalrous ideal as portrayed in literature is, of course, only one side of the coin. Equally, the conclusions of modern historians about the grim realities of medieval knighthood produce an incomplete and distorted picture. Fictional ideal and historical reality must be seen together. Medieval commentators were themselves aware that there were bad knights, who brought knighthood into disrepute. In romances, too, the hero knights encountered their sinister mirror images, the wicked knights who terrorized the helpless peasants, dishonoured ladies, even desecrated churches. Just as these "black knights" certainly had their counterparts in real life among the robber barons, freebooters and mercenaries of medieval Europe, so too it is clear that thousands of knights felt themselves contributing to a tradition of chivalry stretching back hundreds of years.

Here is one of the few instances in which it can be clearly seen that life imitated art. As early as 1223 we hear of knights taking part in a tournament in Arthurian dress in Cyprus to celebrate the knighting of the son of the

RIGHT *The work of writers and artists such as the British novelist Sir Walter Scott makes knights seem familiar figures – deceptively so, since most of us know little of how they lived. This splendid Victorian engraving shows a combat between De Bois Guilbert and the disinherited Black Knight, from Scott's most famous novel,* Ivanhoe, *set in twelfth-century England. Scott was a passionate enthusiast about medieval history and culture, and wrote a series of successful historical novels which did much to promote the nineteenth-century fascination with chivalry and medieval life.*

crusader baron, John of Ibelin; the first of many such tournaments in costume. The aristocracy and gentry of medieval Europe were fascinated by the idea of chivalry, even though many of its most popular and enduring literary expressions, such as the romances of Chrétien de Troyes, showed knights in a context far removed from the actual function of the warrior élite, that is, making war. Equally the rulers of medieval Europe exploited the desire of their retainers to emulate this ideal, organizing rituals and ceremonies, designing vows and accoutrements intended to enhance the allure of knighthood, despite its attendant obligations of military service and the sometimes crippling expense it entailed. Thus in 1306 we hear of the Feast of the Swans, held by King Edward I of England, a magnificent and highly romantic ceremony at which the king knighted his eldest son, together with 300 or so other young men of noble birth. After the dubbing ceremony there was a great banquet, during which

> ... two swans were brought before King Edward I in pomp and splendour, adorned with golden nets and gilded reeds, the most astounding sight to the onlookers. Having seen them, the king swore by the God of Heaven and by the swans that he wished to set out for Scotland and, whether he lived or died, to avenge ... the breach of faith by the Scots.

This same oath was then pledged by all the other nobles present, and the newly created knights, thus providing Edward with a substantial number of fighting men for his intended campaign against the Scots. It also provided him with an excellent opportunity to levy a special tax: the same chronicler, the anonymous author of *Flores historiarum*, records that "for the knighting of the king's son, the clergy and people ceded a thirtieth part of their goods to the king, and the merchants a twentieth".

In contrast to the high ideals which are constantly honoured in romance and chronicle, and in the grand rituals and ceremonies with which knights celebrated their deeds and their station, history also provides us with tales of savagery perpetrated by knights throughout the Middle Ages. Thus, when the First Crusade reached its triumphant conclusion in 1099 with the recapture of Jerusalem from the Seljuk Turks, the great crusader lord, Godfrey of Bouillon, was chosen as its first ruler. He was honoured from the early fourteenth century onwards by being considered the ninth of the Nine Worthies. (The Nine Worthies were a collection of biblical, classical and historical heroes supposed to be the greatest examples of chivalry and they included Alexander the Great, Julius Caesar, Arthur and Charlemagne.) Yet we now know that, at the taking of Jerusalem in 1099, he presided over the massacre of every single person in the city, with the exception of the Saracen commander and his personal retinue who were given a safe conduct.

We can see, also, as the medieval period went on, that there were forces at work which undermined any idealism or high-mindedness associated with the practice of knighthood. Knights in romances spent much time engaged in quests designed to test their knightly qualities, or prove them worthy of their ladies, rather than fighting battles to protect or advance their society or serve their lord. Real knights, unlike their literary counterparts, were obliged to be in the field at short notice, heavily armed and mounted on an expensive horse. If a knight was captured, he could expect to pay a huge ransom, in

RIGHT *A late copy of a medieval illustration depicting the Jousts of St Inglevert. These took place near Calais in May 1390 when, over a period of four days, some forty knights jousted against one another before large crowds. Such events provided an opportunity for the display of knights' skill in combat, and often participants and spectators would travel from all over Europe to attend. Jousts were especially popular when, as in this case, they took place during a truce in the all too frequent wars of the period.*

TOURNAMENT at INQUELVERT, by 3 FRENCH KNIGHTS, against all comers

addition to losing his horse and his armour, the legitimate prize of his captor. More important knights, especially those with estates of their own, were expected to maintain their position with style. This involved supporting other knights in their retinue, as well as squires, pages and perhaps a herald, all of whom had to be fed, clothed, armed and given costly gifts from time to time. A successful knight could make an immense fortune, as we shall see from the example of William the Marshal and others, but for ordinary knights it could be an expensive calling.

One or two romances touch on the financial problems experienced by knights. Examples include Marie de France's *Lanval*, in which the knight's

LEFT *A Samurai warrior of fourteenth-century Japan. Though many societies have produced warrior elites, the Samurai were the closest in every way to the knights of medieval Europe. From purely military beginnings they too developed an ethos based on traditions of loyal service and the pursuit of honour.*

poverty is magically relieved by his fairy mistress, or the anonymous Middle English *Sir Amadace*, who, having been all but bankrupted by his knightly generosity, sets forth to repair his fortunes by adventure, only to spend his last forty pounds on a deed of charity – burying the decaying corpse of an indebted merchant whose creditors are denying him burial. For this, of course, he is later rewarded.

During the thirteenth and fourteenth centuries it became more difficult, and then impossible, for kings and great magnates to maintain armies in the field comprising men motivated solely by their desire to fulfil their feudal obligations to their lords. The cost of a knight's equipment and horses had become prohibitive and, increasingly, it became necessary to pay knights for their service, or at least to tempt them to fight with promises of great booty to be looted from the vanquished.

The later Middle Ages saw the rise of a new kind of "knight" who was a professional adventurer, motivated by nothing higher than gain – a mercenary, in fact. By the mid-fourteenth century there were large numbers of these men in Europe, with no place in society other than as soldiers of fortune. One of the greatest scandals of the age resulted from the recruitment of such men into the army of King Peter of Cyprus in his "Crusade" against the city of Alexandria in 1365. The mercenaries sacked the city, slaughtered thousands of its inhabitants (including many Christians), stole as much loot as they could carry and then went home, with the result that the city fell back into the hands of "the Infidel" within days of its conquest.

So, after the rise of chivalry and its "golden age" in the eleventh and twelfth centuries, we see the operation of two conflicting trends. On the one hand are the efforts of knights themselves and their lords and kings to glorify and elevate the status of knights, and make knighthood more socially exclusive; on the other, social and political pressures which tended to debase and brutalize knights. But in searching for the truth behind the glittering image, we shall see that the exacting concept of knighthood, which was early recorded in the *Ordene de Chevalerie*, was a real influence on the knights of the time.

Many of the medieval romances, from all the countries and languages of Europe, were largely drawn from three great cycles: the *Matter of Rome*, whose stories were drawn from classical antiquity ("Rome" referred to the supposed "authority" from whose works the tale had been drawn, rather than the subject matter – the stories themselves came equally often from Greek literature or myth); the *Matter of France*, which concerned the deeds of Charlemagne and his twelve "peers" in their eighth-century conquests of the Saracens; and the *Matter of Britain*, which was the story cycle of King Arthur and his knights of the Round Table in sixth-century Britain. Thus, most of the romances written from 1150 to 1450 were set in the distant past. Those lords and knights who participated in the Arthurian dress tournaments which achieved such a vogue in the thirteenth and fourteenth centuries were looking to the past just as surely as were the Victorian ladies and gentlemen who, inspired largely by the medieval romances of Sir Walter Scott, took part in the disastrous medieval tournament held at Eglinton castle in 1839 when heavy rain turned the lists into a bog.

The difference was that, in the Middle Ages, people did not view themselves, as we do now, as the culmination of centuries of civilized development, but rather as the degenerate remnants of a far greater past. They did not, however, see the past as essentially different from their own time, only better. The past was in most respects an ideal mirror of present society. This is why we find in medieval illustrations the heroes of the Trojan war represented in contemporaneous dress and arms, and even fighting with the latest medieval battle techniques.

Medieval knights – their aspirations, their experiences, their stories – are familiar to us. This is partly because many of their values have been incorporated into the ethos of the "gentleman" in western culture, but it is partly because the natural desire to form, and to be seen as, an élite group, bound by common goals and acknowledging certain rules of behaviour, has resulted in the creation of similar groups at other times and in other societies. The most striking analogy is of course the Samurai of medieval Japan.

The aim of this book is to reach an understanding from a perspective both historical and human of a phenomenon which most people experience only as a kind of cultural cliché and I shall focus as much as possible on the records, memories and opinions of real individuals. This is not a discussion of an abstract concept or code of "chivalry" but an exploration of the world of knights in the Middle Ages, covering a period of roughly five hundred years, from about AD 1000 to shortly after AD 1500. In discussing knights, not only as a potent social and cultural force but as living people, I shall emphasize the importance of ethical and emotional aspects of being a knight as much as political and historical ones.

ABOVE *Perhaps the archetypal Knight in Shining Armour, complete with white charger – a beautiful and sensitive painting of Sir Galahad by George Frederick Watts. Sir Galahad was a late addition to the world of medieval romance (the original hero of the story of the Holy Grail was in fact Sir Perceval), but he appealed to the Victorians, who preferred his absolute purity and integrity to the more flawed and human character of his father Sir Lancelot, by far the more popular figure in the Middle Ages.*

CHRONOLOGICAL TABLE

MILITARY AND POLITICAL HISTORY

1030s Muslim Spain breaks up; much territory gained by Christian kingdom of North Spain.
1032 Duchy of Burgundy becomes part of German Empire.
1037 The Seljuk Turks begin dramatic expansion in the East.
1048 Seljuks sack Armenia.
1060 Robert Guiscard completes the Norman conquest of Southern Italy.
1061 Robert Guiscard begins conquest of Sicily.
1066 William Duke of Normandy gains throne of England at Battle of Hastings.
1076 Norman conquest of Salerno; becomes capital of Norman Sicily. The Seljuk Turks capture Damascus and Jerusalem from the Fatimids.
1084 Seljuks capture Antioch; Robert Guiscard rescues Gregory VII from Emperor Henry IV.
1085 Christians capture Toledo; Normans capture Syracuse.
1091 Normans complete conquest of Sicily.
1094 El Cid captures Valencia from Moors.
1095 Pope Urban II preaches the Crusade.
1096 First Crusade sets off for Holy Land.
1097 Crusaders defeat Seljuks at Nicaea and Dorylaeum.
1098 Siege of Antioch; falls to Crusaders.
1099 Crusaders capture Jerusalem.

1098-1100 Crusaders establish three states in Holy Land: Kingdom of Jerusalem, Principality of Antioch, and the County of Edessa.
1109 Crusaders capture Tripoli, and found fourth state.
1129 Roger of Sicily takes over Southern Italy.
1144 Geoffrey Plantagenet ("The Fair") of Anjou captures Normandy.
1140s Civil war in England between the Empress Matilda and Stephen of Blois.
1145 Edessa captured by Emir Zangi. Second crusade fails to recapture it.
1152 Henry Plantagenet marries Eleanor of Aquitaine; 1153 becomes King of England and the richest and biggest landowner in Europe.
1158 Emperor Frederick I (Barbarossa) restores Imperial rule to Northern Italy.
1160-2 Henry the Lion, Duke of Saxony and Bavaria conquers Wends of the lower Elbe.
1169 Saladin conquers Egypt; 1174 declares himself Sultan.
1170 Frederick Barbarossa defeated by the Lombard league of North Italian cities at the Battle of Legnano.
1180 Henry the Lion dispossessed by Frederick; Saxony divided, Bavaria given to Otto of Wittelsbach.
1187 Jerusalem lost to Saladin after the Battle of Hattin.
1190 Third Crusade: Richard I conquers Cyprus and
1191 establishes Kingdom of Acre.
1192 Richard captured and held for ransom in Germany.

1201 Fourth Crusade sets off and
1204 Sacks Constantinople.
1204 Philip Augustus takes Normandy from England.
1206 Rise of Genghis Khan.
1212 Christian Kings of Spain defeat Muslims at Battle of Las Navas de Tolosa
1214 Philip Augustus defeats John of England and Otto IV of Germany at Battle of Bouvines; Frederick II is Emperor.
1215 John signs the Magna Carta.
1218-21 Fifth Crusade captures Damietta in Egypt.
1228 Emperor Frederick II obtains Jerusalem by negotiation for the King of Acre.
1229 Albigensian crusade ends; heresy is destroyed, southern France economically shattered.
1236 Ferdinand III of Castile captures Córdoba.
1242 Alexander Nevsky defeats Teutonic Knights.
1244 Jerusalem lost again.
1249 Louis IX captures Damietta on Seventh Crusade.
1268 Mamluks capture Antioch.
1270 Louis IX dies during Eighth Crusade.
1277 Edward I begins conquest of Wales.
1283 Conquest of Wales completed.
1291 The Mamluks over-run Acre – last remnant of the crusader kingdom is lost.

KNIGHTS

1000-1050 The mail shirt which formed the basic armour of a Dark Age warrior is refined and extended to become a knee-length hauberk, sometimes supplemented by leggings and mittens of mail.
1050-75 Development of technique of charge with couched lance, basis of knights' military supremacy.
1084 Pope Gregory VII names the knights of Robert Guiscard 'Knights of Christ'.
1096 Military activity specifically linked to religious goals in the First Crusade.

1119 Knights Templar founded.
1128 First recorded dubbing, of Geoffrey of Anjou.
1130 Council of Clermont forbids tournaments.
1140s Knights Hospitaller incorporated as a military order.
1164 Foundation of the Order of Calatrava.
1175 Recognition of the Order of Santiago.
1183 Foundation of the Order of Alcantara.
1190 Foundation of Teutonic Knights.

1219 Death of William Marshal.
1223 First recorded tournament in Arthurian dress.
1227 "Venusfahrt" of Ulrich von Lichtenstein.
1233 Teutonic Knights found Kulm and Thorn and set out to conquer Prussia.
1237 Teutonic Knights absorb Brethren of the Sword.
1240 "Artusfahrt" of Ulrich von Lichtenstein.
1240-50 *The Ordene de chevalerie* written.
c.1241 80 knights suffocated at tournament at Neuss.
c.1250 First surviving heraldic Rolls written.
1273 The "Little Battle of Chalons" tournament.
1285 Tournament at Chauvency.
c.1290 Heraldic treatise *De Heraudie* written.

ART AND LITERATURE

1036 Beginning of church at Jumièges, Normandy. Major programme of church-building especially in Norman kingdoms.
c.1100 Composition of the *Chanson de Roland*.

1100-20 Duke William IX of Aquitaine writing troubadour lyrics.
1136 Geoffrey of Monmouth writes *History of the Kings of Britain*.
c.1155 Wace writes *Brut*.
c.1160 *Eneas*; Thomas *Tristan*.
c.1165 Benoit de St. Maur *Roman de Troie*.
c.1170-90 Poems of Chrétien de Troyes.
c.1184-86 Breton lais of Marie de France.
c.1185 Andreas Capellanus *On the Art of Honest Love*.
c.1190 Béroul *Tristan*.

c.1200 Wolfram von Eschenbach *Parzifal*.
1207 Per Abbat *Poema de Mio Cid*.
c.1210 Gottfried von Strasburg *Tristan und Isolde*.
1200-35 Development of the French prose Vulgate Cycle of romances.
c.1215 Geoffrey de Villehardouin *The Conquest of Constantinople*.
c.1220 Layamon *Brut*.
c.1220s Matthew Paris *History of the English*.
c.1235 *Roman de la Rose I*.
c.1270 *Arthour and Merlin*.

RELIGION AND LEARNING

1009 The Church of the Holy Sepulchre in Jerusalem destroyed by order of Hakim, sixth Fatimid Caliph of Egypt.
1016-1030s Peace of God and Truce of God legislation.
1059 Pope Nicholas II recognizes Normans as rulers of Southern Italy.
1088 Construction begins on final version of Cluny Abbey.
1098 Cistercian Order founded by St. Robert at Cîteaux.

1115 Abbey of Clairvaux founded by St. Bernard.
1122 Agreement between Pope Calixtus II and Emperor Henry V over investiture of bishops.
1158 Founding of Bologna University.
1159 Regulation of University of Paris.
1170 Thomas Becket murdered; 1173 canonised.
1182 Philip II expels Jews from France.

1208 Pope Innocent III preaches crusade against Albigensian heresy in Southern France. Places England under interdict.
1200-10 Recognition of University of Oxford.
1209 Franciscan Order founded.
1215 Dominicans founded.
1222 University of Padua founded.
1224 University of Naples founded.
1246-8 Ste Chapelle built by Louis IX.
1290 Jews expelled from England.

1314 Robert Bruce defeats Edward II at Bannockburn, confirming independence of Scotland.
1315 Leopold of Austria defeated by Swiss Confederation at Battle of Morgarten.
1337 Edward III of England claims the throne of France; start of Hundred Years War.
1340 English naval victory over French at Sluys.
1346 English victory at Crécy.
1347 Edward III captures Calais.
1346-50 Black Death decimates population of Europe – down by 25-30%. Widespread persecution of Jews, especially in Germany.
1351-3 Swiss confederation joined by Zurich, Glarus, Zug and Berne.
1356 King John of France captured at Poitiers.
1360 Treaty of Brétigny - brief respite in Hundred Years War.
1362 Philip the Bold becomes Duke of Burgundy.
1365 Siege of Alexandria led by Peter of Cyprus.
1366 Throne of Castile in dispute; France supports Henry of Trastamara, England Peter the Cruel. Edward the Black Prince defeats Henry and captures Bertrand du Guesclin at Najera. Hundred Years War starts up again.
1370s English lose ground in France.
1381 Peasants Revolt in England.
1385 Portuguese defeat Castile at Aljubarotta; Visconti rules Milan and Northern Italy.
1390s Expansion of Ottoman Empire under Sultan Beyazit.
1396 Battle of Nicopolis; Christians beaten by Beyazit.

1411-14 Civil War in France between Orléanists and Burgundians; Sigismund of Hungary becomes Emperor of Germany.
1415 Battle of Agincourt.
1420 Henry V of England recognized by Charles VI as heir to the throne of France.
1422 Henry V dies; war begins to go badly for the English.
1425 Florence and Venice form alliance against Visconti of Milan.
1429 Charles VII crowned at Orléans.
1431 Joan of Arc burnt at stake.
1434 Cosimo de Medici becomes ruler of Florence.
1436 Emperor Sigismund recognized as King of Bohemia after long struggle against nationalist Hussites.
1453 English have lost all French possessions except Calais. End of 100 Years War. Ottoman Turks finally capture Constantinople.
1454 Milan, Venice, Florence and Naples make peace.
1455 Start of Wars of the Roses over English crown.
1470 War between Switzerland and Austria.
1475 War between Charles the Bold of Burgundy and the Swiss – 1477 The Swiss win.
1479 Aragon and Castile united under Ferdinand and Isabella.
1480 Ottoman Turks attack Rhodes.
1486 End of Wars of Roses, Henry VII marries Elizabeth of York.
1492 Granada surrenders to Ferdinand and Isabella.

1513 Emperor Maximilian and King Henry VIII of England invade France.
1519 Charles I of Spain is elected Emperor Charles V of Germany.
1523 Sweden becomes independent of Denmark, elect Gustav Vasa as King.
1526 Ottoman Turks invade Hungary.
1555 Charles V abdicates and is succeeded as Emperor by his brother Ferdinand, King of Hungary and Bohemia, and Archduke of Austria.
1558 French capture Calais from English.
1558 Elizabeth I succeeds to throne of England, Protestantism returns.
1559 Henry II of France killed during a joust.
1562 Conflict in France between Huguenots and Catholics.
1566 Revolt in the Netherlands.
1571 Battle of Lepanto: Spanish and Venetian naval force defeats Ottoman Turks.
1572 More revolt in the Netherlands. Massacre of St. Bartholomew's Eve in Paris.
1579 Dutch provinces unite in the Union of Utrecht, in rebellion against Spanish rule.
1588 Defeat of the Spanish Armada.
1593 Henry of Navarre becomes Catholic and then Henry IV of France.
1597 Spanish forces defeated by Dutch at Turnhout.

1307 Knights Hospitaller settle on Rhodes.
1309 Teutonic Knights capture Danzig.
1310 Knights Hospitaller occupy Rhodes.
1312 Knights Templar suppressed by Pope Clement IV under pressure from Philip IV.
1314 Grand Master and others burnt at stake.
1330 Secular orders of knighthood: Order of the Band founded by Alfonso XI of Castile.
1348 Order of the Garter founded by Edward I of England.
1351 Order of the Star founded by John the Good of France.
1352 Order of the Knot founded by Louis of Naples.
1355 Order of the Golden Buckle, by Emperor Charles IV.
1362 "The Great Company" besiege Avignon.
1370 Bertrand du Guesclin made Constable of France.

1410 Battle of Tannenberg – Teutonic Knights defeated by Poles, their power shattered.
1430 Order of the Golden Fleece founded by Philip the Good, Duke of Burgundy.
1434 Passo Honroso held by Suero de Quiñones.
1435 Hospitallers successfully repel Turkish attack on Rhodes.
1454 The Vows of the Pheasant at Lille.
1457 Poles take Marienburg from Teutonic Knights.
1466 Teutonic Knights give Western Prussia back to Poland at the Treaty of Thorn.
1468 Tourney and feast at marriage of Charles the Bold of Burgundy.
1480 Hospitallers once more repel Turkish assult on Rhodes by Ottoman Turks.

1520 Field of the Cloth of Gold tournament near Calais.
1522 Hospitallers dislodged from Rhodes by forces of Suleiman the Magnificent – move to Malta, 1529.
1525 Teutonic Knights turn Lutheran and secularize their state.
1565 Hospitallers successfully defend their fortress on Malta from an attack by the massed armies of the Ottoman Empire.

1309 Jean de Joinville *History of St Louis*.
1307-21 Dante *Divine Comedy*.
c.1320 *Guy of Warwick*.
1349-50 Boccaccio *Decameron*.
1362 William Langland *Piers Plowman* (A text).
1366 Petrarch *Sonnets*.
c.1375-1400 *Sir Gawain and the Green Knight*.
1382-5 Chaucer *Troilus and Criseyde*.
1387 Gaston of Foix *Livre de la Chasse*.
1387-1400 Chaucer *Canterbury Tales*.
1394 Thomaso of Saluzzo *Chevalier Errant*.

1400 Death of Chaucer.
1408 Donatello's *David* (bronze statue).
1440s Fra Angelico active.
1450s Piero della Francesca active.
1461 François Villon *Le Grand Testament*.
1460s Fra Filippeo Lippi painting.
c.1470 Malory writes *Le Morte Darthur*.
1474 Andrea Mantegna painting.
1477 Botticelli's *Primavera*.
1485 Caxton prints *Le Morte Darthur*.
1495 Leonardo da Vinci *The Last Supper*.

1509 Erasmus *In Praise of Folly*.
1513 Nicolo Macchiavelli *The Prince*.
1516 Lodovico Ariosto *Orlando Furioso*. Thomas More *Utopia*.
1528 Baldassare Castiglione *The Courtier*.
1532 Rabelais *Pantagruel*; 1534 *Gargantua*.
1536 Michelangelo *The Last Judgement* in Sistine Chapel.
1540s Titian active.
1574 Torquato Tasso *Gerusalemme Liberata*.
1590 Edmund Spenser *The Faerie Queene*.
1599 William Shakespeare *Julius Caesar*.

1306 Jews expelled from France.
1320-50 Development of guns.
1348 Prague University founded by Emperor Charles IV.
1378 The Great Schism – Urban VI rules from Rome, supported by Italy, Germany and England; Clement VII rules from Avignon, supported by France, Spain, Sicily and Scotland.
1380 Wyclif translates Bible into English.
1385 Heidelberg University founded.
1388 Cologne University founded.

1412 Huss excommunicated. University of St. Andrews founded.
1415-17 The Great Schism ended by election of Pope Martin V; Jan Huss burned at stake.
1455 Gutenberg prints the Bible.
1460 University of Basle founded.
1478 Ferdinand and Isabella establish the Spanish Inquisition.
1492 Jews expelled from Spain. Columbus lands in the West Indies.

1517 Martin Luther nails his theses to the door of Wittenberg church.
1520 Luther declared a heretic, burns the Papal Bull of Condemnation.
1531 Henry VIII of England declares himself head of the Church of England.
1536 Dissolution of the monasteries in England.
1545 The Council of Trent initiates the Counter- Reformation.
1598 Henry IV of France grants freedom of worship to Huguenots.

CHAPTER ONE

THE ORIGINS OF KNIGHTHOOD

By AD 732, just one hundred years after the death of Muhammad, his Muslim followers had established a huge empire with astonishing speed. Egypt, Palestine, Syria, Persia, North Africa and Spain had all fallen to them in succession. The Caliphs ruled over half the known world, and were eager to conquer the rest. Fanatical followers of the Prophet posed a grave threat to Christendom. The Muslim army that invaded Spain in 711 and killed Roderick, the last king of the Visigoths, had penetrated deep into the South of France. In 720 they occupied Narbonne as a base for raiding parties into the neighbouring kingdom of the Franks. In 732 a raiding party sacked Bordeaux and was marching north towards Poitiers. However, on the way they were confronted by the Frankish army, led by Charles Martel, and totally destroyed.

Historians disagree about the military significance of this victory, but its consequences were crucial. The advance of the Muslim empire was halted and Charles Martel, Mayor (leader) of the Franks, gained such prestige and support as to make him a respected and permanent ruler. He requisitioned

FRENCH CAVALRYMAN, C. 900

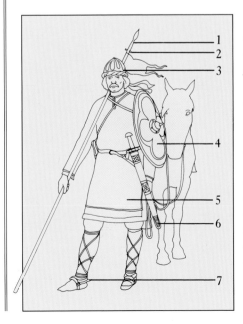

This Carolingian warrior on patrol wears a chain mail hauberk (5) which is slit at the sides. This suggests that he is accustomed to fighting on foot as well as on horseback. He wears a simple conical helmet (3) which, however, is decorated. His lance (1) has lugs (2) beneath the blade, which indicate a thrust and parry style of fighting. Although his horse has a framed saddle and stirrups, the technique of charging with couched lance is still 150 years or so in the future. He carries a round shield (4) with a spiked boss in the centre which could also be used as a weapon, and on his feet he wears leather shoes with a simple prick spur (7). His sword (6) is of the early type with a rounded end to the blade, designed for cutting rather than stabbing.

from the Church many grants of land and used them to reward his followers. They in return swore to fight for him on demand, equipped with horse and spear as well as sword and shield. Charles's power base was secure enough to unify the various tribes and provinces of the Franks into a credible kingdom; after his death his son Pepin the Short succeeded him as Mayor, but ten years later was elected King. Pepin drove the Muslims out of their remaining strongholds in the south of France, and his son Charlemagne (Charles the Great) was spectacularly successful, enlarging the Frankish kingdom into an empire which stretched northwards to include Saxony, westwards to Bavaria, and southwards to Northern Spain, Lombardy and half of Italy.

CHARLEMAGNE AND THE FRANKS

It is Charlemagne who can with certainty be credited with the development of the famous heavy cavalry of the Franks. The mounted warriors who formed these élite troops were necessarily drawn from among the Frankish nobility and landed gentry, as they had to provide themselves with horses, coats of mail, helmets, swords and lances. Charlemagne ensured that his warriors were properly equipped. In 806 he wrote to one of his vassals:

> You shall come to the Weser with your men prepared to go on
> warlike service to any part of our realm that we may point out; that is,
> you shall come with arms and gear and all warlike equipment of
> clothing and victuals. Every horseman shall have shield, lance,
> sword, dagger, a bow and a quiver. On your carts you shall have ready
> spades, axes, picks, and iron-pointed stakes, and all other things
> needed for the host. The rations shall be for three months, the
> clothing must last for six.

Building on that early success at the Battle of Poitiers in 732, the Franks employed the tactic of charging their enemies in close formation, spears bristling forwards. When this terrifying onslaught had shattered the enemy ranks, the Franks dispatched them with their swords.

The combination of Frankish superior numbers, their greater skill and reputation for savagery overwhelmed most of their opponents, but there

ABOVE *Carolingian soldiers, from the ninth-century St Gall Psalter. All have saddles with stirrups, some are wearing mail-coats, and all are armed with fearsome lances, which have hilted blades to prevent them from penetrating too deeply into the bodies of enemies.*

LEFT *Spanish infantry on the march, from a fresco showing the campaigns of King James I of Aragon against the Moors. A troop of crossbowmen precedes a troop of lancers.*

were occasions in which the cavalry was defeated by more lightly armed troops, and these are almost as revealing as the victories. In 778, while Charlemagne was leading his victorious army back into France after a successful campaign against the Spanish Muslims, his baggage train, full of looted goods and provisions, was ambushed in the pass of Roncesvalles by Basque soldiers. By the time Charlemagne realized the peril and arrived with reinforcements, the loot had been stolen, all his rearguard had been slaughtered, and the Basques had melted away into the woods and rocky terrain. One of the dead commanders was Count Roland of the Breton Marches, later to be immortalized in the great *Chanson de Roland*, which turned even this crushing defeat into a kind of victory.

Only four years later, at the battle of Suntelberg in 782, it seems that over-confidence in the technique which had so often proved their superiority led the Frankish commanders to disaster when, without the discipline necessary to the success of this shock tactic, they charged an armed camp of rebel Saxons. The Saxons were able to surround isolated units of cavalry and cut them down.

The empire created by Charlemagne did not, as he had hoped, form the basis for a united European state, a credible successor to the Roman Empire,

BELOW *An illustration from a medieval encyclopedia of warfare by Hrabanus Maurus, dated 1028, which shows early knights using lances as throwing weapons, stabbing weapons and "couched" (holding the lance much nearer to the blunt end, clamped against the body by the right arm). The fleeing knight's chain mail has not protected him from the heavy blades of the lances.*

CHARLEMAGNE – AN IDEAL CHRISTIAN KING

On the death of Pepin the Short, his kingdom was divided between his two sons, Charlemagne and Louis, according to the custom, but in 771 the younger brother Louis died and Charlemagne became the sole ruler of the Franks. Charlemagne inherited a great kingdom from his father, and when he died he had almost doubled it in size. He was a remarkable man who deserved the great fame and reverence in which he was held throughout the Middle Ages. As a capable and successful military leader he organized about 60 campaigns, half of which he directed in person. His most difficult task was the subjugation of the Saxons, who refused to be converted to Christianity despite the consistent use of extreme violence to persuade them. They managed to resist conquest for almost thirty years. In between his expeditions against the Saxons, however, Charlemagne responded to the Pope's appeal to subdue northern Italy (Lombardy), to add the huge kingdom of Bavaria and a sizeable portion of northern Spain to his dominions before being crowned Emperor by Pope Leo III in AD 800. Though modern commentators have found his tactics in Saxony unnecessarily brutal, his destruction in 796 of the ferocious Avars, the dominant tribe at the time between the Black Sea and the Adriatic, certainly benefited their victims, the Slav peoples of eastern Europe.

Perhaps the most remarkable thing about Charlemagne, however, was not his military genius but his keen interest in intellectual and cultural revival. He had a brilliant administrative mind, as his surviving "capitularies" (detailed letters of instruction and advice to his many vassals and officers) show, and he worked closely with the Church in his attempts to organize new political structures. He was himself insatiably curious about almost every subject, valued scholarship and promoted all branches of learning in his kingdom.

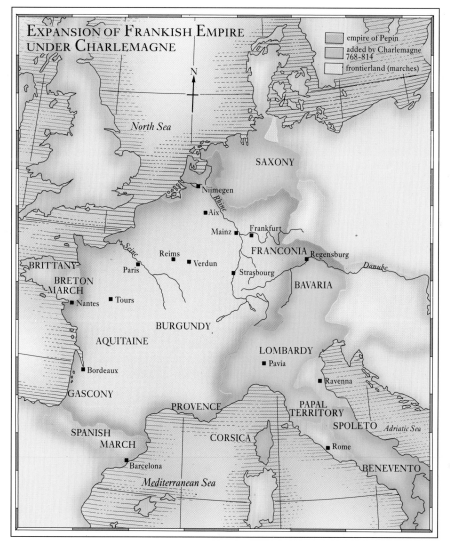

EXPANSION OF FRANKISH EMPIRE UNDER CHARLEMAGNE

empire of Pepin
added by Charlemagne 768-814
frontierland (marches)

North Sea

SAXONY

Nijmegen
Aix
Mainz
Frankfurt
FRANCONIA Regensburg
Reims
Paris Verdun
Strasbourg
BRITTANY
BRETON MARCH
Nantes Tours
BAVARIA
Danube

BURGUNDY

AQUITAINE

LOMBARDY
Bordeaux Pavia
GASCONY
Ravenna
PROVENCE
PAPAL TERRITORY
SPOLETO Adriatic Sea
SPANISH MARCH CORSICA
Rome
Barcelona
BENEVENTO
Mediterranean Sea

ABOVE *The earliest known portrait of Charlemagne and his wife, dating from about AD 820, from a codex in the monastery of St Paul in Carinthia. Painted within ten years of the Emperor's death, it shows him in his prime, rather than as the white-bearded patriarch familiar from later portrayals.*

ar sun chier mes œ ouel lices uart.
n bær temer palœent ouitre part.
ue œuancent por mi legiant œ sart.

asent lipor a les naus teœ mmart.
τ chant il su œ tens la giant baubart.

He established the famous Palace School at Aachen, where he collected many notable scholars from Ireland, Northumbria, Spain and Italy as well as his own country, headed by the great teacher Alcuin of York. Charlemagne was himself the most important pupil of this school, and many of Alcuin's surviving letters to the King contain the answers to his questions, ranging from the meaning of a word to the basics of medieval astronomy.

But the school also educated many young men (at the king's expense), from the sons of noblemen to poor scholars, who later became teachers themselves and helped form the traditions of learning and teaching which developed into the first great universities at Paris, Bologna, Padua, Oxford, and Cambridge. Another of the tasks undertaken by the scholars was the preservation and dissemination of existing knowledge. A massive programme of book copying was undertaken and a new style of handwriting, "Carolingian minuscule" developed which was easier to read. Charlemagne also had a great collection of ancient Germanic songs and poems written down (though these were later destroyed by his son, Louis the Pious). He sponsored the building of new churches, such as the cathedral at Aachen, which were the largest buildings to be erected in these countries since the end of the Roman Empire. Though the empire he created did not become the basis for the unified Europe he had envisaged, his energy and personality, as well as his ambitions, made a lasting mark on European culture.

in which military power would support a strong central government. The empire was divided between his grandsons, and quarrels between them and between their successors, and further subdivisions, ensured the gradual decline of the Carolingian Empire. In the tenth century a confederacy of duchies and counties in what had been the Germanic, western part of Charlemagne's dominion, developed into a unified German kingdom, and in 962 its king, Otto I, was crowned Emperor of the "Holy Roman Empire of the German Nation". Charlemagne, however, provided inspiration for Otto and successive medieval rulers in that his reign became an almost mythical symbol of the ideal Christian state. Charlemagne himself, and some of his famous warriors, were honoured and celebrated in stories and in art during the succeeding centuries as models for the rapidly developing feudal relationship of ruler and vassal.

The Values of Feudal Society

Feudalism, as it developed in early medieval France, was not new but evolved naturally out of the social conditions which had existed for hundreds of years in western Europe, where settled Christian states were almost always under threat from invasion by hostile Norse or Muslim nations from north and south, or destructive raids by Slav and Magyar tribes from the east. The fundamental two-way contract of feudalism, in which a lord protected his people in exchange for services, was the obvious way to structure a society which was heavily rural and agricultural, where there were few towns, and "government" consisted of agreement between the most powerful noblemen in the land. The obligation of the lord to protect his society generally and the people who worked his land and provided his wealth in particular was desirable in such conditions. Just as the peasants were required to work on their lord's lands a certain number of days in the year, the lord himself was required to be a trained warrior, capable of turning out, ready and equipped to fight, at the command of the overlord from whom he held his lands. If the lord had an extensive holding, his obligation would extend to the provision of a number of trained fighting men in addition to himself, and the wealthier he was, the larger, better equipped and more highly skilled had to be the force he provided.

Every lord held his lands in fief from an overlord who, in turn, held his from a great and powerful noble family, who held their patrimony from the king. Each link in this chain had made an oath to the effect that his tenure of the land was conditional on the service he rendered his overlord. The relationship was symbolized by the act of homage, in which the lord would kneel and place his hands between the hands of his overlord and swear an oath to serve him.

In theory this system enabled a well-regulated kingdom to mobilize an efficient fighting force against a common enemy for the protection of society. In practice, particularly in France, where the authority of the monarchy was weak, it meant that the great nobles, Counts of large regions such as Anjou and Blois, could mobilize efficient fighting forces against each other and conduct what amounted to private wars within the kingdom. The tenth- and eleventh-century legislation known as the Peace and Truce of God was an attempt by the Church to limit the sufferings caused by these wars.

RIGHT *The feudal estate was a self-sufficient economic unit, depending on intensive year-round agricultural labour. Here, the tasks of the month of February are illustrated, from the* Très Riches Heures of Jean, duc de Berry; *peasants are ploughing, sowing, pruning fruit-trees and herding sheep. Of course not all feudal estates were as large or as grand as this fifteenth-century castle with its spotless fields.*

Europe in the thirteenth century was recognizably the same shape and size as the Europe of today; it stretched from the British Isles in the west to the kingdoms of Hungary, Bohemia and Poland in the east, and from the recently converted Scandinavian countries in the north to the Iberian peninsula in the south. What made the Europe of the thirteenth century different from the Europe of today was that all its constituent countries felt themselves to be members of a unified Christian state. They acknowledged one faith, that of the Holy Roman Catholic Church, which wielded spiritual and, increasingly, temporal authority over the whole region, and in theory at least, the overlordship of the Holy Roman Emperor.

Divisive nationalistic movements and successful religious dissent did not occur until the later Middle Ages, when Europe fragmented into nations and Christendom into the different Christian theologies. In the thirteenth century Christendom was united against the threat of Islam; this was the age of the crusades, when the Church could mobilize vast armies drawn from all parts of Europe against specific pagan enemies – the Turks or Egyptians in the Holy Land, the Prussians and Lithuanians in Northern Europe, or in the case of the Albigensian crusade, heretical sects within their own Christian community.

The men and women of the ruling class were members of an international confederation of extraordinary mobility; they travelled widely to visit their friends and relations or to go to war with them, and it was not uncommon for noblemen of one area to be invited to take up vacant thrones in quite another. They were, however, known by the territory which was their main holding, from great magnates such as Geoffrey of Anjou or Eleanor of Aquitaine, to simple knights who took their name from one village or estate. During the time span covered by this book, and indeed during the thirteenth century, there were many changes of boundary and fortune within Europe, but a map such as this of medieval Christendom should help to place some of the individuals named in this history.

THIRTEENTH–CENTURY EUROPE

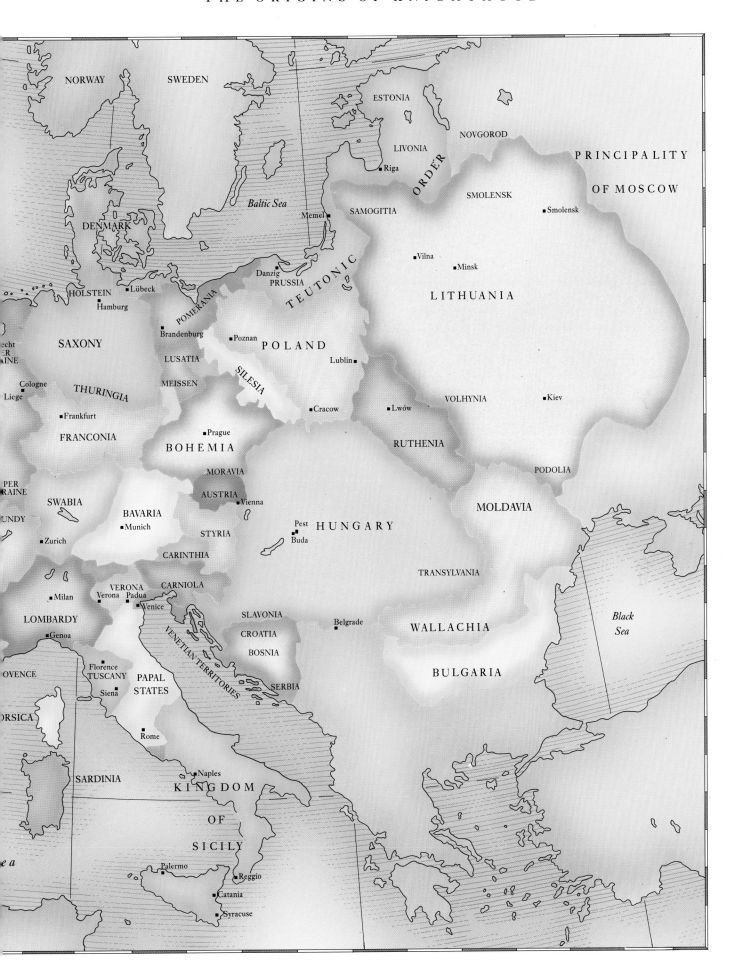

The practical aspects of feudalism – the fact that a lord often trained and equipped his own body of fighting men – were mirrored in its ethos, which had developed directly from the intense loyalty of much earlier Germanic warrior societies. We may compare the evidence of the Roman historian Tacitus, writing in the second century, with much later Germanic tribal groups in ninth- and tenth-century England, as described in the *Anglo-Saxon Chronicle* and the poem *The Battle of Maldon*. These sources indicate that the loyalty between a chieftain and his *comitatus*, his group of personal household warriors, remained essentially unchanged for a period of eight hundred years or so. Tacitus wrote of the tribes inhabiting what the Romans called "Germania" that:

> Real distinction and strength belong to the chief who always has
> around him a band of chosen warriors to be a glory in peace and a
> protection in war ... When the fighting begins, it is shameful for a
> chief to be outdone in bravery, and equally shameful for the
> followers not to match the courage of the leader: to survive one's
> chief and return from battle is a foul disgrace that lasts as long as life.
> To defend him, to support him, to turn one's own deeds to his glory,
> this is the main oath of their allegiance.

This relationship was fostered by bonds of tradition, of common upbringing between the young warriors, often also of kinship within the small tribal group. It was a two-way relationship. To earn this devotion from his young men, a good chieftain must be generous with expensive gifts of weapons and armour, while the young warriors' eagerness for these gifts was not so much the desire to be rewarded as to be honoured.

The tribes referred to by Tacitus – the Saxons, Goths, Lombards and Franks – settled large areas of western Europe after the power of the Roman Empire had declined; the Saxons in England, the Goths in southern France and Spain, Lombards in northern and central Italy ("Lombardy"), and the Franks huge areas in what is now northern and central France and the Low Countries. The values of their society, in which government was almost entirely based on oaths of personal loyalty and service sworn by men to their lord, were central to the developing feudal systems of these lands.

Tacitus' remark that it is a foul disgrace to return alive from a battle in which your chief has been killed is borne out by two examples – one historical, one literary – from Anglo-Saxon England. In 757, the *Anglo-Saxon Chronicle* tells the story of a feud between Cynewulf, the king of Wessex, and Cyneheard, a prince whose brother Sigeberht had previously been king of Wessex until he was deposed and banished by Cynewulf "for unlawful actions". Cyneheard discovered that Cynewulf intended to banish him, too; and he ambushed the king one night when he had gone with only a small retinue of men to visit his mistress. Cynewulf was attacked in the bedchamber by Cyneheard and his men and killed. His small band of men was woken by his mistress's screams and they rushed to attack the superior force of Cyneheard's men:

> ... and the prince offered each of them money and life, and none of
> them would accept it, but they all went on fighting continuously until
> they all lay slain.

26

In the morning, the tables were turned when the dead king's loyal thanes, Osric and Wigfrith, arrived with the rest of the king's warriors and surrounded the house. Cyneheard offered them money and land if they would accept him as king, and he mentioned that he had with him some kinsmen of theirs, in the hope that they would not attack him if it meant killing members of their own families:

> They replied that no kinsman was dearer to them than their lord,
> and they would never follow his slayer, and then they offered to let
> their kinsmen depart unharmed.

But the kinsmen did not think highly of this suggestion, and refused to desert their lord "any more than your comrades who were slain with the king". The king's thanes then attacked the house and Prince Cyneheard and all his men were killed (except for one who was Osric's godson, and he, the chronicler points out, was badly wounded).

The poem *The Battle of Maldon* celebrates an event which took place in 991, when the Norwegian Anlaf with ninety-three ships full of men was raiding the coasts of Kent and East Anglia. The king at this time was Aethelred, the famously unready, but the coast was defended by the Ealdorman of Essex, Byrhtnoth. He caught the invading army at Maldon. The battle commenced quite favourably for the English, who were able to keep the stronger force at bay because they were defending a narrow spit of land. But eventually Byrhtnoth, "because of his pride", fell back so as to allow more of the Vikings to cross over and fight. At this point the battle turned disastrously against the English when Byrhtnoth was decapitated. Despite the Battle being a serious defeat for the English, the poem was written to celebrate the great loyalty and bravery of a few of Byrhtnoth's men, who decided to fight on by their fallen leader, even though this meant certain death:

> Byrhtwold grasped his spear and spoke.
> He was an old companion. He brandished his ash-spear
> And with wonderful courage exhorted the warriors
> "Mind must be the firmer, heart the more fierce,
> Courage the greater, as our strength grows less.
> Here lies our leader, dead,
> An heroic man in the dust.
> He who now longs for escape will lament forever.
> I am old. I will not go from here,
> But I mean to lie by the side of my lord,
> Lie in the dust with the man I loved so dearly".

Thus we can see that, long before the appearance of the knight proper, there had been an ancient tradition of a warrior élite whose idea of honourable conduct was bound up in a nexus of noble qualities, such as courage and prowess, stemming from the absolute loyalty and personal devotion they felt for their leader. These were important stepping stones towards the knight's sense of identity, both individually and as a member of a international band of like-minded brothers.

ABOVE *A twelfth-century decoration on the capital of a pillar in the church at Clermont-Ferrand, showing the symbolic struggle between Vice and Virtue. Embedding their lances in two prostrate bodies, the embattled knights have kite-shaped shields, conical helmets and full chain-mail suits.*

FEUDAL LORDS AND SERF-KNIGHTS

The feudal system established in northern and central France enabled its great lords, the counts and dukes who controlled large territories, to gain power at the expense of the monarchy. Fiefs were originally granted to a lord for his lifetime in return for service to the crown, and were supposed to revert to the crown on the lord's death. By the eleventh century, however, it had become accepted that both service and lands were hereditary. On a lord's death, his heir was entitled to take possession of his estates, provided that he acknowledged the overlordship of the king by doing *homage*. But in reality this meant that large areas of France, which had once been under the direct personal control of the king, had been alienated from him. His "overlordship" was in most cases merely a formality; he retained control only of a small area of central France. In the mid-twelfth century the greatest landholder in France was in fact the King of England, Henry II.

In the German Empire, though the feudal system itself was essentially similar to that of northern France, this did not happen because successive emperors had been careful not to entrust key roles in their administrations to individual nobles and their families. Instead they had cultivated a close relationship with the Church, giving high office to bishops and abbots – men who had been appointed by the emperor in the first place (at least until Emperor Henry IV's great dispute with Pope Gregory VII over investitures in 1076). This meant that offices could not become hereditary, and the imperial family retained control of its own extensive territories.

The emperor and the men who served him in government needed reliable and efficient administrators to run their estates for them. These were the "serf-knights", known as *ministeriales*. They were "serfs" because technically they were unfree and tied to the lands of the lord they served. They could not marry outside their lord's domain or hold estates from other lords without his permission; their status was

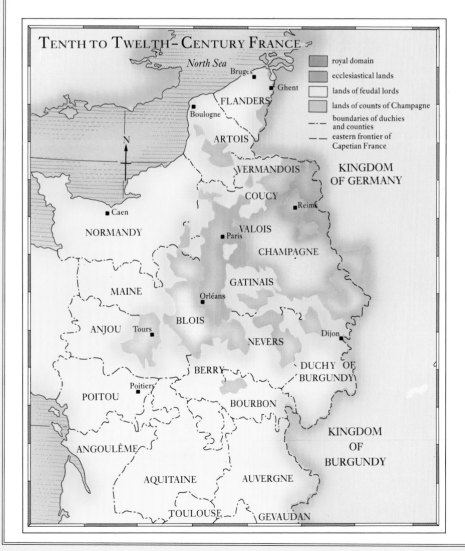

TENTH TO TWELFTH-CENTURY FRANCE

North Sea

Bruges
Ghent
FLANDERS
Boulogne
ARTOIS
VERMANDOIS
COUCY
Reims
Caen
NORMANDY
VALOIS
Paris
CHAMPAGNE
GATINAIS
MAINE
Orléans
BLOIS
ANJOU   Tours
NEVERS
Dijon
BERRY
DUCHY OF BURGUNDY
Poitiers
POITOU
BOURBON
KINGDOM OF BURGUNDY
ANGOULÊME
AQUITAINE   AUVERGNE
TOULOUSE   GEVAUDAN

KINGDOM OF GERMANY

Legend:
- royal domain
- ecclesiastical lands
- lands of feudal lords
- lands of counts of Champagne
- boundaries of duchies and counties
- eastern frontier of Capetian France

ABOVE *Walther von der Vogelweide (c1170–c1230), the greatest of the early* minnesinger, *was descended from* ministeriales, *unfree retainers in the households of German magnates.*

LEFT *This map shows how little direct control the early Capetian kings of France had in the territory of their own kingdom. In fact they reigned over a small part of central and northern France, leaving the greater part of the kingdom in the hands of their major vassals, the counts and dukes who presided over huge fiefs. In practical terms, the Plantagenets of Anjou, Maine and Normandy were more powerful than the Capets.*

RIGHT *A noble lord sits down to his dinner and is served by knights in his household. His butler (by the tankards on the left), his seneschal (standing beside him), and his pantler (lifting the curtain), were all high-ranking household officers, who would in eleventh-century Germany have been serf-knights. The carver (giving bread to the dog) and the ewerer (with the hand-towel over his shoulder, beside the ship which is in fact a basin of water) are probably squires.*

BELOW *Emperor Frederick I (Barbarossa) saw the serf-knights becoming more powerful, emancipated and wealthy. His own* ministerialis, *Werner von Bolanden, was spectacularly successful, and when he died, held lands from more than forty different lords.*

defined by the laws of the domain to which they belonged and they had no legal rights outside it. However, their "service" was like that of a knight to his feudal lord; they served him in hall, they administered his estates and, since they were mounted and trained in arms by the lord, they gave military service too. The serf-knights at any court would occupy the important positions of marshal, chamberlain and seneschal (the steward in a great house).

By the mid-eleventh century it had become generally accepted that *minis-teriales* could own property and many had acquired their own holdings, wealth and status. Though the German aristocracy was more rigidly defined and stratified than elsewhere in Europe, the *ministeriales* managed to make the transition from "serfdom" to its lowest ranks as independent knights. During the investiture dispute and the civil wars which followed it they emerged as a crucial element of continuity and stability in enabling the emperor to maintain control of his lands. They began to hold fiefs from, and do homage to, other lords as an ordinary member of the *Edelfreie* (lesser nobility) might. In the first half of the twelfth century they began to view themselves as a distinct social group; they held assemblies and acted collectively. Eventually they merged with other members of the lesser nobility to form the class of Knights (*Ritterstand*).

THE THREE ESTATES

Together with the development of feudal society and the ethos that it fostered, there grew up another important and influential concept – that of the three estates, which together formed the natural order of society. This was an idea with a pedigree going back to classical times, and it was taken up again in the Middle Ages as the ideal social image. The three estates were the clergy, the workers, and the warriors, or, in medieval terms, the Church, the peasantry and the knights. The Church's function was to pray and to care for the spiritual well-being of the people, the knights' to defend and protect the other two estates, and the peasants' to work the land to provide food for everyone.

King Alfred the Great of England was one of the first medieval writers to promote this idea in his translation of the works of the much admired sixth-century philosopher Boethius, made about 894. Later ecclesiastical commentators, such as Adalbero of Laon and Gerard of Cambrai, also had much to say on the subject. Etienne de Fougères, Bishop of Lisieux, is probably the first writer to identify the warrior class specifically as knights ("la chevalerie") in the 1170s. This continued to be a powerful idea through-out the Middle Ages and still finds clear expression in the fourteenth-century allegorical poem *Piers Plowman*. In a famous passage Piers instructs others in how each must do his part in the right ordering of society:

> "And all manner of men that live by meat and drink,
> Help those who win your food to work strongly."

At this point a knight steps forward and offers to help Piers with his ploughing:

> "By Christ," said a knight then, "he tells us what is best,
> But truly, I was never taught how to handle a team.
> But teach me," said the knight, "and by Christ I will try."
> "By St. Paul," said Perkyn, "You make such a fair offer,
> That I will swink and sweat and sow for us both,
> And labour all my lifetime for your love,
> In covenant that you keep Holy Church and myself
> From wasters and from wicked men that destroy this world ..."
> Courteously the knight then uttered these words:
> "By my power, Piers, I plight you my troth
> To fulfill this agreement, even if I have to fight;
> As long as I live I shall maintain you."

RIGHT *The armed knight ready to do battle in defence of the Church, depicted on a capital in the twelfth-century cathedral of Monreale, from the Norman kingdom of Sicily.*

The important point about this idea is that it links the knight's purpose in life, his deeds and the credit to be attached to them, to the common weal of the whole of society. In conjunction with the feudal system, it broadened a knight's responsibilities and extended his role beyond relationships governed by loyalty to kin and lord into a great interdependent structure of obligations extending, in theory, from peasant to king. The knight's *raison d'être* was to protect all the others, something not articulated in the earlier Germanic heroic ethos, where it was seen to be a nobler thing to die uselessly with your lord than to return and fight another day. As we shall see, the oaths a knight

swore on being knighted often included specific obligations which related to this more altruistic role – to defend the Church, to support and protect women, widows and orphans, and others, such as the sick and the elderly who were unable to defend themselves.

At the same time, almost all commentators who discuss this idea then go on to say how far short of it the reality was. As they are in the main ecclesiastical commentators, they are often scathing on the aptitude of knights to disobey the Church, use their superior force to rob the defenceless poor and live only for luxury and vice. Thus Peter of Blois in about 1170:

> Knights of old bound themselves by oath to support the state, not to flee from battle, and to put the public good before their own lives. But all goes by contraries, for nowadays, from the moment they are honoured with the knightly belt, they rise up against the Lord's anointed and rage against the patrimony of the crucified. They rob and despoil Christ's poor, afflicting the wretched miserably and without mercy, that from other men's pains they may gratify their unlawful appetites and wanton pleasures. They who should have used their strength against Christ's enemies fight now in their cups and drunkenness, waste time in sloth, moulder in debauchery, and dishonour the name and office of knighthood by their degenerate lives.

This and many similar writings in the same vein paint a grim picture of the realities of knighthood; but we should note two things about Peter's outburst. The first complaint he makes about knights is that they rebel against the authority of the clergy (the Lord's anointed) and that they resent the fact that the Church owned and controlled so much land, for which knights were always hungry. Many of the Church's fulminations, while obviously based on reality, must be seen in the context of medieval conflicts over secular and spiritual power. The Church and knights in particular did not always see eye to eye on the true role of the knight, as we shall see in more detail later. The second interesting thing about the passage is that Peter is contrasting bad modern knights with good knights of old; he has not lost faith in the idea of knighthood or its potential as a crucial element in the right ordering of society. He also firmly believes that there had been good knights in the past who did live up to their vows. For Peter, writing in the 1170s, knights were an accepted part of society and had been for so long that it was unthinkable to question their continued existence. But it was really during the eleventh century that the mounted warrior of the early Middle Ages evolved into a knight, as part of a number of other major social and intellectual developments taking place at that time.

THE GREAT CHANGE

The knight of the eleventh century onwards can be distinguished from his early medieval predecessor by the fact that he had been "dubbed" to knighthood in a special ceremony and acknowledged a certain code of behaviour, including specific obligations to defend the weak. His emergence must be seen in the context of the other major developments in all areas of life which took place at roughly the same time. Here we may look at two aspects which particularly affected knights – one social, one military.

We have already seen that the society of early medieval Europe was engaged in a continual struggle for survival against hostile forces. At the time it was not at all clear that this struggle would be won, and many people confidently expected the Day of Judgement to occur on the 1st of January 1000, particularly in England, where the depredations of the Vikings seemed much like the disasters predicted in the Revelation of St John as presaging the end of the world. Successive waves of barbarian tribes, displaced from their own homelands by invasion, or in search of new, more fruitful land, made the eighth, ninth and tenth centuries a time of instability, violence and the constant threat of destruction. The idea of the knight as protector of society developed in response to these pressures.

However, from the late tenth century onwards this was no longer, or so much, the case. The majority of foreign invaders had been decisively defeated or absorbed into the Christian society of western Europe. The conversion to Christianity of, successively, Russia (989), Poland (1000), Hungary (1001), Denmark (1104), the Slavs (1147) and Sweden (1164), effectively extended Christendom and meant the cessation of constant hostilities with their peoples. Released from these pressures, the civilization of western Europe underwent extraordinary developments in a comparatively short space of time. Government and economic conditions stabilized; trade and commerce grew rapidly, leading to increased prosperity, the

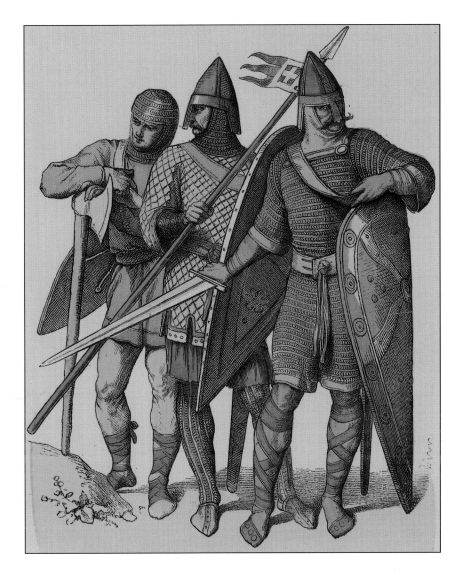

RIGHT *This nineteenth-century engraving shows two knights and man-at-arms of the First Crusade, the supreme expression of the idea of the interrelated social responsibilities of the Three Estates, and particularly of the duty of knights to fight on behalf of the Church.*

growth of towns and cities, and an astonishing burgeoning in social, intellectual and artistic areas. The population expanded and, in order to feed it, forests were felled and great tracts of land never previously cultivated were brought under the plough.

It was a period of growth and consolidation for the Church. Successive movements for internal reform, and an increasingly sophisticated organization for legal and governmental administration, enhanced the prestige and power of the Church. Enjoying the position of sole spiritual leader throughout the whole of Europe, the Church came increasingly to play a part in more secular matters, and the popes to claim authority both as political and spiritual leaders.

During the eleventh and twelfth centuries a revolution in thought and ideas took place, inspired by great intellectual curiosity. Schools were established where the great minds of the period exercised themselves in questioning, investigating and arguing. The great universities of Europe developed from these schools, first established at Paris and Bologna. The most important result of these activities was the development of intellectual method, and its application to previously unquestionable truths. Even biblical texts were submitted to the rigours of logical analysis and discourse. To distil a clear and orthodox meaning from these often contradictory texts, a

massive body of literature of previously undreamt-of subtlety and complexity was created.

In everyday life too there were significant developments. Professor R. W. Southern in his book *The Making of the Middle Ages* characterizes the result of these as "the emergence of the individual from his communal background". He compares the architecture of the early medieval Great Hall, where the lord and his household lived, ate and slept together in one great open hall, with the evolving medieval castle, where different areas were devoted to different activities and, for the first time, there were individual chambers where people could be by themselves.

For the knight the castle is of crucial importance. Here the lord lives, and his wealth and prestige attract to him as members of his household landless knights to form his retinue, clerics to administer his estate and a host of servants needed to support his activities. The wealthier the lord, the more inclined he was to social display, and the more his household took on the character of a court, a centre of wealth and patronage, attracting minstrels and men of letters, who celebrated in a new, sophisticated courtly literature the aristocratic values and activities of the lord and his associates.

When not on campaign, the knight was likely to be at a court, where, besides the rigorous physical training which was part of his daily round, he was also exposed to the literature and culture of his class – the epic *chansons de geste* and their tales of martial prowess, or, increasingly, the new romances with their tales of knights and ladies, discreet amours, dangerous quests and devilish enchantments. A court was a centre for intellectual and creative activity which was in many ways the secular equivalent of a monastery or a cathedral school. At court we see the emergence of a culture associated specifically with knights, defining their virtues and qualities, their aspirations to fame and wealth and, last but certainly not least, honour.

Another major factor affecting the development of knighthood was the new developments in military technology and tactics, which occurred in the

ABOVE *The English fought on foot at the Battle of Hastings, and their most fearsome weapon was a four-foot battle-axe, which could inflict devastating wounds. This encounter shows how a charge with couched lance could cancel that advantage.*

TOP *In this scene from the Bayeux Tapestry we can see Norman Knights using their spears to throw over-arm and under-arm. The knight on the extreme left, fleeing from the English archers, seems to have his lance "at rest" preparatory to couching it for a charge. Note the reinforced pommels and cantels at the front and the back of the saddles to give greater stability in combat.*

second half of the eleventh century. These were largely related to the use of the lance by knights. In the early Middle Ages, mounted warriors appear from the remaining pictorial evidence not to have used saddles or stirrups. Both of these were introduced by contact with the barbarian horsemen of the east, such as the Magyars of Hungary, and were in use by the ninth century. Stirrups in particular enabled the cavalry man to have much greater control over his horse, and much greater stability in the saddle. It is difficult to deduce from the small remaining evidence exactly how the early cavalry soldiers fought; they charged their enemies and they carried lances, but it is not until the later eleventh century that we see any contemporary representations of a charge with "couched" lance. Before that we only see warriors with lances throwing them overarm, underarm, or stabbing downwards with them.

The technique of charging with couched lance (that is, holding the lance much nearer to the blunt end, clamped against the body by the right arm), was a revolutionary development and became the standard technique of medieval cavalry. In conjunction with the use of a saddle with a raised and reinforced back, which prevented the knight being thrust backwards off his horse by the impact when he struck his target, this technique enabled a

BELOW *This ornamental bronze shield boss of about AD 600, shows a Lombard horseman, riding out to hunt with neither saddle nor stirrups. Originating in China, these crucial innovations did not reach Western Europe until the late eighth century.*

WILLIAM THE MARSHAL – A BRILLIANT CAREER

William Marshal was probably born in about 1144. His father John was a minor landholder who held the hereditary office of marshal in the King's household. John Marshal substantially improved his family fortune by repudiating his first wife and marrying a lady of property whose brother became the Earl of Salisbury. William was the fourth of his six sons so, though he was born into the knightly class, he had no money or property to inherit and had to make his own way in the world.

We know so much about William's life because he became so wealthy and famous that his biography was written within a few years of his death in 1219. Though the life story is in the form of a verse romance, it contains many fascinating and humorous details of a knight's life in the twelfth century.

England was in a state of civil war, following the death of Henry I and the accession to the throne of his daughter Matilda. Her cousin, Stephen of Blois, also claimed the throne with the support of about half the barons and lords of England. William had a narrow escape from death while still a child. His father, who was on the side of the Empress Matilda, was besieged by her rival, King Stephen. John Marshal had asked for a truce, and the King had granted it in exchange for a hostage – William, who at this time was about eight years old. John broke the terms of the truce by using it to refortify the castle, and Stephen threatened to kill the little hostage. William's father unfeelingly replied that he should go ahead, since he "still had the hammer and anvil on which to forge a better son than that one". One of Stephen's officers proposed putting William in a catapult and throwing him over the castle wall, but Stephen was too kind-hearted to murder him and instead kept him prisoner for two months.

William was brought up from the age of about twelve in the castle of a family connection, William of Tancarville. He learned there all the essential qualities of knighthood, and was fond of listening to romances. He was knighted in 1164 on the eve of a battle at Drincourt. He acquitted himself well in the battle, but unfortunately his horse was killed and he had to pawn the new robe which the lord of Tancarville had given him in order to buy another. Soon he was attending tournaments, which in William's day consisted of two "teams" of knights attacking one another for sport over a wide range of countryside. The object was to take prisoner as many knights from the opposing team as possible, though it appears that

knights were very often wounded and killed at these events. A captured knight forfeited his horse, and possibly his armour too, and had to pay a ransom to be released. William was extremely successful and realized that he could make his fortune at tournaments. He entered into an agreement with a Flemish knight, Roger de Gaugi, in 1177, that they would travel from tournament to tournament together, helping each other to capture knights, and splitting the ransom money equally between them. In ten months they took 103 knights prisoner.

William by this time had grown rich enough to equip his own team of knights, and the biographer records that he was generous with gifts to them. On one occasion he was dining with friends at an inn when he saw a knight fall from his horse in the street and break a leg. William rushed out and picked up the wounded man in his arms, armour and all, and carried him into the inn. There he presented him to his friends so that they could pay the bill with his ransom money. How the wounded knight felt about this act of chivalrous generosity is not recorded.

William himself was not immune from the dangers of tournaments. The *History* tells how one day some knights were seeking William after a tournament in order to give him the prize. They couldn't find him, but at last he was spotted in the blacksmith's shop with his head on the

ABOVE *William Marshal unhorses Baldwin of Guisnes at a tournament at Monmouth. This delightful miniature was drawn by the artist and historian Matthew Paris in his* Historia Maior *in 1233.*

anvil, having his helmet hammered back into shape so that he could get it off his head.

William's career really began to take off in 1167, when he had joined his uncle, the Earl of Salisbury, in a campaign to suppress a rebellion in Poitou. Their party was ambushed; the earl was killed, William wounded and taken prisoner. William's courageous conduct in the campaign had however attracted the notice of the great Eleanor of Aquitaine, now Queen of England as well as the overlord of Poitou. She paid William's ransom and in 1169, through her influence, William was placed in charge of her eldest son Henry. William directed the prince's household and supervised his military training. In 1170, when the prince was fifteen, his father, Henry II of England, decided to crown him to ensure a peaceful succession, and from then on he was known as the Young King.

The Young King had inherited his father's ungovernable temper. Jealousy of his youngest brother, John, led him to rebel against his father in 1173. In preparation for a military campaign, the Young King had himself knighted. He chose William Marshal to perform the crucial ceremony of girding on the sword and delivering the ritual blow. The *History of William Marshal* remains discreetly silent about William's part in the rebellion; but at its conclusion he was a party in the negotiations for the peace treaty, and retained his position.

His close relationship with the Young King was maintained until 1182, when he lost favour with both Henrys because of a malicious rumour that he was having an affair with the Young King's wife, Margaret of France. William challenged his accusers to single combat (then a legitimate legal process for determining the truth in a dispute) but the Young King forbade it and allowed William to leave the court unharmed.

So great was William's fame and prestige at this point that, as soon as it was known that he was no longer in the service of the Young King, three great lords offered him property and a pension if he would become their man. But William had no wish or need for their protection.

He went on pilgrimage to Cologne instead, and waited until he could be reconciled with the Young King. This happened in 1183 when the Young King and his brother Geoffrey launched another rebellion against their father. The young Henry sent for William who joined him on his journey south, just in time to see his master die of a fever. On his deathbed, he asked William to discharge for him an unfulfilled vow to go on crusade to the Holy Land. William spent the next two years in Syria, returning home, it seems, just before the capture of Jerusalem by Saladin in 1187.

On his return he was taken into service by Henry II and eventually was rewarded

ABOVE *The face of a hero – the tomb effigy of William Marshal in the Temple Church, London. William had joined the Knights Templar a few months before his death in 1219.*

with the hand in marriage of Isabel de Clare, a rich heiress and daughter of the Earl of Pembroke. He remained at the centre of political life throughout the reigns of Richard I and John, and one last story testifies to his absolute loyalty and honour. When King John died in 1216, his heir, Henry III, was a child of nine years. The country was in turmoil as large areas of the south east acknowledged Prince Louis of France as king. An invasion by the French to subdue the rest of the kingdom was expected at any moment. The few nobles who had remained loyal to King John gathered together. On the initiative of the papal legate, Gualo, Henry was first knighted (by William) and then crowned king. William was then begged to become the king's guardian and protector. At first he refused, saying that he was too old (he was over seventy), but in the end he consented. The position, however, looked hopeless; the *History* records William consulting his friends for their advice:

> "They have entrusted me with an almost hopeless governorship. The child has no money and I am a man of great age." Tears came into his eyes as he spoke, and the others wept too, out of pity. "Yes," said John de Erley, who had understood his way of thinking, "you have undertaken a task that must be carried through at all costs. But when we reach the end, I tell you that, even putting things at their worst, only great honour can come of it ... No man will ever have earned such glory upon earth."
>
> "By God's sword," said William Marshal, "this advice is true and good. It pierces my heart. If everyone else abandoned the king, do you know what I would do? I would carry him on my shoulders, step by step, from island to island, from country to country, and I would not fail him, even if it meant begging my bread."

William captured and dismantled all the castles held by Louis in the east of England; Louis retreated to France in 1217 and the kingdom was secured for Henry III. William joined the military religious order of the Knights Templar (with whom he had served in Syria) shortly before he died in 1219 and was buried with great honour in the Temple Church in London.

knight to deliver an enormously powerful blow on his opponent, because the lance, held in this rigid fashion, had the collective momentum of the man and the charging horse behind it. A whole line of knights charging in this manner seemed at first to be unstoppable. When Anna Comnena, the daughter of the Byzantine Emperor Alexius, first saw Frankish and Norman knights charging in formation during the First Crusade, she described the result as an "irresistible first shock", adding that "a Frank with a lance in his hand could punch a hole in the walls of Babylon".

The skill and training required to operate this kind of tactic successfully was considerable. To learn to hold the heavy lance steady while wearing full armour and controlling a galloping horse required a great deal of practice. It was thus customary for young boys of good birth to be sent away from home for training to the court of a lord connected with the family. In the early years of knighthood it was possible for anyone to be a knight providing they could afford the expensive horse and even more expensive armour, and were able to spend many hours acquiring the necessary skills in horsemanship and weapon-handling. In practice, however, almost all were from aristocratic or at least "gentle" families.

LEFT *A fourteenth-century wooden statue of a crusader knight, with lance at rest. This is the position in which a lance is held immediately before being lowered for the charge, and therefore expresses hostile intent. It is held close to the blunt end and clamped rigidly against the body by the right arm.*

The knight's chief enemy in battle was an archer, but in the Middle Ages pitched battles were comparatively rare and a knight was much more likely to be injured by the weapons of his knightly opponent in a tournament or mock battle. To protect himself from the blows of lance, sword (and arrows) it was essential for him to wear a mail-shirt. This garment had to be constructed in a painstaking and laborious manner. All the links had to be made by hand (by winding wire round a rod and then cutting down one side of it). The ends of the open links were then hammered flat, and when they had been linked together the ends were pressed over one another and riveted. A complete coat of mail, covering a man from head to knee, contained thousands of individual links and could cost a great deal. Money was not often used in the eleventh century, but there is a record of one lord, Langry Gros, giving a *mansus* (a piece of land capable of supporting a household of people) to the great Abbey of Cluny in 1080 in exchange for a suit of mail. Such armour was often an important item of family property and handed down from father to son.

Possession of expensive equipment, and training in the use of arms at the court of a lord in the company of his peers and elders, where he would also learn the manners and values of knighthood, set the knight apart from the lower orders of society more than mere wealth could do. He was part of a special caste, with its own values, its own customs, its own history and literature, its own technology and skills. Knighthood was not so much a rank to which those lower in the social scale aspired and from which those possessing it could graduate to higher states, as the sign of membership of a great international noble association. To be a member of this brotherhood was an honour equally to the landless bachelor squire and to the king's heir. One more thing remains for us to examine, which defines the emergent knight – his initiation into the state of knighthood by undergoing the ritual dubbing.

THE DUBBING CEREMONY

For many centuries throughout Europe it had been traditional for a young warrior to be publicly and ceremonially presented with arms on the occasion of his coming-of-age, which was usually also the time at which he officially entered the war-band of his lord. Gradually this ceremony became more elaborate and the presentation of arms, originally intended to mark a young man's majority, came to acquire a broader significance – that he was entering a new "state" or "order" of knighthood.

The first record of what we would recognize as a proper dubbing ceremony is John of Marmoutier's account of the dubbing of Count Geoffrey the Fair of Anjou. This took place in 1128, when Geoffrey was fifteen years old. He had been selected by King Henry I of England as a suitable husband for his daughter and heir Matilda, and it was seen to be appropriate for the young man to be knighted on the eve of his wedding. Thirty of his companions were knighted with him. The ceremony took place at Rouen, in the presence of King Henry.

> As the next day was dawning, Geoffrey was prepared for his solemn bath, as custom demands of a young man about to become a knight. When the king learned from his chamberlains that the Angevin* and

ABOVE *A young man is given the ritual bath which, from the earliest times, was the traditional means of physical and spiritual purification, essential before entering a new state. In the earliest account of a dubbing ceremony, written in the mid-twelfth century, the bath is seen as a long-established custom for the candidate to knighthood.*

LEFT *Matthew Paris's drawing of a young man being knighted. He is dressed, spurs are fixed to his heels, and a sword is girded around his waist by the great lord (or in this case king) who confers knighthood, and is then presented with his own arms on surcoat, banner and shield.*

those who had come with him had arisen from the ewer, he summoned them to his presence. After cleansing his body, the noble offspring of the count of Anjou was wrapped in crisp linen, dressed in a ceremonial robe interwoven with gold and covered with a cloak, dyed purple in the blood of oyster and murex. He was shod in silken shoes which had soles that were decorated with lion-cubs. His comrades, who were expecting to receive the gift of knighthood with him, were likewise clothed in linen and purple. Decked out in such finery as I have described, the king of England's future son-in-law proceeded from a secret chamber into public view, accompanied by the assembled nobility of his country, bright like the flower of the lily and covered in red like a rose.

The horses were drawn up, the arms brought and distributed to each as was appropriate ... then the young man was fitted with a cuirass second to none, whose double layer of mail could be pierced by the blow of no lance or javelin, and with iron boots which were so reinforced with two thicknesses of compact mail; his feet were bound with gold spurs and a shield covered in gold motifs of lions was hung from his neck. On his head was placed a helmet, resplendent with many precious stones ... very last of all a sword from the royal treasury was carried out to him. It had been preserved from long before, when it had been carefully crafted by that master, Weyland.

* The "Angevin" is a member of the ruling House of Anjou.

RIGHT *The Victorian painter Edmund Blair Leighton's intensely romantic portrayal of a dubbing, "The Accolade". The title refers to the blow on the neck – the* collée *– which actually conferred knighthood. In practice this was almost always done by another knight, or a lord – certainly not by a woman. Later knighthood could only be conferred by a monarch (even a female one, as in the painting) and the blow was made on the shoulders with a sword.*

The rest of the day was spent in "the practice of military games" and the celebrations continued for seven days and nights.

There are several important things to notice about this passage. The ceremonial associated with knighting had already become a highly sophisticated ritual accompanied by great pomp and expense and obviously intended to confer honour on the participants. As we can see, it had already become customary for the young knights to take a ritual bath as a preparation for the ceremony. But basically this was still just a grander version of the ancient presentation of arms; the more serious moral and religious overtones which were later to characterize the ceremony are conspicuous by their absence. This is an entirely secular affair; Geoffrey and his companions are dressed and armed in the presence of the king and nobles in the hall of the royal

palace. They do not seem to go to church at any point to pray, it is not recorded that they or their arms are blessed by any priest or bishop and, more important, they do not make any oaths or promises regarding their future conduct as knights. John of Marmoutier does not mention the *collée*, or blow, which actually confers knighthood in later texts, and altogether gives the impression of the glittering ceremony without any of its serious meaning.

Very different is the next account we shall examine, an anonymous poem written some time before 1250, called the *Ordene de Chevalerie*. This is a treatise on what it means to be a knight in the form of a story, which tells how Hugh, Count of Tiberias, is captured during the campaigns of the Third Crusade by the pagan prince Saladin. Although Hugh is worth a large ransom, Saladin agrees to release him on condition that Hugh will show him how a man is made a Christian knight. Hugh agrees to this and the rest of the poem describes the ceremony of dubbing to knighthood, explaining in great detail the moral significance of each feature. As the following paraphrase will show, the actual steps of the ceremony are almost identical to the ritual dressing and arming of Geoffrey of Anjou a hundred or more years before, but now the ceremony has been transformed by the addition of a symbolic meaning to each element.

ABOVE *The tomb effigy of Geoffrey the Fair of Anjou, a brightly coloured enamel on the lid of his sarcophagus at Le Mans cathedral. Geoffrey died in 1154 but, like many medieval lords, made elaborate arrangements for his burial, and had commissioned the tomb three years earlier.*

> First Hugh dressed Saladin's beard and hair, and then he brought him to a bath: this is a bath of courtesy and bounty, he said, and should recall to you the baptism of the child, for you must come out of it as clean of sin as the infant from the font. Then he brought him to a fair bed, to signify the repose of paradise, which is what every knight must strive to win by his "chivalry". Raising him, he dressed him first in a white robe, signifying the cleanness of the body; over that he threw a scarlet cloak, to remind him of the knight's duty to be ready to shed his blood at need in defence of God's church. Then he drew on brown stockings to remind him of the earth in which he must lie in the end, and to prepare in life for death. After that he bound about Saladin's waist a belt of white, signifying virginity, and that he should hold back lust in his loins. Then came the gold spurs, to show that the knight must be as swift to follow God's commandments as the pricked charger. Last, he girded him with the sword, whose two sharp edges are to remind the new knight that justice and loyalty must go together, and that it is the knight's task to defend the poor from the strong oppressor. There should have followed one more thing, the *collée*, a light blow from the hand of him who had girded the new knight, but this Hugh as Saladin's prisoner would not give. But he did give him four commandments to which a newly made knight must be bound for the rest of his life. He must not be consenting to any false judgement, or be a party in any way to treason; he must honour all women and damsels and be ready to aid them to the limit of his power; he must hear, when possible, a mass every day, and must fast every Friday in remembrance of Christ's passion.

This poem was both popular and influential, copied and imitated many times throughout the Middle Ages. It may be over-particular in stressing specific meanings for each act in the ritual, but in general it undoubtedly gives an accurate picture of the ceremony by means of which most knights entered the state of knighthood.

ABOVE *The medieval knight in all his glory; Sir Geoffrey Luttrell is armed, prior to setting off for a tournament, by his wife and daughter. From the fourteenth-century Luttrell Psalter.*

It was not until much later in the Middle Ages, and for reasons which we shall be discussing in chapter three, that the ceremony was taken over by the Church; in its original form, it consists of a ritual arming which is conducted in a hall or public place by a layman, preferably a noble lord or a renowned knight. Since the elements of the ceremony described by John of Marmoutier are essentially the same (except for the *collée* and the oath) as those in the *Ordene*, namely the bath, the dressing in the white robe and the red (or purple if the knight was royal or noble) mantle, and the arming with belt, spurs and sword, it is likely that these elements and their symbolism had fully developed during the latter part of the eleventh century, along with so much else crucial to medieval knights.

Circumstances did not always permit the ceremony to be conducted in its full magnificence; we learn from the biography of William Marshal, a phenomenally successful knight, who rose from comparative obscurity to become one of the most powerful men in the land, that when, as in his case, a young man was knighted on the eve of battle, the ceremony could be shortened to the wearing of the mantle, the girding on of the sword, and the *collée*, all given to William by his patron, the lord of Tancarville.

But in whatever form, and however thoroughly understood by its participants, we can see the emergence of a rite which is clearly and uniquely designed for entry into the state of knighthood and which confers a new status and new obligations. By taking part in this ceremony, a young man at the turn of the twelfth century was at once distinguished from his contemporaries, who simply served the lord who gave them arms. At the same time this ceremony is quite distinct from the homage paid by a vassal to his overlord. He is a Knight in the full consciousness of the tradition of knighthood.

CHAPTER TWO

THE RISE OF ROMANCE

Arguably the most lastingly influential aspect of medieval knighthood was its idea of itself, as depicted in contemporary literature. In this literary review of knights we find various kinds of material; the eleventh-century *chansons de geste*, then the love poetry of the troubadours of southern France, and the emergence of a major new literary mode – the narrative verse romance. At the same time there are medieval treatises on knighthood, containing detailed instructions for young knights on how to live up to the high calling they have chosen. In more practical terms, treatises on warfare, rule books for tournaments, and manuals on "venery" (hunting) all add to the complex literary portrait of the knight.

THE EPIC *CHANSONS*

In eleventh-century Europe, particularly France, poems in the vernacular (as opposed to Latin) became popular, recounting the heroic exploits of great warriors from the past. At first these poems were composed orally and performed by professional minstrels, or *jongleurs*, who travelled from castle to castle. Their French name, *chansons de geste*, means "songs of deeds", and this is primarily what they are; celebrations of the martial feats of national heroes, especially the deeds of Charlemagne and his twelve "peers", such as

KNIGHT IN QUEST OF ADVENTURE, C. 1180

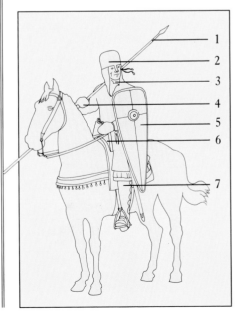

This knight carries a lance (1) which he may couch to charge his opponents, but since it is not decorated with a pennon or banner he could also throw it, a technique equally favoured at this date. His helmet (2), with round top and nasal bar, is of a style introduced around 1100. His mail hauberk or byrnie has been extended; it now incorporates a hood or coif; a loose flap (aventail) (3) hanging in front of his throat can be pulled up and secured by thongs to helmet or brow to protect his face, and the sleeves are now lengthened into mittens (4). He carries the characteristic kite-shaped Norman shield (5) and rides in a saddle with raised pommel (6) and cantle (behind) to give him an extra secure seat during combat. His shins are protected by mail greaves (7).

LEFT *Medieval minstrels* – histriones *in Latin,* jongleurs *in French – sang and played musical instruments, as well as recounting stories. It seems likely that when they recited poems they did so to musical accompaniment. Here two Spanish minstrels are playing a rebec and a lute in an illustration from the* Cántigas de Santa Maria.

Girart de Roussillon or *Ogier li Danois.* Other nations celebrated their own heroes, for example the Spanish epic *Poema de Mio Cid,* whose subject was Rodrigo Diaz de Vivar, a very successful and brilliant general. He began his career in the service of Sancho II of Castile but was exiled on the accession of Sancho's brother Alfonso. He served the Moorish kings of Saragossa for almost ten years before capturing the Moorish city of Valencia and ruling it as an independent state until his death in 1099.

The earliest *chanson de geste* to survive is the greatest of all: the *Chanson de Roland,* which was composed in about 1100. This is unlikely to have been the first poem of its kind, however, since it shows the sure handling by a great artist of techniques which had clearly become established conventions of the genre by this time. This makes it an excellent example for showing the characteristics of the *chansons* and their epic nature.

The destruction of Charlemagne's rearguard by a Basque ambush in 778 was recorded by his biographer, Einhard, in about 830. In the battle, Einhard records, "died Eggehard, who was in charge of the King's table, Anshelm, the Count of the Palace, and Roland, Lord of the Breton Marches, along with a great number of others." By the time the *Chanson de Roland* was composed, this brief mention has been greatly elaborated; Charlemagne has twelve great "peers" – warlords of noble birth, of whom the greatest is his nephew Roland. Roland's closest friend and companion is Count Oliver, who is also the perfect foil for Roland's hot-tempered and impetuous personality (the poet comments "Roland is fierce, but Oliver is wise").

Roland also has an enemy: his stepfather, Ganelon. Ganelon's enmity is aroused early in the poem, when Roland nominates him for a dangerous mission; he must be Charlemagne's messenger to the pagan King Marsile, who has just sued for peace. The last two ambassadors sent by Charlemagne were killed, and Ganelon sees this as nothing less than an attempt on his life by Roland. He consequently devises a plan for revenge – he betrays his own king and country by plotting with Marsile to ambush the rearguard of the

French army as it crosses the Pyrenees on its return to France. Reunited with Charlemagne, Ganelon nominates Roland to lead the rearguard, which will protect the retreating army and its baggage through the narrow mountain passes. Everyone knows this is a position fraught with danger, but Roland reacts with characteristic pride; he swears that Charlemagne will not lose so much as a pack-mule, cannot be dissuaded from taking command, and refuses to accept reinforcements – the usual 20,000 soldiers will suffice.

This poem, like many epics, is tragic in the classical sense. Roland is a great hero, but his personality has a fatal flaw – his immense pride in his noble blood and in his personal reputation for bravery and prowess. When Oliver sees the pagan forces coming in arms against them, he points out that the French are outnumbered five to one, and begs Roland to summon help from Charlemagne by blowing his ivory horn, Olifant. But Roland refuses:

> "Now God forbid," Roland makes answer wroth,
> "That living man should say he saw me go
> Blowing of horns for any Paynim foe!
> Ne'er shall my kindred be put to such reproach.
> When I shall stand in this great clash of hosts
> I'll strike a thousand and sev'n hundred strokes,
> Blood-red the steel of Durendal* shall flow.
> Stout are the French, they will do battle bold.
> These men of Spain shall die and have no hope."

> * Durendal is the name of Roland's sword.

Battle is joined and described in bloodthirsty detail, with many cleavings down the middle with swords and thrustings through the body with lances. Roland, Oliver and the other Peers perform wonders of fighting, and the hundred thousand strong Saracen host is cut down in thousands; "Of hundred thousand scarce two will fight again" the poet comments. But then King Marsile draws up with twenty more huge battalions. Battle is rejoined, but the French know that they are doomed. One by one the Twelve Peers fall; for each death Roland and Oliver exact a terrible revenge. The pagan Prince Grandoyne strikes down four of the Peers, then meets with Roland:

> The Prince Grandoyne was a good knight and gallant,
> Strong of his hands and valorous in battle;
> Athwart him now comes Roland the great captain;
> He'd never met him, but he knew him instanter
> By his proud aspect, and by his noble stature,
> His haughty looks, and his bearing and manner.
> He cannot help it, a mortal fear unmans him;
> Fain would he fly, but what's the good? he cannot.
> The Count assails him with such ferocious valour
> That to the nasal the whole helmet is shattered,
> Cloven the nose, and the teeth and the palate,
> The jaz' rain hauberk and the breastbone and backbone,
> Both silver bows from off the golden saddle;
> Horseman and horse clean asunder he slashes,
> Lifeless he leaves them and the pieces past patching.
> The men of Spain fall a-wailing for sadness:
> The French all cry: "What strokes! and what a champion!"

ABOVE *Charlemagne mourns at the tomb of Roland, who has been ceremoniously interred in a suitably elaborate tomb in this fourteenth-century manuscript.*

POETS AND THEIR PATRONS

When the Jersey-born poet Wace wrote *Brut*, his French verse translation of Geoffrey of Monmouth's *History of the Kings of Britain*, in c.1155, he dedicated it to Eleanor of Aquitaine. She was the grand-daughter of Duke William IX of Aquitaine, the famous troubadour, and was herself renowned as a generous patron of troubadours. Her courts in Aquitaine and Poitiers were influential centres of wealth and patronage, and Eleanor and her two daughters, Marie and Aelis, who married Count Henry I of Champagne and Count Thibaut of Blois respectively, spread the influence of the witty, sophisticated southern French courts northwards.

Marie, Countess of Champagne, in particular was a famed and respected patron of the arts. Chrétien de Troyes, the greatest poet of the time, was probably a member of her court, working under her protection. On at least one occasion she requested him to write a poem on a particular subject. This poem was the *Lancelot*, and explored the theme of a lover's perfect subjection to his mistress, engendering conflict with his desire for personal fame and honour.

Marie and the other ladies of her court were said to enjoy debating intellectual questions on the subject of love. In the 1190s Andreas Capellanus (the Chaplain) composed a work entitled *On the Art of Honest Love*, meaning love outside marriage. This represented ladies and knights (including Marie herself) holding mock-trials to pass judgement on lovers' conduct in a variety of challenging situations, and contained a code of thirty-one rules for the behaviour of lovers, including such gems as the lover's obligation to turn pale and tremble when his beloved enters the room. The main premise of the first two parts of the treatise, which Andreas attributes to Marie herself, is that true love cannot exist between married couples because it cannot exist without jealousy and there can be no jealousy within marriage.

Until recently all this was taken seriously by medieval scholars, despite the fact that the third part of the book consists of a complete retraction of the rest; but now his intention is perceived as satirical.

A crucial factor in the relationship between medieval authors and their patrons was that it provided mutual benefit: the patron rewarded the writer with gifts and money, and the writer bestowed fame and glory on his patron. Writers attached

to a particular court or noble household often produced an account of the family history, such as Lambert of Ardres' chronicle of the lords of Ardres, or might celebrate an event, such as a betrothal or marriage, a great feast or tournament, or compose elegies and eulogies of the dead, such as Jean de Condé's funeral eulogy for his patron William I of Hainault in 1337. In a large court, several authors might be employed. Christine de Pisan records in her *Book of the Deeds and Excellent Customs of the Wise King Charles V* that the king recruited the most talented and well-respected writers in France to his court, and that he kept a team of them constantly employed on books he had commissioned.

Many little poems have survived from the Middle Ages in which the writers express their strong desire for a present from their forgetful or niggardly patrons, but it was not normal for a writer to be employed permanently in that capacity. Usually they held some official post and wrote in their spare time. Chaucer was a customs official; Andreas Capellanus and John of Trevisa were chaplains. Christine de Pisan was exceptional in being a full-time professional writer.

ABOVE *A Spanish and a Moorish minstrel in an illustration from the* Cántigas de Santa Maria.

OPPOSITE *A sixteenth-century Italian banquet in progress – the kind of occasion at which the recitation of family histories, or eulogies of illustrious family members, composed by a court poet under the lord's patronage, would form an acceptable entertainment.*

ABOVE *The month of April from the* Très Riches Heures *of Jean, duc de Berry, shows a betrothal between a richly dressed lord and lady, an event certain to be celebrated by their respective court poets.*

But time has run out for the French. Four assaults have been withstood, but at enormous cost; only sixty French knights remain alive. Roland at last consents to blow the horn and summon Charlemagne with the main army, if only to ensure that the fallen have Christian burials. With his last strength he winds the horn, giving such a powerful blast that the blood bursts through his temples. Oliver, mortally wounded from a treacherous spear-thrust in the back, dies. Roland weeps for him. At last only Roland and the warlike Archbishop Turpin of Rheims are left; Roland gathers together the bodies of the Twelve Peers, and swoons. While trying to revive him, Turpin dies of his wounds. Roland tries to shatter his sword so that no Saracen can steal it when he is dead; but the steel is too sound. So he lays the sword and Olifant the horn beneath his body and, turning his face towards the enemy, gives up the ghost.

Roland's death occurs only just half-way through the poem, and the rest is concerned with its aftermath – Charlemagne's grief and rage on finding the bodies of the slain, his revenge on the fleeing pagan hordes (God holds the sun still in the sky so that there is time enough for all the pagans to be slaughtered), and lastly the trial and horrible execution of the traitor Ganelon and thirty members of his family.

Chansons de geste continued to be written in the twelfth century and clearly their bloodthirsty ethos continued to have a broad appeal to the warring knights, who were their audience and often their subjects. The qualities celebrated in them are, however, principally in an older, more primitive style than those emerging in the courts of France. As a hero, Roland evidently had many great qualities – his prowess as a warrior, his loyalty to Charlemagne, his love for his companions – but these qualities hark back to an age of feudal, military society. Some of Roland's characteristics – his boastfulness, the overweening pride which is clearly to blame for the destruction of 20,000 of the king's finest soldiers and knights, his tendency to jeer at the dead bodies of his opponents – would not be seen as recommended for knights in the years that followed.

THE TROUBADOURS AND THE CULT OF LOVE

In the southern part of France, society was not subjected to the stresses of invasion and strife to the same extent as in the north. The legal and intellectual heritage of the Roman Empire was much stronger there, and peace and prosperity enabled a civilized courtly culture of considerable sophistication to develop. At these courts, from the late eleventh century onwards, we hear of the "troubadours" – literally "finders" – who discovered, or rather invented, a new kind of poetry. The poems of the troubadours present the first medieval treatments of "romantic" love, where the subject is the beauty and excellent qualities of the beloved lady, coupled with the agonies of unfulfilled love on the part of the poet.

Troubadours themselves seem to have come from a wide variety of social backgrounds, but the greater number of them were from the knightly class. We know more about troubadours than about the anonymous authors of the *chansons de geste*, because several of them had a short biographical sketch, known as a *vida*, added to manuscripts of their poems after their

BELOW *A manuscript miniature portrait of the troubadour Bernart Ventadour. He wrote love poetry to Eleanor of Aquitaine and many later scholars supposed them to have been lovers. Like a number of other troubadours, Bernart was of humble origins – his father had been a servant who stoked the baking ovens at the castle of Ventadour.*

ABOVE *Knights and ladies dancing the "carolle" in the Garden of Love, a late fifteenth-century manuscript illustration of the famous allegorical poem the* Roman de la Rose.

deaths. The troubadours, younger sons originally destined for the Church, or simply young men with a penchant for making verses, were educated, worldly, witty characters who were highly valued at court and by their peers. Most were attached to the household of a lord, though some travelled from court to court in search of patronage. Occasionally one hears of a troubadour being rewarded for his services with lands of his own, such as Perdigon who was awarded the status and the maintenance of a knight by the Count of Auvergne, even though he was the son of a poor fisherman. Some troubadours were noble lords in their own right, such as Duke William IX of Aquitaine, Alfonso I of Aragon, Enric I of Rodez, William of Les Baux or Albert de Malespina. Even King Richard I of England, who lived for many years at the worldly and sophisticated courts of his mother Eleanor of Aquitaine, tried writing poems. The *vidas* also record the existence of eight women troubadours, all beautiful, noble and well-educated.

The first troubadour whose poems have survived was Duke William IX of Aquitaine, who lived from 1071 until 1127. Duke William was a man who lived very much for his own pleasures and did not much concern himself with the strictures of the Church; criticized by contemporary religious writers as "godless and wicked", he kept a large number of mistresses, and his surviving poems often celebrate their charms in coarse language. But by the

51

mid-twelfth century, poets such as Arnaut Daniel or the great Marcabru were writing sophisticated lyrics in which the complexity of the verses was mirrored by their elaborately stylized sentiments.

The subject of these poems was almost always love, as a powerful motivating force, which refines and improves the good qualities of the lover until he has proved himself worthy to be granted the love of his lady. His lady is usually married, and usually somewhat above him in social status – the wife of a great lord. She is a distant, elevated being, beautiful and virtuous, and an expert in the manners and customs of courtly society. The poet always approaches his lady as an inferior, as a humble supplicant, who desires to serve her in order to be rewarded with her love. To love is an exquisite pain and yet gives great joy; the lover suffers greatly but would not give up his love for anything, as the following lines from a poem by Arnaut Daniel declare:

> I continually improve myself,
> For I serve the gentlest lady
> In the world (and say so openly)
> I am hers from head to toe,
> And even amid cold winds,
> The love raining within my heart
> Keeps me warm in harshest winter ...
> ... I do not want the Empire of Rome,
> Nor to be elected Pope,
> If I cannot return to her
> For whom my heart burns and cracks;
> And if she does not cure my ills
> With a kiss before the New Year,
> She'll kill me and condemn herself.
> Yet in spite of the ills I suffer,
> I shall not desist from loving ...
> ... I am Arnaut who gathers the wind
> And hunts the hare with the ox
> And swims against the incoming tide.

The lady is sometimes kind and generous to her devoted lover, sometimes capricious and cruel, but she is the dominant and more powerful partner. The poet/lover offers her worship and devoted love service; she can advance and reward or reject and spurn him. It is unlikely that many of the "loves" celebrated in the troubadours' poems were consummated in real adulterous love affairs; such a course would be extremely dangerous for the lover, since one of the greatest treasons any vassal could commit was to sleep with his lord's wife. But physical consummation is undoubtedly the goal aspired to in many of the poems and, in this fictional world, rules were developed to regulate the behaviour of lovers; this is the "Courtly Love" made famous by the nineteenth-century French critic Gaston Paris, who assumed that the poems referred to a genuine cult of adulterous love widely practised in the courtly society of France.

Modern writers prefer the view that the adoration of noble ladies expressed the social and emotional aspirations of the troubadour knights; but whether a literary convention or an account of real-life illicit love affairs, there can be no doubt that the cult of love and the quasi-religious worshipping of highborn ladies was to be hugely influential to the emergent literature of romance.

THE RISE OF ROMANCE

The manners and morals of a wealthy, leisured, sophisticated court society such as that which gave birth to the troubadours could not have offered greater contrast to the more rugged poetry and values celebrated in the *chansons de geste*. Troubadours were quickly imitated in northern France (*trouvères*) and Germany (*minnesinger*). From the mid-twelfth century, however, a new kind of poetry began to be written, in which the knightly hero's martial prowess was complemented by refined manners and romantic motivations: the narrative verse romance.

The hero of a *chanson* had much in common with the hero of a *roman*, but there are also important differences. The epic hero is typically seen performing a role essentially related to protection or advancement of his

ABOVE An early fifteenth-century painted Italian tray, showing six legendary lovers venerating Venus triumphant. Lancelot and Tristan are among the devout worshippers. A characteristic medieval blend of the explicit and the mystical makes this object a powerful image of the continued fascination for the Cult of Love.

society, usually in warfare. His values are based on a communal bond of loyalty – to his peers, to his country, to his God, and, overwhelmingly, to his lord. This loyalty finds expression in his great courage and prowess in combat, and is absolute; no greater test can be imposed on it than that of fighting on in the face of certain death, and for this reason the hero of an epic will often be found fighting to the death against overwhelming odds. Epic writing often displays an attitude towards experience of a deeply fatalistic kind; the hero-warrior consents to his fate, and displays his superiority not necessarily by triumphing over his enemies but by embracing a glorious death.

In romance, on the other hand, the hero is essentially solitary and does not engage in combat for the purpose of protecting his lord and society so much as seek adventure with a view to proving himself. He is conscious of living up to a standard of behaviour, which embraces the more refined qualities expressed in the term *courtoisie* – polished manners, a high moral sense, and knowledge and skill in the social arts of courtly life as well as in combat. Because the adventures which befall a romance hero are often designed specifically to test some aspect of his knightly character, he tends to be successful in the end. He may fall short of perfection, or he may fail in his task at first and then learn from his mistakes, but he profits by experience and ultimately triumphs.

Further, while the epic world is one of military comradeship, where there is small place for women and for love, in romance Love has become an important motivation for the hero. In the *Chanson de Roland* romantic love is confined to a very few lines describing how the sister of Oliver, Aude, who is betrothed to Roland, swoons and dies on hearing the news of his death. In romances, the knight is proving himself worthy of his lady's love. He tends to be in competition with other knights; he wants to be the best and therefore does not usually experience the great comradeships of the warrior.

This new emphasis on individual aspiration and achievement is paralleled elsewhere in the widespread intellectual developments of the "Twelfth-century Renaissance". Almost from the first, romances gave greater attention to the inner feelings of their characters, their psychological motivations and changes of heart. This is particularly striking in the case of female characters, previously confined in the masculine and warlike world of the epic to passive roles. The *Roman d'Eneas* (c 1160), reworking freely from Virgil's epic poem the *Aeneid*, devotes much attention to the conflicting emotions first of Dido, the tragic Queen of Carthage, and then of Lavinia, the native princess with whom Aeneas ultimately discovers the happiness of *leal amor*, mutual true love.

At about the same time, somewhere between 1155 and 1170, there was written the earliest surviving version of another immensely popular romance story, that of *Tristan*. Here the theme of noble characters torn by the conflicting demands of passionate love and feudal and moral duty is much more fully elaborated. Tristan, the nephew of King Mark of Cornwall, is sent to bring his uncle's bride, the Princess Iseult, from Ireland. On board ship they accidentally drink a love potion intended to ensure the happiness of the

RIGHT *Sir Tristan, fighting in a* mêlée *at court, watched by the Queen and her ladies. Sir Tristan was reckoned to be one of the five "dangerous knights", second only to Sir Lancelot. He is here fighting Sir Palomedes, who later became his friend.*

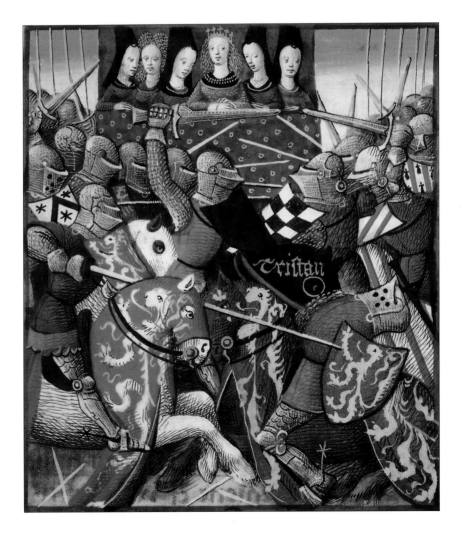

THE STORIES OF KING ARTHUR

King Arthur and his knights grew to their position of supremacy in the mythology of the Middle Ages from very small and obscure beginnings. The only contemporary historian of the period when Arthur was supposed to have lived, Gildas, who died in about 570, did not mention Arthur in his account of the Saxon invasions of England. Not until the last quarter of the eighth century did the chronicler Nennius, in his *History of the Britons*, record that Arthur, a war-leader (*dux bellorum*) resisted the Saxons together with the kings of the Britons in twelve great battles. In the last of these, the battle of Mount Badon, Arthur "alone killed nine hundred and sixty men; and in all the battle he was victorious". No further writings about Arthur have survived from the time between 800 and 1100, but we know that many stories existed and were circulated by word of mouth from the remark made by the chronicler William of Malmesbury in the early twelfth century:

> This is the Arthur concerning whom the idle tales of the Britons rave wildly even today – a man certainly worthy to be celebrated, not in the foolish dreams of deceitful fables, but in truthful histories; since for a long time he sustained the declining fortunes of his native land and incited the uncrushed courage of the people to war.

From the tone of this statement it seems likely that the stories told by the Britons were full of magical happenings and formed the source material both for the Arthurian romances of Chrétien de Troyes and his followers and for the surviving Celtic story cycles in the four ancient books of Wales, which were written down in the twelfth and thirteenth centuries.

It is probably not a coincidence that the man who really immortalized Arthur and made all subsequent romance cycles possible was a Welshman, the historian Geoffrey of Monmouth. In about 1136 Geoffrey wrote, in Latin prose, a *History of the Kings of Britain*, in which the story of King Arthur is greatly elaborated and given many of the elements now familiar to us from numerous retellings. Geoffrey claimed that the source of his material on

BELOW *This famous stone frieze on an archivolt in Modena Cathedral shows the abduction of Guinevere and her rescue by Arthur and his knights. Built in the first quarter of the twelfth century, it predates any surviving medieval romance, and almost certainly predates the composition of Geoffrey of Monmouth's* History of the Kings of Britain – *evidence that Arthurian stories were widely known early in the period.*

RIGHT *A rare depiction of the Round Table. Sir Galahad is presented to the assembled knights, ready to take his rightful place in the Siege Perilous (a place at the table which had always been vacant, reserved for the knight who would succeed in the quest for the Grail).*

Arthur was "a certain very ancient book in the British tongue", which was given to him by the Archdeacon of Oxford. Whether this means a real book, or whether Geoffrey was referring to the "wild ravings" of the oral tradition, his version of the story included Merlin the magician, the seduction of Arthur's mother, Igerna, by his father, Uther Pendragon, his marriage to Guinevere, accounts of his chief knights, Sir Gawain, Sir Kay and Sir Bedivere, the treacherous Sir Mordred who abducts Queen Guinevere and usurps the kingdom, and, after the final battle, Arthur's mysterious departure to the Isle of Avalon for the healing of his grievous wounds.

The book was immensely and immediately popular. Transposing the sixth-century British chieftain to contemporary British king and his court, it pre-figures some of the themes of romance. Arthur "developed such a code of courtliness in his household that he inspired peoples living far away to imitate him". After Arthur's conquest of France his court celebrates with a tournament:

> The knights planned an imitation battle and competed together on horseback, while their ladies watched from the top of the city walls and aroused them to passionate excitement by their flirtatious behaviour.

Not everyone was approving, however. Gerald of Wales, author of *Journey through Wales*, was expressing a view held by many churchmen when he told this delightful anecdote of a man afflicted by demons:

> When he was harassed beyond endurance by these unclean spirits, Saint John's Gospel was placed on his lap, and then they all vanished immediately, flying away like so many birds. If the Gospel were afterwards removed and the *History of the Kings of Britain* by Geoffrey of Monmouth put there in its place ... the demons would alight all over his body, and on the book too, staying there longer than usual and being even more of a nuisance.

French and then English versions of the *History* were made by Wace and Layamon; the elaboration of the tales of Sir Lancelot and of the Holy Grail by Chrétien de Troyes, and the popularity of the tale of Sir Tristan, which was also considered part of the Matter of Britain, paved the way for an enormous body of Arthurian romance produced in every European country for the next five hundred years.

RIGHT *One of the most famous and enduring episodes in the Arthurian myth: the mortally wounded Arthur waits at the lakeside while faithful Sir Bedivere casts Excalibur back into the lake, where it is caught and brandished by a mysterious hand.*

ABOVE *An expression of devotion; a knight kneels before his lady on a painted fifteenth-century Flemish shield, designed for the parade before a tournament. Death hovers behind the knight, waiting for the moment when the knight's continual quest for danger leads him astray. The notch at the top left is for resting the lance on.*

married couple. Unable to bear life apart from each other, the lovers are compelled to resort to dishonourable tricks and stratagems to conceal their love from the elderly and jealous King Mark. The normal moral standards of life in a feudal society are turned on their heads. Tristan and Iseult are admired for their goodness and loyalty to each other in maintaining an adulterous love which leads them to lie and plot the deaths of those who would betray their secret. The barons who reveal their adulterous passion to the king are condemned as envious, spiteful and wicked men.

The love-cult of the troubadours had transformed the value system of the martial epic. In romance, where the hero is a lover, it is his lady who is the focus of his loyalty and for whom he seeks to prove his worth; it is his greatest motivating force and largely replaces the desire of the epic hero to deserve the praise of his lord and his companions. "Worth" is an important concept in romance and must reflect the concerns of real contemporary knights. The natural ambition of the knight for pre-eminence, not only in arms but in the social qualities of *largesse* (generosity), *pité* (compassion), *franchise* (independent spirit), and *courtoisie* (courtly behaviour, especially towards women), lead him to seek worth, to enhance his reputation in the eyes of others. His worth will enhance that of the lady he loves; her worth, in terms of her beauty, virtue and social status, will also enrich him. This is well expressed in the lyric poetry of Ulrich von Lichtenstein, the famous jouster and poet:

> Knights who seek for honour, you should make sure
> Of serving when you're armed ladies of worth
> If you wish to use your time
> In knight's ways, with honour,
> Pay court to fairest women.
>
> Your courage should be high as you bear shield
> You should be polished, bold, blithe and gentle
> Serve knighthood with all your skill
> And be glad, set love high,
> Thus shall you win high praises.
>
> Think now of the greetings of great ladies,
> How sweet they make the life of their dear friends.
> He who wins ladies' greetings
> Wins honour, his desire;
> His joy is all the sweeter.
>
> The knight who with his shield will ward off shame
> Should always strive to use his utmost strength
> For deeds of arms bring honour.
> Worth and praise are his due,
> But both are dearly purchased.
>
> Bring my shield here! Today you shall see me
> In the service of my dearest lady.
> I must strive to win her love;
> She shall greet me or I
> Perish as I strive to serve.

Most romances related stories from three great cycles of subject matter: the *Matter of France*, stories of Charlemagne and his twelve peers and their battles

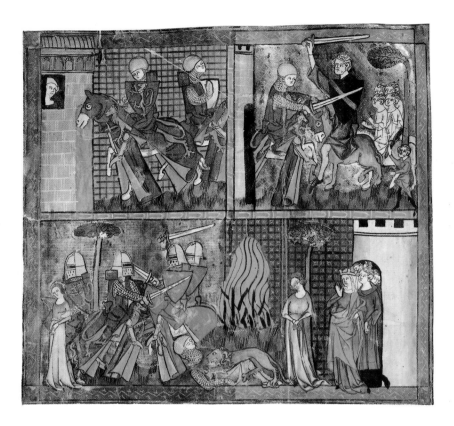

ABOVE *A composite illustration of scenes from* Yvain *by Chrétien de Troyes. Yvain discovers his faithful helper Lunete imprisoned in a chapel at the top left; at the top right Yvain kills the evil giant Harpin; at the bottom left he rescues Lunete who is about to be burnt alive for treason; Yvain's lion disembowels the wicked seneschal who had falsely accused Lunete; Lunete is reconciled with Yvain's wife Laudine.*

against the evil Saracens; the *Matter of Rome*, stories drawn from classical (usually Latin) authors, such as the stories of Troy, of Aeneas, and of Alexander the Great; and the *Matter of Britain*, the most popular and often retold of all, the stories of King Arthur and his knights of the Round Table.

There were romances on other subjects too; individual knights not connected with either Arthur or Charlemagne whose noble qualities or heroic exploits were celebrated. Sometimes these were national heroes supposed to have existed in history, such as *Richard Coer de Lyon*, or *Chevalère au Cygne* (the Knight of the Swan, a fictional hero of the First Crusade). Sometimes the story has been converted from a saint's life into a romance, as in the many versions of *Sir Ysumbras* which are based on the life of St Eustace; or it could be a story told to prove a moral point, for example *Amis e Amilun*, the tale of two faithful friends – one saves his friend's life by taking his place in a judicial single combat although a supernatural voice has told him that if he takes part in the fight, he will contract leprosy: the other then slaughters his own children so that his friend can be cured by bathing in their blood. Many short romances are based on ancient Celtic stories which feature supernatural characters and events; these are known as Breton Lais, and several of the best of them were composed by a poetess, Marie de France, in about 1160-70. But by the final quarter of the twelfth century the new literary mode in France had already found a master who would never be surpassed.

CHRÉTIEN DE TROYES AND THE GOLDEN AGE OF ROMANCE

Between 1170 and 1190 Chrétien de Troyes wrote his five surviving poems, *Erec et Enide*, *Cligès*, *Yvain* (sometimes called *Le Chevalier au lion*), *Lancelot* (sometimes called *Le Chevalier de la charrette*), and *Perceval*, or *Le Conte du*

ABOVE *From a manuscript of* c *1300, the first kiss of Lancelot and Guinevere. The poem is a later French version of the story of Sir Lancelot, recounting more of the history of his love affair with the Queen than was divulged by Chrétien de Troyes.*

graal, which he left unfinished at his death. We know virtually nothing about Chrétien himself; he mentions his name in the prologue to *Erec et Enide* and, at the beginning of *Lancelot*, informs us that he is writing at the express wish of Marie, Countess of Champagne, from which it is presumed that he was attached to her court. He dedicated the unfinished *Perceval* to Count Philip of Flanders, a great patron of the arts.

All of these poems, long verse narratives, are subtle and complex explorations of the difficulties of reconciling various ideals of behaviour; they provide a depth of psychological analysis of their characters combined with a vivid picture of aristocratic and courtly life and a richness of poetry which has rarely been equalled in any age. The two most influential of the poems were the *Lancelot* and the *Perceval*. Chrétien mentions that both the subject matter and the treatment of it for the *Lancelot* were suggested to him by the Countess of Champagne, something which he may have found creatively irksome since he left the poem to be finished by someone else. It was imitated, translated and re-worked throughout Europe (with the exception of England, where its hero was never popular and remained little known until Malory's *Morte Darthur* in 1485), and was subsequently incorporated into the huge compilation of French prose romances covering the rise and fall of the Round Table known as the Vulgate Cycle.

Sir Lancelot was often seen as an archetype of the perfect knightly lover, and all subsequent portrayals of his character are ultimately derived from Chrétien de Troyes' poem. His Lancelot is a complex man whose passion for Queen Guinevere dominates his personality; in true troubadour fashion he venerates Guinevere with a religious intensity which verges on blasphemy, while Guinevere herself alternates between tenderness and appalling cruelty.

At the opening of the poem, Guinevere, under the protection of the incompetent Sir Kay, is abducted by the evil knight Sir Meleagant. Sir Gawain, riding in pursuit of her, comes across a nameless knight whose horse has been killed. The knight is, of course, Lancelot, but his name is not revealed until half-way through the poem, after 3,500 lines. Nor is his initial lack of identity merely accidental; it reflects the fact that the knight "has no strength or defence against love which holds him in its sway; his thoughts are such that he totally forgets himself, and he knows not whether he is alive or dead, forgetting even his own name, not knowing whether he is armed or not, or whither he is going or whence he came". Lancelot has been brought to this state of near insanity by the abduction of the Queen, and does not fully recover until the two are reconciled half-way through the poem.

The incident which gave the poem its other name – *The Knight of the Cart* – occurs not long after the appearance of the Knight. After his second horse falls dead under him, he meets with a hideous dwarf who is driving a cart. The dwarf offers to reveal news of the Queen's whereabouts if the Knight will ride in the cart. In those days, the narrator explains, it was a serious matter to be seen riding in a cart:

> Whoever was convicted of any crime was placed upon a cart and dragged through all the streets, and he lost henceforth all his legal rights, and was never afterward heard, welcomed or honoured in any court. The carts were so dreadful in those days that the saying was then first used "When you see and meet with a cart, cross yourself and call upon God, that no evil may befall you".

The Knight is reluctant to associate himself, and his rescue of the Queen, with the shame and ignominy which will certainly follow if he gets in the cart. For two steps he hesitates, but then jumps in since this is the only way in which he can learn where the Queen has been taken. Through all his subsequent adventures (and there are many), everyone greets him as "the Knight who rode in the cart" and he is taunted and despised as a man in disgrace.

Sir Gawain catches up with him again, and before long the two learn that the land where the Queen has been taken can only be entered by one of two perilous bridges across a dangerous river; one is underwater, and the other is made from the blade of a sword. Gawain, courteously given the choice by Lancelot, opts for the less perilous water-bridge; Lancelot himself, crawling across the sword-bridge on bare hands and knees, is badly wounded. He allows himself only one night to recover before doing battle with Meleagant, whom he defeats and would have killed if his father, King

ABOVE *Sir Lancelot rides in the cart, accompanied by Sir Gawain and a squire. At this point in the poem he has not been named, and is henceforth referred to as "The Knight of the Cart".*

BELOW *Sir Lancelot crosses the sword-bridge, lacerating his hands and knees, then tackles the lions on the other side (which, however, turn out to be magical illusions) before doing battle with Sir Meleagant while Guinevere and King Bademagu look on.*

Bademagu, had not requested Guinevere to intercede for him. After disarming, Lancelot hurries to present himself to the Queen. She refuses to speak to him or even look at him. Lancelot, not surprisingly, is dumb-founded. He leaves the court to meet Gawain; musing, he decides that the Queen's reason for hating him must be that he rode in the cart, thus tainting her with disgrace.

Meanwhile, a false report has reached Guinevere that Lancelot has been killed. She reproaches herself bitterly for her baseness and cruelty, and when Lancelot returns she greets him with flattering warmth. She then informs him that her former cold behaviour was a punishment, not for riding in the cart but for hesitating to get into it. He begs her forgiveness, and she invites him to speak with her at her chamber window that night. The window is barred, a precaution by the noble King Bademagu to protect her from Meleagant; but, inspired by love, Lancelot wrenches the bars from their sockets, cutting his fingers to the bone. He spends the night joyously with the Queen and at dawn leaves her, carefully replacing the bars. Unfortunately his blood has stained her sheets and in the morning the beady-eyed Meleagant accuses her of committing adultery with Sir Kay, who has been sleeping in her room while recovering from his wounds.

This gives Lancelot an opportunity to defend Guinevere in a trial by combat. He is well able to do this because, of course, Guinevere is innocent as charged – she did not go to bed with Sir Kay. Lancelot makes an oath on holy relics that she did not, Meleagant that she did; naturally Meleagant gets the worst of the contest, but once again King Bademagu, who loves his son even though he has no illusions about his character, asks Guinevere to stop the fight. Even though he has sworn on holy relics to have no mercy on Meleagant, as soon as Lancelot hears the Queen agree to this request, he refuses to strike his opponent.

One more incident from the romance serves to demonstrate Sir Lancelot's absolute subjection to the whim of his beloved. The ladies of Arthur's court hold a tournament, with the intention of giving themselves in marriage to the knights who do best. Lancelot attends the tournament in disguise and, at first, performs wonders. The Queen recognizes him and sends a message by a maiden that he is to "do his worst". Lancelot begins to miss his opponents, and eventually spends his time running away from them, and all the other knights despise him for a coward.

This lasts all day, and on the following day he receives the same message, and agrees to it with the same humility. This is the kind of paradox which the witty and well-educated lords and ladies of Marie of Champagne's court relished; the hero, instead of striving to win in order to please his lady and honour her with his high reputation, has to act completely against his normal character and do badly – a much keener test of his love for her, since it contradicts his self-love. Of course, it also gives Lancelot a splendid opportunity to "come from behind". The Queen eventually relents and bids him do his best, and he finishes the tournament as the acknowledged victor. More importantly, it completes the thematic exploration of love within the structure of the poem; Lancelot here atones for his earlier fault, when he hesitated at the cart to expose himself to shame and ridicule for Guinevere's sake. It is probably significant that it was shortly after this episode that Chrétien left the work to be finished by Godefroi de Leigni.

ABOVE *Another scene from the later romance* Lancelot du Lac. *The Holy Grail appears to the Knights of the Round Table (Lancelot is sitting under the canopy), draped in samite so that they cannot see it clearly. This episode triggers off the Quest for the Holy Grail.*

RIGHT *Scenes from the life of Sir Galahad, son of Sir Lancelot. At the top left Galahad is knighted in a chapel; top right, he draws the sword from the magically floating stone before Camelot; bottom, he takes part in a tournament mêlée before Arthur and Guinevere.*

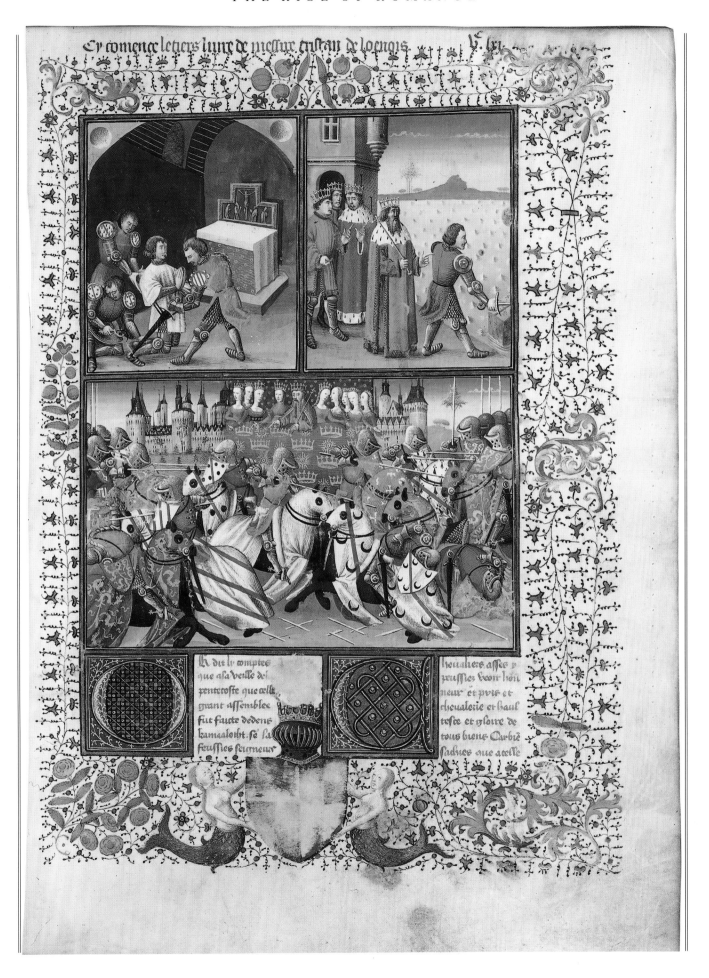

RAMON LULL – THE CODIFIER OF CHIVALRY

Ramon Lull's *Book of the Order of Chivalry* was probably the most popular treatise on the subject in the Middle Ages. It was translated into all the European languages and became the standard text, outside Germany. The author was an extraordinary man with a vast literary output, including manuals of instruction, debates and dialogues on the Christian faith, encyclopedic compendia on religious topics, theological treatises, mystical lyrics, and a religious romance, *Blanquerna*. As an eminent writer, and still more as a Christian missionary and martyr, Lull was venerated from his death in 1316 and we know an unusual amount about his remarkable life.

In 1229 King James I of Aragon recaptured Majorca from the Moors. Ramon Lull, the father of Ramon, fought in this expedition and was rewarded with numerous estates on the island. His wife Elisabet joined him shortly after; Ramon Lull, his only child, was born near Palma in about 1232. Of noble blood on both sides of his family and heir to considerable wealth, young Ramon seemed destined for a distinguished court career when he entered service in the King's household as a page at the age of about 14, and later became tutor to the King's younger son, Prince James. This relationship was to stand him in good stead all his life and he successively became the Prince's seneschal and majordomo (steward and chief household officer).

As a young man, Ramon was intensely interested in knightly pursuits, and wrote troubadour-style love poetry. He was a genial person, with lax morals. Though he married a lady named Blanca Picany in 1257 he was constantly unfaithful, and later remarked:

> "The beauty of women, O Lord, has been a plague and a tribulation to my eyes, for because of the beauty of women have I been forgetful of Thy great goodness and the beauty of Thy works."

One incident related that he was so enamoured of a lady that he followed her

ABOVE *Hermit instructing a squire. An illustration from Ramon Lull's* Book of the Order of Chivalry.

into a church to seduce her, still riding on his horse, and was ejected by an angry crowd.

One day in 1263 he was sitting in his room composing an amorous song when, glancing to his right, he saw a vision of Christ hanging on the cross. Ramon went to lie down until his composure was restored, but a week later the vision re-appeared. Ramon did not at first know what this visitation meant, but after the silent, suffering figure had appeared to him five times, he gave himself up to the will of God and underwent a complete change of life. After many days of deep thought, he resolved to devote himself to the conversion of those Muslims who still occupied part of Spain and all of North Africa. This enormous task, he thought, should be tackled in three ways: first by writing books in which arguments would overcome the false beliefs of the infidels, second by founding colleges to train missionaries who would convert the Muslims in person, and third by himself actively travelling to North Africa as a missionary and suffering a martyr's death in the cause of the Christian faith.

Ramon provided for his wife and his two children, then sold the rest of his estates and gave his wealth to the poor. He

began to write, and to learn Latin and Arabic. He produced his vast *Book of Contemplation*, the *Great Art* (of converting heathens), then the *Book of the Order of Chivalry* in 1275, followed by *Doctrine for Boys*, written for his young son, Dominic.

In 1276 his old friend and pupil, James II of Aragon, succeeded to the throne of Majorca and other territories. Almost at once, and probably as a result of Ramon's persuasion, he founded a missionary college at Miramar. Thirteen friars were to live there studying Arabic, then go forth and preach Christianity to the Moors. Ramon himself taught at the college for a time, but soon left for years of wanderings around Europe, soliciting help for missionary work from kings, princes and popes. He travelled to Paris, Bologna, Rome, Perpignan, Montpellier, Genoa and many other places. He made his first mission to North Africa in 1292. He arrived at the great city of Tunis, sought out the most learned men of the Muslim faith and offered to be converted to Islam if they could prove to him by argument that their faith was truer than his. Needless to say, he refuted all their arguments and began to convince them with his own. His success led to his denunciation to the Caliph, who had him banished.

On his second visit to North Africa, in 1307, his proceedings were less tactful; he appeared in the market-place of Bugia and shouted loudly that "the law of Christ is holy and true, and the sect of the Moors is false and wrong, and this I can prove". This resulted in a six-month imprisonment, but it did not deter him from returning for a third time, in 1314, when he was more than eighty years old. This time he took the precaution of bringing a letter of introduction and protection from his old friend, King James II of Aragon, to the King of Tunis. For a while he enjoyed peace and success; he held daily disputations and undertook preaching tours in surrounding villages. Then he left Tunis for the less tolerant atmosphere of Bugia, where early in 1316 he was beaten and stoned to death by an angry mob.

Within a few years of being written, almost all the great early French romances had been translated into German by a group of brilliant young knight-poets – *Tristan* by Eilhart von Oberg and later by Gottfried von Strassburg, *Eneit* by Heinrich von Veldeke, *Erec* and *Iwein* by Hartmann von Aue and, the greatest of them all, *Parzifal* by Wolfram von Eschenbach, written between 1198 and 1210.

Parzifal is of particular interest because at the beginning of the story its hero knows nothing of knighthood and has to learn, gradually, what it means to be a knight. In order to save him from the dangers of a knight's life, his mother, Herzeloyde, has brought him up in the depths of the forest far away from civilized life, and he has had no education. When he sees knights for the first time in their shining armour, he believes himself to be gazing upon gods. On learning the truth, his knightly ancestry makes him yearn to be a knight himself, and he leaves his mother to seek King Arthur. Though he quickly acquires a horse and a suit of armour, it is the moral and intellectual attainments of knighthood which are lacking in the young Parzifal; he behaves in a rude and boorish way, not thinking of the consequences of his actions and guided by little beyond his own desires. However, a wise old lord, Gurnemanz, undertakes to instruct Parzifal in the behaviour and principles fitting for a knight. He must have a strong sense of right and wrong, he must have compassion for the unfortunate, he must be generous, kind and humble. He must be free-handed but not a spendthrift. He must be discreet, truthful, in answering questions, always give mercy to his defeated opponents if they ask it; he must be manly and cheerful in spirit, courteous and honourable towards ladies, and (an interesting detail) clean and elegant in his person:

> "You will frequently have to wear armour. As soon as it is removed,
> see that you wash your hands and around your eyes to get the iron
> rust off. That way you will be of love's colour, and women's eyes will
> note that."

Gurnemanz then teaches Parzifal how to handle his horse and arms, something which does not come by nature even to one of knightly stock:

> "The way you came riding here to me! I have seen many a wall where
> I found the shield more properly hung than yours was around your
> neck. It is not too late: let us go out on the field and learn some skills."

Gurnemanz shows Parzifal "how to bring the horse out of the gallop with a sharp dig of the spurs, how to urge it to the charge by a pressure of the thighs, how to lower the spear properly, and how to bring up the shield in front against a spear thrust". Parzifal excels at once.

Chrétien's Gurnemanz at the same point fastens on the hero's spurs, girds his belt about his waist, and salutes him, saying, "I have given you with this sword the highest Order that God has created and ordained, which is the Order of Chivalry, which must be without villainy". This is an exaggerated version of a view which was clearly held by many knights. The idea that chivalry was a noble order in an almost mystical, quasi-religious sense, which had been ordained by God for the right regulation of society, was a

ABOVE *Scenes from Books Fourteen and Fifteen of Wolfram von Eschenbach's* Parzifal: *top, a feast to celebrate the betrothal of King Gramoflanz to Sir Gawain's sister Itonje; middle, Parzifal encounters his pagan half-brother Feirefiz and they do battle; bottom, Feirefiz and Parzifal reveal their names to one another and are reconciled.*

LEFT *The commander of Châteauneuf du Randon surrenders the keys to the town in 1380 to Bertrand du Guesclin, constable of France, who lies dying. An unromantic figure who had little use for the extravagant notions of knight-errantry, Du Guesclin was nevertheless the stuff of legends, and became the hero of a* roman *soon after his death.*

very important factor in the way knights saw themselves and their purpose.

It would certainly be a mistake, however, to give the impression that all medieval romances were literary masterpieces. For every Chrétien de Troyes or Wolfram von Eschenbach there were a dozen less gifted writers producing much less demanding, more "popular" products; the Jeffrey Archers and Robert Ludlums of medieval literature. These poems, too, have much to tell us about the way knights were seen. One of the most typical is the Middle English *Guy of Warwick*. The earliest surviving English version, probably composed between 1300 and 1325, is a clever adaptation of an Anglo-Norman original which is about a hundred years older. The poem was extremely popular, for reasons which are not now clear, and continued to be retold well into the nineteenth century as a children's story. Its opening section gives a classic account of a young knight's progress from tournaments to more serious involvement in warfare, echoing the earlier real-life career of William Marshal and prefiguring the instructions of Geoffrey de Chargny.

The first part of the poem describes the education of the hero; he falls in love with Felice, the daughter of his lord, the Earl of Warwick, and gradually realizes what he must do to prove himself worthy of her. Guy is the son of the

Earl's steward, and therefore Felice's social inferior. At the beginning of the story he is a naive young man. Though he is well-loved for his courtesy and generosity, all this squire has to recommend him to Felice are good looks and passionate devotion. He declares his love to Felice in an outpouring of enthusiastic romantic clichés; Felice pours the cold water of common sense onto the bonfire of Guy's passion and tells him to be off or she will reveal his presumption to her father. This does not prevent Guy from returning a short time later to renew his pleas, when the excess of his emotions causes him to swoon at her feet. Felice, regarding the prostrate form of Guy, begins to relent and when he awakes she informs him that:

> "No man may I love,
> Unless he be truly a knight ...
> ... when thou hast undertaken arms,
> and I have heard of it,
> Then thou shalt have my love,
> If thou be such as I think thee."

Felice, impressed at last by Guy's determination, perceives that whether he is of lowly birth or not, he possesses qualities which may make him a suitable match for her. She wants him to be the best knight, a man who, living in accordance with the knightly code, will become its perfect embodiment, famed for his strength and bravery.

Unfortunately Guy understands her to mean that he has only to be knighted and the improvement in rank will make him worthy of her. Re-

BELOW *The heroes of medieval romance did not allow scruples to deflect the physical consummation of their love. Here Sir Lancelot is tricked into sleeping with the daughter of the king of Norgalles, believing her to be his true love Queen Guinevere (the wife of his overlord King Arthur). This is how Sir Galahad was conceived; his illegitimacy brought no stain upon his knightly perfection.*

covering from his love-sickness with astonishing speed, he sets off to court to ask Earl Rohaut to knight him. After the ceremony, he returns to Felice and claims her love in accordance with her promise. Felice informs him that he has only the name of knight; he must now go and earn himself a reputation that shows him to be worthy of it. Guy's first attempts to prove himself show that his idea of knighthood is still somewhat limited. He spends a year travelling round Europe attending tournaments, winning the prize at each, gaining friends and a reputation for courtesy and generosity as well as for prowess. At the end of his successful year Guy again returns to claim Felice's love, but once again he has underestimated her exacting standard. In fact, he has just done well enough to show how much better he could do if he really applied himself, and Felice declares that she is unwilling to hinder him from achieving his great potential. Guy himself is not convinced that he can ever attain this peerless eminence but he sets out on his travels once more. Soon he begins to be drawn into more serious adventures, in which he is fighting in real wars for the sake of justice and championing the oppressed. First he helps a certain Duke Segyn, wrongfully accused of murdering his lord's nephew, and reconciles the quarrelling lords after many brave deeds of arms. Then he comes to the relief of the Emperor Ernis, the Greek or Byzantine emperor, besieged by Saracens. For his third adventure he returns to Europe to restore the lost inheritance of his friend Tirri. In each of these adventures Guy asks the advice of his older and wiser friend, Heraud. Asked whether he thinks it will be a good idea to aid Duke Segyn, Heraud replies:

> "I give counsel, and good it is;
> A man shall do well to help those
> That have greatest need of help.
> For fame and renown you shall win there,
> And praise for yourself and all your kin."

Heraud appears here rather like an actor's agent, telling him which parts will further his career, which parties to attend and which premieres to be seen at. The implication of his advice is that, whatever the merits of the case, it is better for one's reputation to champion the underdog. Later, and rather more sure of his own mind, Guy asks Heraud about the relief of Emperor Ernis:

> "Heraud, my friend, will we go?
> ... Into Constantinople I will go
> To help the emperor in his troubles,
> Who is besieged by the Sultan.
> Men of that country say
> That the land is destroyed and men cast down,
> And Christendom greatly damaged."

These selected passages show that one of the themes of *Guy of Warwick* is the same preoccupation with what a good knight should be and do that we have seen in other romances, and though some of the stylistic features of this popular poem, such as the sing-song rhymes, the well-worn, clichéd descriptions, the tedious and repetitious battle-sequences, made it the butt of Chaucer's devastating satire on romance, *Sir Thopas*, at heart it shares the same concerns and the same ideological background as its greater predecessors.

Before we consider treatises and manuals of instruction on knighthood, it is worth pointing out an aspect of the romances that often escapes the attention of modern readers: their sense of humour. Knights and courtly society in general enjoyed reading about the characters and exploits of heroes like Lancelot, but that did not mean that they were unaware of the absurd aspects of their lover-like behaviour. Even Chrétien's *Lancelot* contains moments in which the hero's feelings are so extreme as to topple over into comedy, such as when he glimpses Guinevere from an upstairs window and is transported with joy, only to be plunged into a suicidal gloom as soon as she is out of his sight. Lancelot toys with the idea of throwing himself out of the window; luckily the sensible Gawain is at hand to hold him back and remind him of his duty.

Chrétien is not above having a little fun at the expense of the romance convention of magical gifts. Lancelot and his companions are lured into a castle and trapped between the gate and the portcullis. However, Lancelot has a magic ring, given to him by the fairy Lady of the Lake who reared him, with the property that whoever gazes at its stone will be freed from any enchantment. Lancelot accordingly gazes at the ring and begs the Lady to help him. A delicious anticlimax follows:

> But after appealing to her and gazing upon the ring, he realises that there is no enchantment here, but that they are actually shut in and confined.

Parzifal also contains a scene which brings the required behaviour of romantic lovers into the realms of comedy. Parzifal catches sight of three drops of blood on the snowy ground. This reminds him forcibly of the complexion of his beloved wife, Condwiramurs, and he immediately falls into a trance-like state of adoration. Unfortunately he is close to where King Arthur and his knights are encamped with their armies, about to go to war, and Parzifal has halted in his saddle with his lance held upright, an attitude expressing a hostile challenge. Sir Segramors and then Sir Keie both attempt to joust with Parzifal, who ignores them completely until some accident removes the blood drops from his line of vision, upon which he responds to his attackers ferociously – both are unhorsed, and Keie's arm and leg broken. After each encounter Parzifal returns to his contemplation of the blood on the snow. Fortunately the next knight to appear is the quick-witted Gawain, who instantly realizes that Parzifal is in a love-trance, and brings him out of it by draping a yellow scarf over the blood drops. Parzifal is then able to converse like a rational person.

A masterly comic treatment of romantic love can be found in the Provencal romance *Flamenca*. The hero has fallen in love with a beautiful lady whose jealous husband keeps her locked up in a tower and only releases her to attend church on Sundays, when she is concealed behind a screen. The hero pretends to be a priest so that he can talk to the lady, but they can only say two words each Sunday, as he hands her the sacramental host. Nevertheless, within a few weeks of these blasphemous, clandestine conversations they have arranged an assignation.

No real knight is likely to have behaved like the paragons of knightly virtue portrayed in the romances, nor would he ever have to contend with malicious dwarfs, bridges made of sword-blades, magical beds which burst

ABOVE *The knight-poet Wolfram von Eschenbach, author of the German masterpiece* Parzifal, *from the Manessa Codex.*

into flame in the middle of the night, or any of the other supernatural paraphernalia which abound in romances. But the fact that this kind of reading material was popular has much to tell us about the self-image and the aspirations of contemporary knights, which is also borne out in non-fictional books which knights wrote about themselves.

KNIGHTLY NON-FICTION

The instructions given by Gurnemanz to Perceval in Chrétien's poem clearly influenced the ideas expressed in *L'Ordene de Chevalerie*, which we looked at in the previous chapter. The prose *Lancelot* of the Vulgate Cycle elaborated further, when the Lady of the Lake explains to the young Lancelot that knights first came into being as a sort of divinely-appointed police force, when envy and greed corrupted the world.

> "They were the tall and strong, the handsome and robust, the loyal, the valiant and the bold ... A knight must be merciful without wickedness, affable without treachery, compassionate towards the suffering, and openhanded. He must be ready to help the needy and to confound robbers and murderers, a just judge without favour or hate. He must prefer death to dishonour. He must protect Holy
> Church for she cannot defend herself."

The Lady further explains the significance of each item in a knight's equipment, including his horse, which symbolized the people who must support the knight by providing him with his livelihood, just as his horse must carry him.

The symbolic meanings of the knight's equipment, the origins of the "order" of knighthood, and the true character of a knight, are all reflected in the many treatises on chivalry which have survived the Middle Ages. By far the most popular of these was written by the Spanish knight, poet, and later missionary, Ramon Lull, in about 1275 – the *Book of the Order of Chivalry* (*Libre del ordre de cavayleria*). Like the *Ordene*, this opens in the form of a story, in which a young squire is riding through a forest on his way to be knighted. He strays from the path but then comes across an old hermit. The hermit, who was once himself a noble knight, questions the squire about knighthood, and finds him (like the young Parzifal) ignorant of its true nature and its high purpose. He begins to instruct the squire, reading from a little book which he then presents to him so that he can in turn instruct other aspirants to knighthood.

This is the "Book" referred to in the title. It begins with a history of chivalry, which is very like the account given by the Lady of the Lake to Lancelot. The tone is that of the dedicated enthusiast and teacher; its message is that there is more to knighthood than military prowess – the ethics of chivalry are of crucial importance, too much neglected in the author's own day, and should be taught in schools. The book next discusses the duties of the knight: first, to defend his faith and protect the Holy Church, second to defend his lord and protect the weak, including women, widows and orphans. A knight should keep himself ready for action by continuous exercise, by hunting, and by attending jousts and tournaments. He should accept office in secular government if the king chooses him, and he should

ABOVE *Not all marriages were matters of contractual convenience. Here a knight and his lady set down a permanent record of their love, in the most romantic tomb effigy in Europe, the Greene Monument at Lowick. Evidence that romantic love influenced real-life relationships.*

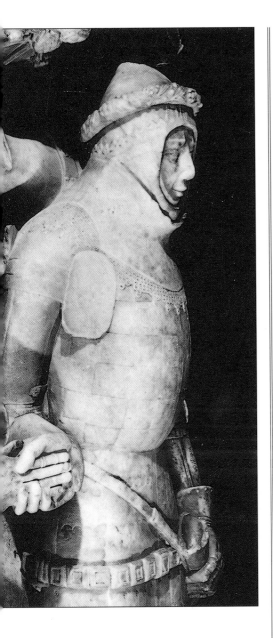

act as judge or magistrate in local justice courts. It is his duty to pursue criminals and bring them to justice.

The next chapter is based around the idea that every candidate for knighthood should be examined to determine whether he is worthy of it. A squire wishing to become a knight must first of all be fit and healthy, of a proper age, must be of good family and in possession of a patrimony large enough to support him in the rank of knight. He must also possess courage and honour, and must hold an untarnished reputation. His reasons for wishing to become a knight are to be carefully examined – they must be honourable and must not proceed from worldly ambition or vanity.

An account of the actual knighting ceremony follows, which differs from that given in the *Ordene de Chevalerie* in that it must take place in church and be attended by religious preparations and lengthy sermons on the Christian faith. The actual dubbing, however, is to be bestowed by a knight, not by a priest. A long explanation of the symbolism of each piece of armour and equipment follows, then a chapter on knightly vices and virtues, a chapter on the customs of knighthood and a concluding chapter on the honour that should be done to a knight.

Successive treatments elaborating on the same theme continued to be popular throughout the Middle Ages, as in the *Livre de chevalerie/Book of Chivalry* written in the early 1350s by Geoffrey de Chargny. He was an eminent French knight, lord of several great estates, member of the Order of the Star, and bearer in battle and on state occasions of the Oriflamme, the sacred banner of St Denis. He was killed at the Battle of Poitiers in 1356.

Geoffrey de Chargny's work gives a clear picture of the stages in advancement of a good knightly career. As a boy the knight will have enjoyed listening to the tales of the high deeds of old in romances; after proper training he will seek fame and honour in achievement at tournaments, travelling all over Europe to attend and compete with the noblest and most skilled. As soon as he can, he should advance to the real business of knighthood and take part in genuine warfare. He should have studied military treatises which open to him the science of taking castles by siege, or the tactics of pitched battle. To serve one's lord in war at home is the first stage of honourable achievement in arms, but the highest praise is deserved by those who have travelled abroad and fought in distant lands. A knight must never be satisfied with what he has done, but should always wish to achieve more, and he who achieves more is more worthy. It is good for a knight to be in love, for love will spur him on to yet higher achievement because of the honour it will do his lady. A knight should be modest about his achievements; if he is successful, he will be wise to attribute this to the aid of God and the Blessed Virgin. In spite of the importance which Geoffrey attaches to worldly glory as a reward of knighthood, he unambiguously declares that a life in arms regulated by sound chivalric values will be rewarded with eternal rest in paradise.

This is the ethical and ideological background against which the words and deeds of real knights must be seen. We will look in the next chapter at the relationship between knights and the Church, and in this context it is important to remember how confident knights felt about their role in society as a just protector and upholder of law, and how closely they related knightly virtues to Christian principles.

CHAPTER THREE

CHURCH AND KNIGHT

The early Church's attitude to warfare was explicit: killing people, even in battle, was a sin and no Christian could be excused its consequences. In the first three centuries after Christ, this could mean a severe public penance lasting for several years.

THE CHURCH IN EUROPE: KNIGHTS AND PRIESTS

In the fifth century St Augustine evolved the concept of the "just" war and thereafter, particularly in strife-torn medieval Europe, the Church recognized that there were circumstances in which homicide was not only excusable but every Christian's duty. Charlemagne and his successors exacted feudal levies from bishops and abbots, and it was not unknown for churchmen to fight in person – the ferocious Archbishop Turpin in the *Chanson de Roland* had his counterparts in real life, such as Geoffrey, Bishop of Coutances, and Odo, Bishop of Bayeux, who fought in the army of Duke William of Normandy at the Battle of Hastings in 1066.

The consolidation and extension of ecclesiastical power during the eleventh and twelfth centuries affected the knightly class as well as all other parts of society. The Church attempted over a long period to control the often destructive energies of knighthood, partly by legislature and prohibition,

A TEMPLAR AND A HOSPITALLER, C. 1250

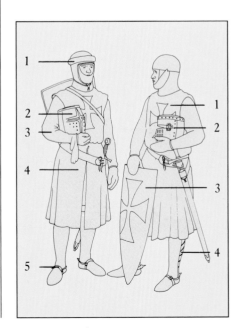

The Templar (on the left) is wearing a padded arming cap (1), on which his helm (2) will rest. His mail hauberk (3) is now worn over a padded undercoat called a gambeson, and under the surcoat (4) of the Order – white, with a red cross on the breast. The loose, knee-length garment is split to the waist at front and back for ease when riding. He has mail leggings and prick spurs (5).

The Hospitaller wears the black surcoat (1) with white cross which was adopted by the Order in 1248; in 1259 this was changed to a red surcoat with white cross. He wears a simple round helmet (2) over his mail coif. Shields (3) have by this time grown shorter and more triangular in shape. The mail leggings (4) are laced behind the knight's calves.

ABOVE *Melchisedech offers the host to Abraham, dressed as a thirteenth-century knight; statues on Reims Cathedral bear witness to the ecclesiastical view of ideal knighthood and its relationship to the Church.*

more successfully by directing martial energies to ecclesiastical ends and by taking over the rituals and ceremonies of knighthood. On the whole, however, the knights resisted this process and continued to justify their existence and their activities in largely secular terms.

It is worth pausing to consider the normal state of affairs between Church and knight. In the society of the Middle Ages, the two were closer to each other than the frequent fulminations of churchmen would lead us to suppose, for both had an interest in preserving the stable order of society. Knights throughout the Middle Ages regarded themselves as equal partners with the Church in performing the important tasks of local government and administration; it was their job to sit as judges in secular courts. No matter how bitter the quarrels between individual prelates and lords might be, they united immediately against the threat of social insurrection from the labouring classes, on whom both depended for their livelihood.

The important officers of the Church were almost all drawn from the same class as knights, that is the land-holders. Whether these were counts, dukes, princes or simple families holding one estate with sufficient revenue to maintain the rank of knight, all land-holders had, essentially, the same interests and felt a class solidarity. The Church offered an honourable career for younger sons and for superfluous daughters of land-holding families. Knights might often have one or more brothers in a monastery or in the priesthood, and history gives us many examples of great lords relying on their relatives, who held high ecclesiastical office, for support. An example is Stephen of Blois, whose brother Henry was the powerful and influential Bishop of Winchester and who usually worked for his brother's cause in the dispute with Empress Matilda over the throne of England.

It is difficult now for us to comprehend the religious sensibilities of a medieval person or to realize quite how important the Church was in everybody's lives. Particularly in the later Middle Ages, with the proliferation of religious orders, no one could walk far without coming across a church, monastery, friary or priory. Every country parish had a church with its parish priest, every city its bishop. Prosperous towns supported a large number of religious communities, and in cities cathedrals were built more splendid than many princes' palaces. Almost all religious foundations had been granted their initial endowments by secular lords, and grew and thrived on continued gifts of money and land.

The Church had its own courts and laws, and a significant hold over education. By far the majority of literate people were clerics of some sort (hence the "benefit of clergy" rule, which meant that an accused man could exempt himself from trial in the secular judicial system if he could prove that he could read). The Church was heavily involved in local and national government. It wielded the power to enforce moral dictums, and its influence over the daily life of every member of medieval society was enormous. Even the most godless of lords were known to undergo sudden repentance and set off on pilgrimage barefoot, or to donate vast sums of money to their chosen monastery.

The Church was a great landlord – many knights held their lands from abbeys or monasteries, and their feudal overlords were abbots or bishops. The closeness and mutual benefit of the knights' relationship with the Church can be seen in surviving medieval churches, where tomb

effigies, stained glass windows, family monuments with banners and achievements, painted altar-pieces, all testify to the importance of piety in the knight's self-image. In addition, penitent or grateful knights donated gifts of plate to church treasuries, or sometimes paid for an entire chapel or a new roof to the church itself.

Another important way in which the Church influenced knights was by the grandeur of church ceremonial, which its rich embroidered robes, incense, awe-inspiring solemnity and sacred objects invested with spiritual significance. This was certainly an unconscious influence, since most of the complaints of churchmen against knights criticize them for their love of finery and the vanity of their self-aggrandizement. There can be no doubt that knights were fascinated by rich robes and solemn rituals. The rituals they devised for themselves – dubbing ceremonies, vowing ceremonies, ceremonial banquets, the ceremonies associated with tournaments – became more and more elaborate as time went by, but must initially have been inspired by the richness of high masses sung at cathedrals, or by state weddings and investitures which they had witnessed.

The willingness of knights to co-operate with the Church's efforts to contribute to, and increasingly to control, its rituals was related to the Church's ability to enhance the honour of knighthood. Many knights were clearly extremely pious, but they retained on the whole a strong sense of their own place and value in the scheme of things, independent of the Church's views.

THE PEACE AND TRUCE OF GOD

The first evidence of a serious campaign by the Church to reform and control the knights of Europe is the ecclesiastical legislation known as the Peace of God and the Truce of God. Enacted between 990 and 1048, these laws were made in response to social conditions which threatened the peace and stability of the community at large, including the Church. The principal source of this disruption was the endless petty wars between rival lords, mainly conducted as a series of guerrilla raids on the territories of their opponents. Parties of armed, mounted men would descend on a village, or

PREACHING THE CRUSADE

The techniques which had been pioneered by Urban II in his first call to arms on behalf of the Church became standard for his successors. The bulk of the work was done on tours by major prelates, preaching sermons which were designed to move their listeners to take the cross. Urban's own sermon was never bettered, just elaborated on. It relied on three strong appeals. First, to move the listener's anger at the injustices and outrages resulting from the occupation of the Holy City by the infidel Turks; second, to make him dissatisfied with his own life, as sinful or dull and leading to damnation; and third, to offer him the way to salvation by fighting against the enemies of God. Urban himself under-took a tour of France after the initial success of Clermont, preaching at Nimes, Tours, Rouen and many other towns and cities, meeting with princes and lords to urge them personally to raise troops for the great enterprise.

Some who joined the crusades were openly cynical, like the poet Aymer de Pegulhan, who expressed himself delight-ed at the opportunity to earn salvation for doing what he liked best:

> Behold! Without renouncing our rich garments, our station in life, all that pleases and charms, we can obtain honour down here and joy in paradise.

But many responded simply and directly to the exhortations of the preachers. Talented preachers, who could arouse genuine enthusiasm, were more success-ful, as is clear from the contemporary accounts of the preaching of the Second Crusade. King Louis VII of France was unable to inspire his nobles to join him in taking the crusading vow, but when he had enlisted the help of the brilliant Bernard of Clairvaux, he was over-whelmed with volunteers.

We are fortunate in having a detailed record of one such tour of recruitment for a crusading army: that of Gerald of Wales, who accompanied Baldwin, Archbishop of Canterbury, on a tour of Wales in 1188, summoning soldiers of Christ to fight with Richard the Lionheart in the Third Cru-sade. Gerald was the son and grandson of Norman knights, and his two brothers were also knights. Gerald himself had been encouraged from an early age to enter the Church, where he was never quite as successful as his natural talents and excellent connections promised.

Gerald, according to his own account, was handsome and clever, a witty conversationalist and a great Latin stylist with several popular books to his name. His works certainly show a man of insa-tiable curiosity, and his *Journey through Wales* is not so much an account of preaching the cross as a collection of anec-dotes on all kinds of subjects – history, folklore, the behaviour of animals, the clothes, language and customs of the local people, weather, demons and incubi and their relations with men, beautiful scenery, family backgrounds, practical jokes; any interesting natural or supernatural phe-nomena that came to his attention.

Nevertheless, we can learn much about preaching the crusade from Gerald's de-lightful book. He and Archbishop Bald-win travelled through Wales for about six weeks in March and April 1188. Besides

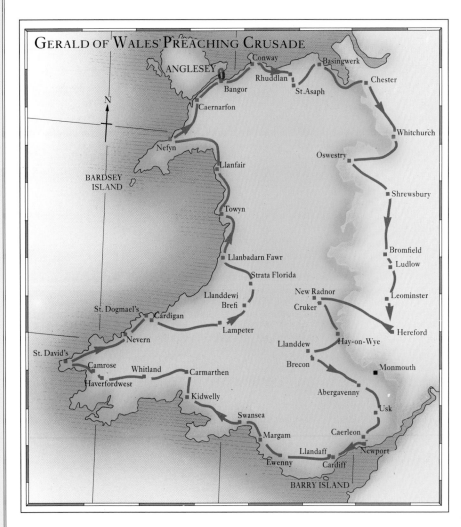

LEFT *A Victorian engraving of Pope Urban II preaching the First Crusade to the assembled crowds at Clermont. In fact the size of the crowds obliged the Pope to make his address in a field outside the town.*

to set an example to others. Next came Einion, Prince of Elfael, who first asked permission from his father-in-law the Lord Rhys ap Gruffydd, the ruler of South Wales. Rhys's own intentions of going on crusade were frustrated, according to Gerald:

> Rhys himself went home quite determined to make the holy journey as soon as the Archbishop should have entered his own territory. The result was that for nearly a fortnight he applied himself with great energy to all the preparations necessary for so long a journey, collecting pack-animals and sumpter-saddles, persuading other men to go with him and raising funds. Then his wife Gwenllian, daughter of Madog ... put a sudden stop to his noble intentions by playing upon his weakness and exercising her womanly charms.

It is obvious that going on crusade was not popular with the wives and families of the fighting men; Gerald tells how, "After the sermon which was given at Hay, we saw a great number of men who wanted to take the Cross come running towards the castle where the Archbishop was; leaving their cloaks behind in the hands of the wives and friends who had tried to hold them back."

Not all the recruits were noblemen, or even ordinary freemen. Gerald was surprised when, after the Archbishop's sermon at Usk, "some of the most notorious criminals of those parts were converted, robbers, highwaymen and murderers." (This is perhaps not so surprising in view of the crusader's immunity from prosecution.) There were also churchmen who took the cross; besides Gerald himself, who was an archdeacon, Peter de Leia, the Bishop of St David's, and Gwion, Bishop of Bangor, both made the vow to travel to Jerusalem. Some men who were too old to go on crusade in person donated money instead, like Cador of Swansea. It was understood that this, too, earned a remission of penance for the donor, just as if he had actually gone on crusade.

giving public sermons exhorting people to take the cross, they had many meetings and interviews with the most important lords and princes of the area. Only one, Owain Cyfeiliog of Powys, failed to appear for his appointed meeting, and as a punishment he was excommunicated. Their efforts were clearly successful:

> We worked very hard to make a success of our mission. About three thousand men were signed with the Cross, all of them highly skilled in the use of the spear and the arrow, most experienced in military affairs and only too keen to attack the enemies of our faith at the first opportunity. They were all sincerely and warmly committed to Christ's service.

The first person to take the cross, at Archbishop Baldwin's first public sermon in Bangor, was Gerald himself, which, he says, was done after mature reflection,

even on a monastery, burn the buildings, kill anyone who resisted, and steal or slaughter their livestock. Even worse were the "robber barons", who held strongly fortified castles and simply extorted goods from the communities of the surrounding countryside by force.

In the first instance, raiding parties engaged in "war" on behalf of their lord had no scruples about attacking churches, monasteries or convents. These had often been endowed or supported by their enemy, and damage done to them constituted damage done to him, just as if they were any other part of his property. The epic *Raoul de Cambrai* makes this clear in a passage in which its "hero", raging against his enemies, the sons of Herbert de Vermandois, instructs his knights:

> "Take arms in haste! Four hundred of you ride speedily and reach Origny before nightfall. Spread my tent in the middle of the church; let my pack-horses be tethered in the porches; prepare my food beneath the vaults, fasten my falcons on the golden crosses and make ready a rich bed before the altar where I may lie. I will lean against the crucifix and deliver the nuns up to my squires. I mean to destroy the place and ruin it utterly because the sons of Herbert hold it so dear."

In the poem, Raoul, driven to the verge of insanity by his hatred, is an exaggerated portrait of the kind of behaviour which all too often resulted from the reprisals and counter-reprisals of a blood-feud. There can be no doubt that in these private wars it was the peasantry who suffered all the consequences of these attacks and were their principal victims. Jacques de Vitry, a preacher in the 1220s, described how "the noble knight devours in an hour all that which it has taken the peasant a year of hard labour to produce. Not content with the spoils of war, nor with his revenues and taxes, he further despoils his subjects by heavy demands and illegal extortions. The poor are exhausted, the fruits of their pain and sorrow stolen from them".

Where the authority of the monarch was too weak to enforce discipline on the rapacious or war-mongering knights, as in France, or where it was weakened by civil war, as in England in the 1240s between Stephen of Blois and the Empress Matilda, the civilian population was at the mercy of the lawless and the greedy. The Laud Chronicle explains how during the troubled reign of King Stephen:

> ...every great man built him castles and held them against the king...By night and by day they seized those whom they believed to have any wealth, whether they were men or women, and in order to get their gold or silver, they put them into prison and tortured them with unspeakable tortures, for never were any martyrs tortured as they were...I am not able to tell of all the atrocities or cruelties which they wrought upon the unhappy people of this country. It lasted throughout the nineteen years that Stephen was king, and grew always worse and worse. At regular intervals they levied a tax, known as "tenserie" (protection money) upon the villages. When the wretched people had no more to give, they plundered and burned all the villages, so that you could easily go a day's journey without ever finding a village inhabited or a field cultivated. Then was corn dear, and flesh and cheese and butter, for there was none in the land...
> ...Contrary to custom, they spared neither church nor churchyard, but seized everything of value that was in it, and afterwards burned the church and all it contained. They spared not the lands of bishops, nor of abbots, nor

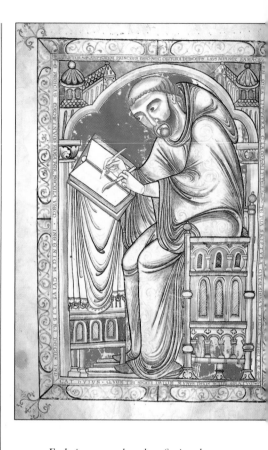

ABOVE *Eadwine, a monk and professional scribe from Canterbury. In the days when literacy was the almost exclusive preserve of clerics, every knight needed to employ the services of at least one in his household. Ideally he would have an almoner, secretary and accountant in addition to his own chaplain.*

of priests, but plundered the monks and the clergy; and every man who
could robbed his neighbour. If two or three men came riding towards a
village, all the villagers fled for fear of them, believing they were robbers.
The bishops and the clergy were forever cursing them, but that was nothing
to them, for they were all excommunicated and forsworn and lost.

The Peace of God and the Truce of God were designed to counter-act such
abuses. The Peace of God was supposed to protect non-combatants, and
the Truce of God to prevent hostilities at certain times. In 989, the
Council of Charroux pronounced that anyone who robbed churches or
attacked an unarmed member of the clergy or stole from peasants would
be excommunicated. The order was soon extended to include merchants,
and in addition prohibited certain acts such as destroying vineyards or
mills. The Truce of God began modestly by reviving one of the
capitularies of Charlemagne, which had forbidden the prosecution of
blood-feuds on Sundays. By the time the Council of Nice sat in 1041, this
had been extended to include Easter and other feast days, and war-making
and plundering were forbidden from Thursday to Sunday inclusive.

The intention was that lords and knights should enter into a pact in
which they would swear a formal oath to observe these restrictions. In
practice, of course, they frequently refused to do so. They regarded the
legislation as unwarrantable interference in their own affairs and there
were many, including even some members of the clergy, who criticized the
Church for assuming a task which clearly related more to secular than to
spiritual matters. It was a bold move for the Church to try to subject
knights directly to its own authority, going over the head of secular
authorities and by-passing secular law-enforcement, such as it was. But
this was the beginning of a period which saw the Church claiming to
assert ultimate temporal as well as spiritual authority in Christendom and
becoming increasingly involved in the struggle for political power.

The movement for the reform of secular authority by the Church,
which produced the Peace and Truce of God, was merely a tentative first
step towards the revolutionary views put forward by Pope Gregory VII.
An outspoken and powerful personality, he claimed uncompromisingly
that all laymen, from peasant to monarch, were subject to the central
authority of the papacy and must serve its interests in every sphere of life.
Knights, said Gregory, were "the vassals of St Peter", and if the interests
of the Church conflicted with the interests of his secular lord, it was a
knight's duty to obey the Church first and foremost.

Pope Gregory completed the transformation of ecclesiastical pacifism
to militancy. Earlier popes, such as Pope Leo IV in 853, had appealed
for military support against the Saracens, the enemies of God and the
Church. Gregory enthusiastically envisaged leading an army in person to
the aid of the Christians of the Eastern Empire against the Turks, and to
liberate Jerusalem. Instead, he became embroiled in a bitter quarrel with
Emperor Henry IV over who should control the investiture of bishops in
the German Empire. He excommunicated Henry and invited other
applicants for the post of Emperor. Henry retaliated by declaring him
deposed and created an alternative Pope – Clement III, a sixteen-year-
old relative. With the Imperial army at his command, Henry captured
Rome itself in order to install Clement. Gregory meanwhile retreated behind

the massive walls of the fortress of Sant' Angelo and summoned to his aid the army of Robert Guiscard, the Norman adventurer who had conquered southern Italy and Sicily. Robert repulsed Henry and released the Pope. Eventually a compromise over investitures was reached, which meant in effect that the Pope had triumphed. But he had done more than that; he claimed, for the first time, that knights fighting for him against the accursed emperor would be rewarded with St Peter's blessing, "in this life and the life to come".

THE FIRST CRUSADE

Pilgrims had travelled to Jerusalem to worship at the scenes of Christ's life and death for centuries, and they continued to do so long after

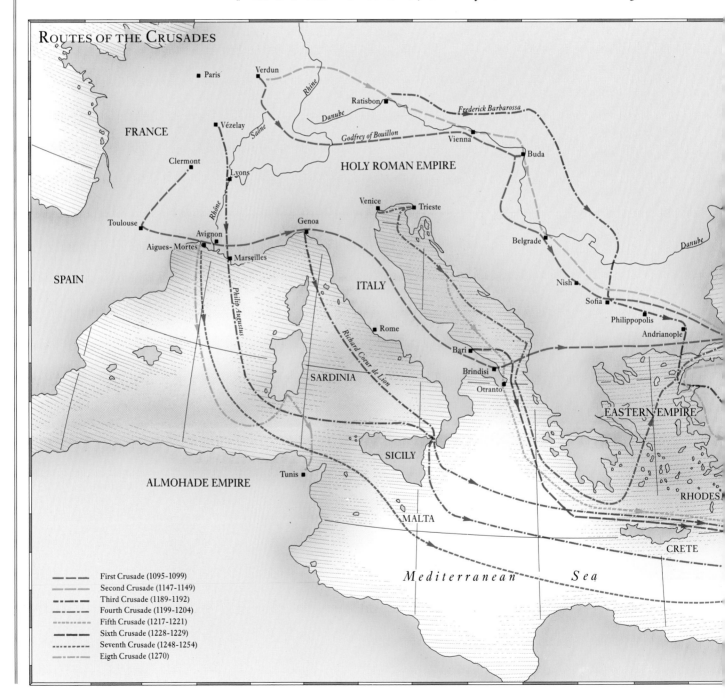

ROUTES OF THE CRUSADES

First Crusade (1095-1099)
Second Crusade (1147-1149)
Third Crusade (1189-1192)
Fourth Crusade (1199-1204)
Fifth Crusade (1217-1221)
Sixth Crusade (1228-1229)
Seventh Crusade (1248-1254)
Eigth Crusade (1270)

Jerusalem had been captured by the Arabs. A Christian community was permitted to remain in Jerusalem; Harun-al-Rashid, the famous Caliph of Baghdad featured in *The Thousand and One Nights*, acknowledged the right of Christians to maintain the Church of the Holy Sepulchre and made it over to Charlemagne, with whom he conducted a long and amicable correspondence. The status quo was disrupted, however, on the appearance of the Seljuk Turks in the eleventh century. Fanatical converts to Islam, they quickly conquered much of the Arab territories of Asia Minor. They also conquered many provinces belonging to the Byzantine Empire. This was the descendant of the eastern half of the old Roman Empire, ruled by its emperor from Constantinople, and its people practised eastern-style Greek Orthodox Christianity.

Jerusalem was captured in 1071 by the Seljuks, the same year in which the Sultan Alp Arslan won a decisive victory over the Byzantine Emperor Romanus IV Diogenes and his vast army at Manzikert. Thereafter, Christian pilgrims to the Holy Places might be arrested, imprisoned, even sold as slaves. It was reports of these abuses which inspired Pope Gregory VII in his desire to lead a Christian army to the rescue of Jerusalem.

In the event, a more roundabout route led to the First Crusade. The Byzantine Emperor, Alexius Comnenus, who had ascended the throne in 1081, was determined to recover the lost provinces from the Seljuks but found his resources unequal to the task. During the 1080s and 1090s he wrote to the Pope and to numerous great lords and princes of the west, requesting them to raise armies and come to Constantinople. The Byzantine Empire, he argued, must be preserved against the inroads of the Turks, to protect the objects and places which were sacred to eastern and western Christians alike. One of his letters, written in 1093 to Count Robert of Flanders, has survived. It contains an extraordinary mixture of enticements and appeals. He begins by describing in detail some of the atrocities committed by the Turks:

> I shall merely describe a very few of them ... the enemy has the habit of circumcizing young Christians and babies above the baptismal font ... Then they are forced to urinate into the font ... Those who refuse are tortured and put to death. They carry off noble matrons and their daughters and abuse them like animals ... Then, too, the Turks shamelessly commit the sin of sodomy on our men of all ages and all ranks ... and, O misery, something that has never been seen or heard before, on bishops ...

He explains that Constantinople itself is now threatened by the evil Turks, and that it must never fall into the hands of the pagans because of all the important relics in the city. "It would be better that Constantinople falls into your hands than into the hands of the pagans", he remarks, and adds that besides the holy relics the city is crammed with gold and treasures. "In your coming you will find your reward in heaven," he tells Robert, "and if you do not come, God will condemn you". Alexius thought of the Franks as little better than barbarians, however, as is clear from his parting injunction:

> If all this glory is not sufficient for you, remember that you will find all those treasures and also the most beautiful women of the East. The incomparable

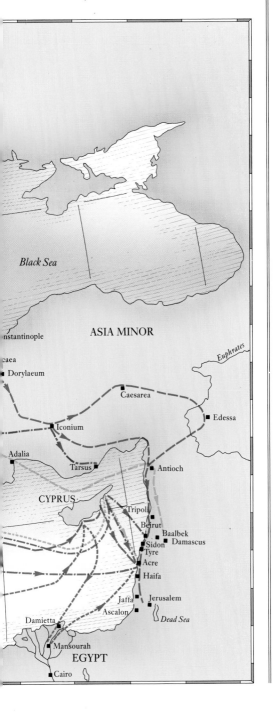

BELOW *The vision of establishing Christian rule in the lands where Christ had lived, inspired eight Crusades. The knights and soldiers who crossed Europe were often genuinely motivated by piety though some were certainly more interested in acquiring territory.*

Black Sea

ASIA MINOR

nstantinople

caea

Dorylaeum

Caesarea

Euphrates

Iconium

Edessa

Adalia

Tarsus

Antioch

CYPRUS

Tripoli

Beirut

Baalbek

Sidon   Damascus

Tyre

Acre

Haifa

Jaffa   Jerusalem

Damietta

Ascalon

Dead Sea

Mansourah

EGYPT

Cairo

beauty of Greek women would seem to be a sufficient reason to attract the
armies of the Franks to the plains of Thrace.

Pope Urban II was deeply moved by his letter (which presumably did not
contain the parts about beautiful women) and saw that the threatened
destruction of the Christian Byzantine Empire would be an appalling
disaster. He was concerned about the atrocities perpetrated by the Turks, but
equally he was concerned about the depredations of Christian knights in
their own countries. He therefore sought to unite the quarrelling lords
behind one great cause, under the leadership and authority of the Church.
He determined to carry out his predecessor's plan to provide military aid to
the beleaguered Christians of the East, and set in motion one of the most
extraordinary events in the history of western Europe.

Texts of his main speech and news of his intentions had been circulated
through the courts of Europe, and advance notice was given of his visit to
Clermont, in November 1095. This was a council of bishops and other
prelates, at which church business was conducted. Among this business,
Urban confirmed yet again the Peace and Truce of God. On the 27th of
November he addressed himself directly and publicly to the people. Such a
large crowd had gathered that his address had to be made outside the city in a
field. He, too, began by enlisting the sympathies of his audience, exciting
their sense of outrage by giving grisly details of the atrocities committed by
the Turks against Christians, and their contempt for, and defilement of, the
holiest shrines of Christianity. Urban was a Frenchman, and according to
Robert the Monk, his message was aimed specifically at the Franks:

> Who shall avenge these wrongs, who shall recover these lands if not you? You
> are the race upon whom God has bestowed glory in arms, greatness of spirit,
> physical energy, and the courage to humble the proud locks of those who
> resist you ... O most valiant knights, descendants of unconquerable
> ancestors, remember the courage of your forefathers and do not dishonour
> them!

According to another chronicler, Balderic, the inspired Pope did indeed
address himself especially to the knights, but in a somewhat less com-
plimentary style:

> You, girt about with the badge of knighthood, are arrogant with great pride;
> you rage against your brothers and cut each other in pieces. The true
> soldiery of Christ does not rend asunder the sheepfold of the Redeemer ...
> you, the oppressors of orphans, the plunderers of widows; you guilty of
> homicide, of sacrilege, robbers of others' rights; you who await the pay of
> thieves for shedding of Christian blood – as vultures smell fetid corpses, so
> do you sense battles from afar and rush to them eagerly.

But the knights had a chance to redeem themselves; the Truce of God in the
west could be observed by fighting a holy war in the east. And at this point
Urban gave full expression to the revolutionary concept of the crusading
indulgence – those who fall in the battle against the heathen will have earned
a heavenly reward:

> Christian warriors, who continually and vainly seek pretexts for war, rejoice,

ABOVE *After his initial success at Clermont, Pope Urban II set off on a tour of France and the Low Countries to gather international support for his crusade. Here he preaches to a packed congregation at one of the great cathedrals of France.*

for you have today found a true pretext. You, who have so often been the terror of your fellow men, go and fight for the deliverance of the holy places. You, who sell for vile pay the strength of your arms to the fury of others, armed with sword of the Maccabees, go and merit an eternal reward ... if you must have blood, bathe in the blood of the infidels ... Soldiers of Hell, become soldiers of the living God!

Urban was an evangelistic preacher, raising the emotions of his hearers to fever pitch, appealing to the excited crowds to leave their sinful ways, leave their way of life, and follow in the new path of the soldiers of Christ. There followed a moment of heart-stopping cartharsis: just as he was declaring that those who chose this path would be given the reward of eternal life, the crowd erupted in a deafening roar of "Dieu li volt!" – God wills it. Urban showed a crucifix to the crowds, and announced that this was to be the symbol of their holy pledge. They should wear the cross on their shoulders or breasts to testify that they were soldiers of Christ. Strips of cloth were torn off at once and sewn onto cloaks and tunics in the form of the cross.

In the enthusiasm of the moment, huge numbers of people, knights and peasants, princes and men at arms, "took the cross". It was no trivial matter for a knight to go on crusade. To pay for the journey, the equipment, the horses, the provisions and the staff to get him to the Holy Land, many a knight had to mortgage or sell his estates. A knight named Achard de Montmerle of the Macon region mortgaged his property to the Abbey of Cluny to finance his expedition; higher up the social scale, Duke Robert of Normandy raised a loan of 10,000 silver marks from his younger brother, William Rufus, the King of England, using his duchy as a pledge.

There were some advantages to going on crusade, however. Every knight who took the cross made a vow that he would pray at the Church of the

ABOVE *An illustration from a fourteenth-century version of the life of Saint Louis (King Louis IX of France) showing him embarking with his army on the Seventh Crusade. The saintly King also led the Eighth (and last) Crusade before succumbing to a severe bout of dysentery.*

Holy Sepulchre in Jerusalem. This was very like – and indeed it was called at the time – going on pilgrimage, and meant that crusaders were granted certain privileges. They had temporary clerical status, so were subject only to ecclesiastical jurisdiction. They did not have to pay any taxes, or pay off any debts, or incur any interest on their debts, or perform any ordinary feudal military service, while they were away on crusade. The Church also promised to protect a crusader's property and family against usurping claimants.

The five armies of the official crusade, under the leadership of Count Raymond of Toulouse, Count Godfrey of Bouillon, Count Hugh of Vermandois (brother of the French king), Duke Robert of Normandy (brother of the English king) and Bohemond of Otranto (son of Robert Guiscard), set off late in the summer of 1096 for the Holy Land. It is difficult to estimate the actual numbers, as the accounts left by the chroniclers are exaggerated, but it seems there was a total of about 35,000, of which between three and four thousand were knights. Some knights and soldiers took their wives and families with them, and the chroniclers report stories of great bravery from these women in support of their menfolk.

Pope Urban had nominated his legate, Bishop Adhemar of Le Puy, as the leader of the expedition, in the hope of retaining control on behalf of the papacy. But, though the response to the call to arms had been truly astounding, the knights were not so ready to espouse the authority of the Church over their own business.

This did not mean that the knights were not motivated by religious zeal; it is clear that many were. Though historians often suggest that going on crusade was a splendid opportunity for landless younger sons to make their fortunes and settle down with new estates carved out in the East, in practice the majority of the crusaders returned home not long after the capture of Jerusalem. Some of the leaders were more devout than others. Raymond of Toulouse and Godfrey of Bouillon, for example, were noted for their piety. Bohemond, the Prince of Otranto, however, was known as a wild and godless adventurer, who only a few years before had invaded the western edge of the Byzantine Empire, to whose aid he was now in theory coming. He and Baldwin of Boulogne were certainly more interested in acquiring new territories for themselves than fighting a purely religious war. After Baldwin had established the first Christian state at Edessa, and Bohemond had become the Prince of Antioch, they both stayed in their new cities and left the deliverance of Jerusalem to the others.

The dedication and religious fervour which had launched the knights on the crusade were sorely tested by the harsh conditions they encountered on the campaign. Burning heat and thirst, contaminated water and bad food, led to constant outbreaks of illness among the troops. When the armies eventually reached Jerusalem they found that all the trees had been cut down and the wells poisoned for miles around. The soldiers became maddened by thirst. Raymond of Aguilers, who was chaplain to the Count of Toulouse, recorded how they struggled and fought to drink at the pool of Siloam, a fountain which gushed every three days:

> Those who were strong pushed and shoved their way in a deathly fashion through the pool, which was already choked with dead animals and men struggling for their lives ... those who were weaker sprawled on the ground beside the pool with gaping mouths, their parched tongues making them speechless, while they stretched out their hands to beg water from the more fortunate ones. In the nearby fields horses, mules, cattle, sheep, and many other animals were standing, too weak to move. They shrivelled and died of thirst, rotting where they stood, and filled the air with the smell of death.

But the strength of faith gave the crusaders the will to win even when all seemed lost. Earlier, when they had finally taken the city of Antioch after a gruelling seven-month siege, the crusaders were dismayed to learn that a huge Turkish army was close behind them, ready to recapture the city. The soldiers were exhausted and weakened by illness and starvation, but at this low point in their fortunes their morale was restored by the miraculous discovery of the Holy Lance beneath an altar in the city. Bishop Adhemar, who had seen one of those already in Constantinople, remained sceptical about the find, but he was already sick with the fever which was to end his life and could do nothing to stem the exaltation of the soldiers. Raymond of Toulouse, too, was ill; it was Bohemond who organized a desperate sortie from the city and, carrying the Holy Lance in their midst, the starving Christians defeated and put to flight a much larger Turkish army. This victory seemed little short of miraculous and was attributed to the Holy Lance, and probably without the faith and hope it had inspired they would not have succeeded.

A less acceptable face of the crusaders' religious zeal was shown at the capture of Jerusalem, when they indulged in a terrible frenzy of slaughter and massacred almost the whole population.

ABOVE *One of the leaders of the First Crusade, Count Godfrey of Bouillon, leads his soldiers into battle. Godfrey was elected "Advocate of the Holy Sepulchre" after the successful conclusion of the crusade in 1099, having refused the title "King of Jerusalem".*

THE MILITARY ORDERS

That thousands of knights and men at arms should mount an expedition overseas at the express bidding of the Church was remarkable enough, but out of this strange wedding between warriors and churchmen came an even stranger offspring: the military orders – knights who were also monks. They lived under a monastic rule, which included the usual injunctions to poverty, chastity and obedience (the Spanish order of the Knights of Santiago, whose members were permitted to marry, was the only exception). This separated them from the dynastic concerns which preoccupied so many of their secular counterparts and, though many of the military orders became extremely wealthy, they were prohibited from participating in the more frivolous activities of knightly life, such as tournaments or dancing. In that sense they were out of the mainstream of medieval knighthood, but they developed its military aspects to a high degree, particularly in training and discipline, the construction and defence of castles, and the tactics of siege warfare.

THE KNIGHTS TEMPLAR

For several years before the recapture of Jerusalem in 1099, a group of knights had acted as guides and protectors to Christian pilgrims travelling through the lands of the hostile Seljuks. At the time of the First Crusade they lived in a hostel near the Temple of Solomon in Jerusalem, and when Hugues de Payns and Geoffrey de St Omer had the idea of formally incorporating the knights as a religious order in 1119, they took the name of the Poor Knights of the Temple of Solomon, or the Knights Templar. The Order was formally recognized by the Church at the Council of Troyes in 1128, and St Bernard of Clairvaux, the most influential Churchman of the day, was commissioned to write the Rule by which they should live. St Bernard embraced the cause of the Templars enthusiastically and, at the request of Hugues de Payns, who had become the Order's first Grand Master, followed up the Rule with *De laude novae militiae* (In Praise of the New Chivalry), in which he forcibly contrasted the noble austerity of the Templars with the luxury, vanity, greed and violence of the secular knights.

The idea of the military monk-knights was received with great enthusiasm. A group of Templars toured France and England to recruit members, and also to solicit gifts of money and property so that the Order could support its military activities in the Holy Land. The gifts, especially grants of estates, poured in, and soon there was a Templar Commandery in every province and in most major towns and cities, where the knights were recruited and trained, the estates administered, and religious services sung in the Templars' characteristic round churches.

Their record of service defending the Christian kingdom of Jerusalem was distinguished, though somewhat marred by their relations with their great rivals, the Hospitallers, which by the 1240s had deteriorated to the extent that knights from each Order were fighting openly in the streets of Acre. Because the great majority of knights on the eight crusades to the Holy Land returned home as soon as the military campaign was over, the task of keeping the kingdom against the Turks, and later the Egyptians, fell to the Templars and Hospitallers. They invested huge sums of money in the

ABOVE *An illustration of the Siege of Antioch during the First Crusade, showing the turbaned Turkish defenders firing their short eastern bows down onto the Christian forces. Antioch was besieged for seven months before finally falling because of treachery.*

construction of a chain of massively fortified castles [see map below], some of which were never captured by the enemy, but were abandoned when the knights withdrew from Palestine in 1291. They were famous for the ferocity of their fighting. After the disastrous Battle of Hattin in 1187, Saladin took prisoner about two hundred Templars and Hospitallers, including both Grand Masters, and ordered them all to be executed, on the grounds that they were "the firebrands of the Franks".

Both the Templars and the Hospitallers entered into diplomatic negotiations with various Moslem leaders over the years. Because they had to live permanently in the Holy Land, they often had a different perspective from that of the crusaders who appeared periodically in pursuit of short term

BELOW *The army of the First Crusade set up four Latin principalities. These states were hundreds of miles from their real allies and could only survive with the intermittent support of armies from Western Europe. Religious military orders, such as the Knights of St John and the Templars, filled the place to some extent of reliable military forces to defend them.*

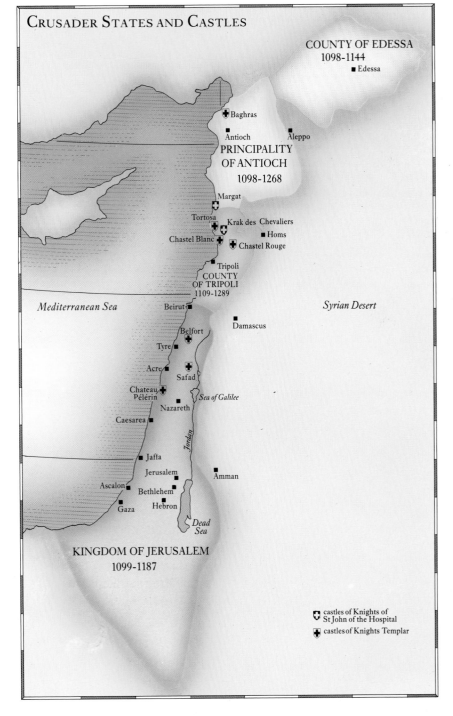

CRUSADER STATES AND CASTLES

COUNTY OF EDESSA
1098-1144
■ Edessa

✚ Baghras
Antioch   Aleppo

PRINCIPALITY
OF ANTIOCH
1098-1268

Margat ♱
Tortosa
✚ Krak des Chevaliers
Chastel Blanc ✚   ■ Homs
✚ Chastel Rouge

■ Tripoli
COUNTY
OF TRIPOLI
1109-1289

Mediterranean Sea   Beirut ■   *Syrian Desert*

■ Damascus

Belfort ✚
Tyre ■

Acre ■
Safad ✚

Chateau ✚
Pélérin
Nazareth   *Sea of Galilee*
Caesarea ■

Jordan

■ Jaffa
Jerusalem ■   ■ Amman
Ascalon ■
Bethlehem ■
Gaza ■   Hebron ■
Dead Sea

KINGDOM OF JERUSALEM
1099-1187

♱ castles of Knights of
St John of the Hospital
✚ castles of Knights Templar

ABOVE *King Philip "the Fair" supervises the burning of some Knights Templar at the stake. Many Templars in France were burned to death after refusing to confess to the charges of heresy and blasphemy, or for recanting confessions extracted under torture.*

military objectives. The Third Crusade came nearest to recapturing Jerusalem, which had fallen to Saladin after the Battle of Hattin. But when Richard Lionheart and his armies were encamped before the city in 1192, the Grand Master of the Templars persuaded him not to attack; and again, in 1228, they were opposed to a negotiated return of the city on the grounds that they could not defend it successfully with the resources available to them.

After the capture of Acre in 1291, the last outpost of the kingdom of Jerusalem had fallen. The Templars withdrew to their European estates. They had lost many of their best knights in the last desperate days of the siege and were demoralized by their failure and by the fact that with the loss of the kingdom they had lost their *raison d'être*. Over the years they had become heavily involved in banking and diplomacy; what had originally begun as a financial facility for pilgrims had grown to an international business which lent large sums of money to kings and governments. The Templars were perceived to be wealthy and corrupt, and they became unpopular.

Their wealth was untouchable because over the years they had won many privileges, including exemption from the payment of taxes and tithes. They were not subject to secular law, and were answerable only to the Pope himself. This made them a law unto themselves in the countries of western Europe where they held lands, and they were very powerful. In 1307, however, King Philip the Fair of France thought of a way to unlock that vast wealth. He and his chancellor, Guillaume de Nogaret, hit on the idea of accusing the Templars of heresy and having the Order abolished. This was done; in 1307 all the Templars in France were arrested (only thirteen escaped) and "interrogated". Under torture or the threat of torture, the knights confessed to a fascinating variety of crimes, ranging from spitting or urinating on the crucifix to sodomy. Later many knights retracted their confessions, but it was too late; the damage to their reputation was irreversible. In 1312 Pope Clement V reluctantly agreed to issue a papal bull suppressing the Order, and Philip had its Grand Master and two senior officers burnt at the stake. The Pope ordered the Templars' properties to be handed over to the Hospitallers, but though this was done in Germany, in France and England most of it went to the crown. In Spain and Portugal the Order was simply refounded under new names.

THE KNIGHTS OF ST JOHN OF THE HOSPITAL

The Hospitallers, as their name implies, had originally been a charitable group which cared for sick and weary pilgrims in the Hospital of St John in Jerusalem. When they had been incorporated as a military order not long after the Templars, they continued to run hospitals, which may explain why they remained popular and respected. Their service in the East was parallel to that of the Templars, and the largest and most famous of the crusader castles – Krak des Chevaliers – was built by them.

After the fall of Acre, they retreated briefly to Cyprus but they had already made plans for their new role. For some years they had built and run a fleet of ships which provided the Christian kingdom with supplies and trade, and also kept down the pirates in the eastern Mediterranean. In 1307 they bought the island of Rhodes and made their headquarters there. They continued their naval operations, fortified the town and harbour of Rhodes,

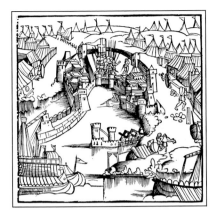

built a fortress for the Grand Master and a large hospital for the sick. They also reorganized themselves so that the knights of each different nationality were grouped together, each in their own "Inn", and each having responsibility for a section of the town and for defending a stretch of the wall.

For most of the fourteenth century they were unmolested, but the Moslems were less than happy to have such a strong Christian power base securely settled in the eastern Mediterranean. In 1435 Rhodes was attacked by the army of Sultan Baybars, but after a month's siege of the town the knights came out unexpectedly and put them to flight. The power of the Byzantine Empire was shattered – rather an own goal on the part of the crusaders who had sacked Constantinople on the Fourth Crusade in 1204, irrevocably weakening the empire – and, when the Turks finally took Constantinople in 1453, the Hospitallers on Rhodes were the only Christian outpost left in the East. In 1480 a huge army of Turks under Palaeologos Pasha landed and prepared to capture the town by pounding the walls with massive cannon. Thanks to the inspired leadership and careful planning of the Grand Master, D'Aubusson, this attack was also repulsed by the knights, though almost half of their number lost their lives in the defence of their city.

The next attempt came in 1522, with the vast armies of Suleiman the Magnificent under the command of his Grand Vizier, Pir Mahomet Pasha. After six months of heroic resistance, the knights surrendered and were allowed to leave the island, having won the admiration of their enemies and of the western world.

Emperor Charles V, who had been moved by their courage though unable to send them help, donated their next home – Malta. In 1565 they were attacked once again by the forces of Suleiman the Magnificent, now an old man of seventy. The story of how the Knights resisted the siege of Malta, under the leadership of their Grand Master, Jean de la Valette, is one of the most thrilling and inspiring of the age. The tiny force, of perhaps 700 knights and 1,500 men at arms, managed to defeat the full might of the Turkish Empire by meticulous preparation and outstanding courage.

THE LIFE OF A TEMPLAR

Towards the close of the thirteenth century, a young knight called Gerard de Caux and two companions applied for membership of the Order of the Knights Templar at the commandery of Cahors. They presented themselves after mass in the morning, and were interviewed by Raymond Robert, the preceptor of a neighbouring commandery, and another Templar. They were asked: "Do you seek the company of the Order of the Temple and participation in the spiritual and temporal goods which are in it?" When they replied "Yes", the brothers warned them of the serious nature of their request:

> "You seek what is a great thing, but you do not know the strong precepts of the Order;

for you see us from the outside, well dressed, well mounted, and well equipped, but you cannot know the austerities of the Order ... for when you wish to be on this side of the sea, you will be beyond it, and vice versa, and when you wish to sleep, you must be awake, and when you wish to eat you must go hungry. Can you bear these things for the honour of God and the safety of your souls?"

The young knights still wished to proceed. They were then asked to establish their eligibility for entry into the Order: they had to believe in the holy Catholic faith, they had to be born legitimate and of knightly family, they must not be married or in holy orders, they must not be in debt, they must be sound in body, and they must not have bribed anyone to gain admission to the Order. Having received their

answers, the two brothers then left the room to report to Brother Guigo Adhemar, the preceptor of the province, leaving the candidates in prayer.

Next they were led into the presence of Brother Guigo and, kneeling before him with bare heads and clasped hands, they were received into the Order. They swore to obey the Master of the Temple and their other superior officers, to "preserve chastity, the good usages and the good

BELOW A late twelfth-century fresco from the walls of a Templar chapel in Cressal showing Templars setting off to fight in the Battle of Brocquel in 1163. The knights were equipped by the Order with horses, armour and their white mantles with red crosses.

customs of the Order", to own no property, to protect, defend and enlarge the kingdom of Jerusalem and never to permit Christians to be murdered or unjustly disinherited, and not to leave the Order without permission.

Brother Guigo blessed the new Templars, raised them to their feet and placed their white Templar mantles with the red crosses over their shoulders, kissed them, and proceeded to instruct them on the rules and customs of their new life. Then, like recruits to an army, they were taken away and given their clothing and equipment: two shirts, a long-sleeved tunic, two pairs of shoes and drawers, a long surcoat open at the front from the waist down, a cape, two mantles, one for summer and one lined with lambswool for winter, a leather belt, a cap and a hat. They were given two towels, their bedding, their armour – suit of mail, helmet, leggings, and white surcoat with red cross – a sword, a lance, a shield and three knives, one for eating with. Each knight was provided with three horses (the sergeants or men at arms had one).

The knight's daily round was based around the religious services laid down in the canons of the Benedictine Rule. At midnight they arose to attend matins, at six in the morning they dressed and heard mass in the chapel followed by prime, tierce and sext, one after another. Then the knights attended to their duties, and exercised, trained and looked after their horses. Their military training was based on strict discipline and absolute obedience to their commanding officers, a factor which made them more efficient troops than ordinary knights. Any knight who attacked on his own initiative was tried by "the justice of the House" and, unless he could show that he acted out of necessity to save a Christian from being killed by a Turk, he would be punished. (by imprisonment, temporary exile or even expulsion from the Order). On one occasion the Commander of the Temple at Acre, Brother Jacques de Ravane, was imprisoned for leading a raid without permission, during which several of his knights were killed.

Dinner was served at midday. Knights ate at their own tables, with the sergeants, squires and, in the Holy Land, native

auxiliaries, at separate tables. Knights were served first. They ate well and, unlike other monks, were permitted to eat the meat of quadrupeds. There would usually be a choice of several different cooked meats at the meal, which was eaten in silence while a priest read from the writings of the Church fathers. The leftovers were given to the poor. Knights needed to stay in good physical condition, and fasting was discouraged because it weakened them, as was illustrated by a story in a sermon preached to the Templars by Jacques de Vitry, who had become the Bishop of Acre in 1216:

ABOVE A splendid expression of the Church militant – Christ, literally armed to the teeth, pictured leading the crusaders in person while God watches from above.

> Once there were certain brother knights of your house who were so fervent in fasts and austerities that they easily succumbed to the Saracens through the weakness of their bodies. I heard about one brother, a most pious knight, who fell from his horse at the first lance blow he received in a skirmish with the infidels. One of his brother knights helped him back into the saddle, at great risk to himself, and the same knight rode again toward the enemy, who again unhorsed him. The other knight, having raised and saved him twice, said "Look out for yourself from now on, Sir Bread-and-Water, for if you get knocked off again, I'm not going to pick you up!"

In the afternoon knights attended the services of nones and vespers at three and six; they could be excused if they were in the middle of performing an important task, such as heating iron in the forge or kneading dough in the bakery. Supper followed vespers, and at nine the brothers gathered for compline, after which they drank a cup of wine and water and received their instructions for the following day. Having attended to their horses, they retired to bed. Thereafter they had to keep silent until prime the following morning.

THE SPANISH MILITARY ORDERS

The Spanish *Reconquista* lasted for more than four hundred years. Though it had some aspects of a Holy War, its main impetus came from the periodic attempts by the kings of the Christian kingdoms of Portugal, Navarre, Castile, Leon and Aragon to drive the Moors from their kingdoms in southern Spain. There was not a permanent state of war with the Moors; the last Moorish kingdom, Granada, managed to co-exist peacefully enough with its Christian neighbours for more than two hundred years after the fall of the kingdom of Cordoba in 1262.

The first military order to be founded in Spain was the Order of the Knights of Calatrava. This came about in a curious way. The Templars and Hospitallers had many foundations in Spain, and in 1134 Alfonso the Warrior of Aragon bequeathed them his kingdom. They agreed, with his heirs, to take possession of a chain of castles instead. The Templars were holding the castle of Calatrava, but because this was a frontier fortress they were repeatedly involved in wars against the Moors of southern Spain. Their main purpose in Europe was to raise money for their operations in Palestine, so they decided in 1157 to abandon the castle and offered it to King Sancho of Castile. He could not find anyone who would hold it against the Moors, until Diego Velazquez, a Spanish nobleman who had become a Cistercian monk, persuaded his abbot, Ramon of Fitero, to move a community of monks to the castle and enlist the help of some knights to protect them. When Ramon died in 1164 the monks moved out, but the knights stayed on and became the Order of Calatrava.

The knights of Calatrava differed from the Templars and Hospitallers because they swore an oath of loyalty to the King of Castile, thus acknowledging a secular overlord, though the Cistercians retained authority over the religious aspects of their lives. This meant, however, that they were not able to resist political pressures from the court of Castile. The King increasingly encroached on the Order's freedom of action and frequently succeeded in getting his own candidate elected as Grand Master.

The Order of Alcantara was a smaller version of Calatrava, formed in 1183, and also living by the Cistercian Rule and loyal to the King of Castile. The most famous of the Spanish military orders was the Order of Santiago, officially recognized by the Pope in 1175, which had developed independently from the others in the tradition of protecting pilgrims travelling to the shrine of St James at Compostela. Unlike the other military orders, they adopted the rule of the Augustinian canons; knights could also marry, though their property belonged to the Order.

Early in the thirteenth century, the Moors assembled a large army in preparation to attack the kingdom of Castile. In response to a general call for help by the Archbishop of Toledo in 1212, many knights from Portugal, Spain, France and northern Italy gathered in Toledo in a spirit of true crusading zeal, wearing the sign of the cross on their shoulders. Unfortunately, most of the foreign knights left after the recapture of Calatrava (which had fallen to the Moors in 1195), leaving the remaining Spanish army greatly outnumbered by the Moorish host. The knights of Calatrava and Santiago, together with the Spanish Templars and Hospitallers, distinguished themselves by their courage in the ensuing battle of Las Navas de Tolosa, though

ABOVE *A page from the beautifully illuminated* Libro de los Caballeros de la Orden de Santiago *which depicts individual named knights of the illustrious Spanish Order of Santiago. This order was unique among the religious military orders in permitting its members to marry.*

THE SPANISH RECONQUISTA

they sustained heavy losses, and this was the most glorious victory of the Reconquista.

Many other orders were formed, including the Order of the Knights of Christ and the Order of the Knights of Montesa, which were created after the suppression of the Templars in 1312, in Portugal and Spain respectively. Though in theory the reconquest continued and was always a Holy War, the Orders did not pursue the initiative begun by Fernando III of Castile and Leon which resulted in the captures of Cordoba and Seville in 1248. During the next hundred and fifty years the Christian kingdoms turned aside from the struggle against the infidels and were more occupied by internal dissensions and civil war. The reconquest was not recommenced against the last remaining Moorish kingdom, Granada, until 1394, when the Grand Master of Alcantara mounted an expedition against it. During this he and his knights were ambushed and massacred in the mountains. Intermittent skirmishes were sometimes successful, however, and some important gains were made from the Moors.

In 1479 Ferdinand of Aragon married Isabella of Castile, uniting the two kingdoms. Granada had been paying tribute to its powerful neighbours as part of a peace treaty, but its sudden refusal to do so provoked the recommencement of the Reconquista in earnest. One by one the great fortresses and cities of Granada were besieged and conquered, and after a nine-month siege Granada itself surrendered and the 700-year occupation of Spain by the Moors was at an end.

As with the fall of Jerusalem, though for a different reason, this left the military orders without a purpose. Though the Portuguese orders continued to fight against the Moors in North Africa, developing their skills at naval warfare as the Hospitallers had done before them, most of the other orders became defunct and secularized.

ABOVE *By the second half of the thirteenth century Moorish power in Spain was reduced to the kingdom of Granada, which survived for over 200 years. Each of the four Christian Kingdoms of the peninsula, Portugal, Castile, Navarre and Aragon, also took on separate political identities.*

THE TEUTONIC KNIGHTS

The Teutonic Knights had also begun as a charitable order, looking after German pilgrims, first in Jerusalem and then running a hospital for wounded German knights outside the city of Acre during its siege by Richard the Lionheart in 1191. They too, when incorporated as the Teutonic Knights of the Hospital of St Mary the Virgin, continued to care for the sick and wounded as well as fighting against the Turks.

The Order contained knights, sergeants (skilled men at arms who were not knights) and priests; the knights had to be legitimate, German and of knightly descent. They continued to fight in Palestine, and Teutonic Knights were killed alongside the Templars and Hospitallers in the heroic last stand at Acre in 1291. But they had already begun to fight the Holy War on a new front: the Baltic states of north eastern Europe. The King of Hungary and the Duke of Masovia had been struggling against ferocious Prussian tribesmen and appealed to the Teutonic Knights for help. The Grand Master of the Knights, Hermann von Salza, agreed to fight in exchange for the outright grant of a territory to the Knights where they could station themselves permanently and build secure fortifications.

The Northern Crusade was launched in earnest in about 1230, though smaller campaigns had taken place before this. The Teutonic Knights soon combined with the smaller local orders of the Brethren of the Sword and the Order of Dobrin, who had been fighting farther north in Livonia (Latvia, Estonia, Lithuania). The conditions under which they fought were very different from the Holy Land, where their enemies were, if anything,

ABOVE *A rather fanciful nineteenth-century interpretation of an encounter between the Teutonic Knights and the pagan Lithuanian tribes during the course of the Northern Crusade.*

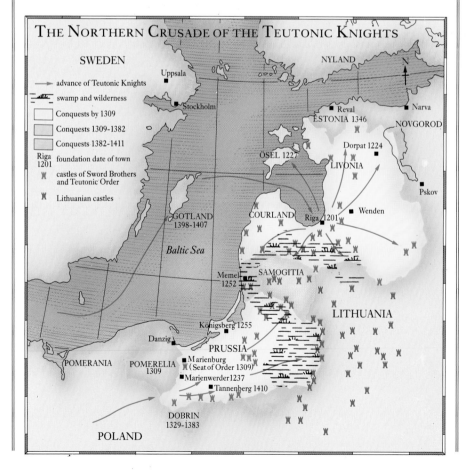

THE NORTHERN CRUSADE OF THE TEUTONIC KNIGHTS

SWEDEN   NYLAND

Uppsala

→ advance of Teutonic Knights

swamp and wilderness

Conquests by 1309

Conquests 1309–1382

Conquests 1382–1411

Riga 1201   foundation date of town

✗ castles of Sword Brothers and Teutonic Order

✗ Lithuanian castles

Stockholm

Reval   Narva

ESTONIA 1346

NOVGOROD

Dorpat 1224

ÖSEL 1227

LIVONIA

Pskov

GOTLAND 1398–1407

COURLAND   Riga 1201   Wenden

Baltic Sea

Memel 1252   SAMOGITIA

LITHUANIA

Königsberg 1255

Danzig

POMERANIA   POMERELIA 1309   PRUSSIA

Marienburg (Seat of Order 1309)

Marienwerder 1237

Tannenberg 1410

DOBRIN 1329–1383

POLAND

LEFT *Crusading zeal was also directed against pagans in Europe. The Northern Crusade was pursued by religious military orders, such as the Teutonic Knights, for over 150 years and as a result, the Germans gradually colonized Prussia, making serfs of the local people.*

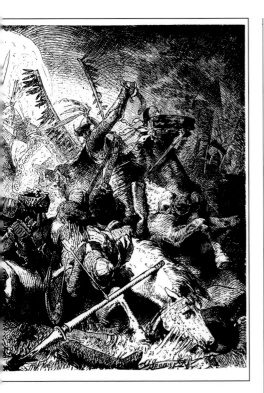

ABOVE: *The German poet Tannhäuser, a member of the Order of Teutonic Knights, from the Manessah Codex.*

superior in civilization and at least equal in military skill and tactics. In the dark, damp forests and bogs of northern Europe they were pitting themselves against savage pagan tribesmen, who fought with unshakeable persistence and ferocity against the armoured knights. The Prussian and Lithuanian tribes were at first resistant to Christianity, and the war quickly became one of attrition in which no prisoners were taken by the knights and even women and children were slaughtered. The knights were outnumbered, but their technology was superior. The Prussians specialized in raids and ambushes but did not have the organization or equipment necessary to besiege a well-defended stone-built fortress.

After initial successes, Germans were invited to move into Prussia and colonize it; the Prussians who had been converted became their serfs. Throughout the thirteenth century remaining pockets of Prussian resistance continued to frustrate the Teutonic Knights for, as soon as they thought a region had been safely conquered, the Prussians would attack in the night, burning new Christian settlements and slaughtering their inhabitants.

The Knights attempted to invade the orthodox Christian states of Russia but were decisively defeated by united Russian armies under Prince Alexander Nevsky in a pitched battle on the frozen surface of Lake Peipus in 1242. The same year saw a major uprising in Prussia, which took thirty years to control. In the fourteenth century they had established firm control of Prussia and were concentrating their efforts against the Lithuanians, now the last remaining pagan nation in Europe. At this point the prestige of the Order was high and it became a proto-military college, where young noblemen and their knights from all the states of Europe could gain experience of real warfare. These campaigns were still dignified with the name of crusades, though with the enemy steadily diminishing in numbers most of the "fighting" consisted of burning and looting native villages and cutting down unarmed civilians.

In 1386 Grand Duke Jagiello of Lithuania converted to Christianity. Renamed Wladislaw II, he set about converting his people, but despite this the Knights viewed him with suspicion. Eventually, successive border disputes and hostilities between Poland and Prussia led to war; Wladislaw gathered an enormous host including Poles, Bohemians, Hungarians, Czechs, Cossacks and Tartars as well as Lithuanians – anyone who had a grudge against the high-handed knights or their Prussian state. At the Battle of Tannenberg in July 1410 the Teutonic Knights suffered a terrible defeat from which they never fully recovered, losing their Grand Master and hundreds of their best knights and men at arms.

From then on the power of the Order and the size of their dominions dwindled. Casimir IV of Poland took the western part of Prussia in 1466 and the Grand Master became his vassal; the Order's territories in Livonia at this point were severed from Prussia and became a secular duchy in 1591.

DUBBING AND TOURNEYING

Since the ninth and tenth centuries, Church pontificals and sacramentaries had contained prayers for the blessing of swords. As time went by, other knightly accoutrements, such as lances and banners, were also blessed by the Church, with the aim of invoking God's aid in battles against pagan invaders:

> Bless this sword ... so that it may be a defence for churches, widows and orphans, and for all servants of God against the fury of the heathen.

The same collections also bear witness to the Church's early versions of the coronation rite, in which this blessing of the sword is united with a ceremony of girding around the waist of the new king, which bestows on him the authority to lead men and the responsibility to defend society from invasion by hostile forces and to maintain its values from within. Sometime during the eleventh century, this rite of girding with the sword was united with the traditional delivery of arms to a young warrior, which as we have seen formed the secular root of dubbing to knighthood. It also introduced both the investment of authority to the knight as a member of the ruling élite, with its attendant responsibilities and obligations – an authority which was, at least in part, bestowed by the Church – and, further, the idea that a religious blessing formed an essential part of the process by which a man was made into a knight.

By the late thirteenth century, an elaborate ecclesiastical ritual for dubbing a knight is found in the pontifical of William Durandus of Mende. This ceremony was performed by a bishop; he took the sword and laid it on the altar, blessing it with a prayer almost identical to the older one quoted above, but supplemented with a soldier's prayer from the Old Testament:

ABOVE *An illustration of a mass dubbing ceremony from a fourteenth-century French psalter, showing the girding on of the sword. This is performed by laymen, not by clerics.*

ABOVE *King Henry II of England does penance at the tomb of his murdered Archbishop of Canterbury, Thomas Becket. Becket's tomb at Canterbury became one of the most popular pilgrim shrines of the Middle Ages.*

Blessed be the Lord God who formeth my hands for battle and my fingers for war. He is my salvation, He is my refuge, He setteth me free.

The bishop then put the sword into the knight's right hand, took it back, gave the knight the *collée* on the neck, as the knight knelt before him, and then girded the sword about his waist. The knight rose and flourished the sword three times; he was then "marked with the character of knighthood". The bishop kissed him on the cheeks and admonished him to perform his duties faithfully and devoutly.

Not all knights were subjected to such an intensely religious ceremony. Many were knighted hurriedly before battles, without the benefit of clergy, but even those who were knighted at leisure during peacetime often created a ceremony equally elaborate but much more secular in its tone. From the evidence of chronicles and romances, it remained more important for the new knight to receive his knighthood from the hands of a knight, preferably a distinguished one, rather than from a priest or bishop. As the Middle Ages wore on, however, dubbing ceremonies were increasingly associated with the Church, took place in a church rather than in the hall of a castle, and were performed in the presence of churchmen, if not actually by them.

So the Church succeeded to some extent in taking over the ritual of dubbing to knighthood. Much less successful were its efforts, conducted over a period of two hundred years, to ban tournaments. The Church's opposition to tournaments emerged early on in their history. By 1130, when the Council of Clermont first decreed that tournaments were forbidden, and anyone who was killed at one would be denied Christian burial, they must already have become popular enough to pose a problem. The grounds for the Church's objections were that tournaments were dangerous and disturbed the peace; many men were killed at them in sport, and they were occasions which encouraged the pride and violence endemic to knights to overflow in deadly sin. In addition, as the Church well knew, they could be very expensive; unlucky knights who were addicted to tourneying often wasted their revenues, even to the point of complete ruin, in order to pay ransoms and replace lost horses and armour.

Tournaments were banned by secular rulers as well from time to time. Henry II banned them in England, but not in his French territories, so that his son, Henry the Young King, and his friend and tutor, William Marshal, had to travel to France in order to take part in them. But despite successive bans and increasing penalties for attendance, tournaments continued to be popular. They were central to the ethos of knighthood, a showcase for knightly qualities as well as a highly enjoyable sport and a possible source of income.

The inescapable conclusion is that, though knights in general were reasonably devout Christians, they only heeded the Church's injunctions which related specifically to them and their activities when it suited them to do so. They had no difficulty in seeing their code as acceptable to God; they saw themselves and the Church as each working in its own way for God's purpose, in harmony but not in either case in subjection to the other. Knighthood was infused in many ways with strong religious sentiments but these were always subordinated to ultimately secular goals.

CHAPTER FOUR

THE
KNIGHT AT PEACE

We have seen from the instructions to young knights written by Ramon Lull and Geoffrey de Chargny, that a definite progression could be observed in the perfect knightly career. From preparation for knighthood, through exercises designed to train the knight in martial skills and chivalrous virtues, then participation and, ideally, success in jousts and tournaments, to fighting in real wars. Wars, too, had an ascending order of importance and worth to a knight, in which the source of greatest honour and glory was fighting for one's faith on a crusade.

NURTURE, FOSTERING AND THE TRAINING FOR KNIGHTHOOD

A knight was most often a member of the land-holding class and his father had usually been a knight before him. During the thirteenth century increased prosperity, especially among the growing merchant class in towns, led to a tightening of the rules for eligibility, limiting knighthood to those who could prove descent from knights. Typically, a knight who had married and started a family was the owner or the feudal holder of at least one estate. In northern France, Germany and England the eldest son inherited his father's lands, and younger sons either had to make a career in the Church or seek their fortunes as freelance knights, as William Marshal had done. In

SIR JOHN CHANDOS, KNIGHT OF THE GARTER, C. 1350

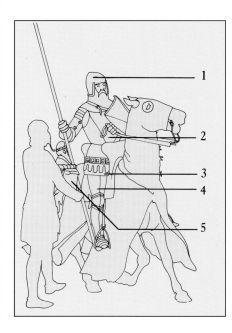

Sir John's armour is interesting since it is somewhere between full mail and plate armour; at this point a suit of mail is worn beneath supplementary pieces of plate armour. His pointed bascinet (1) for instance is attached to a mail aventail by thongs. Over his mail hauberk and breastplate, the surcoat has now become a closely tailored jupon (2) which displays Sir John's arms – argent a pile gules – as do his shield and horse's caparison. Beneath the edge of the jupon the bottom of his short mail skirt (3) can be seen. Plate armour protects his limbs; cuisses (4) on his thighs, poleyns on the knees, greaves on the shins, hinged vambraces on upper and lower arms, with couters at the elbows. The squire carries his great helm (5) which bears his crest.

southern France, Italy and Spain the older system of dividing the inheritance between surviving sons had proved impractical for the knightly class, since it meant ever smaller subdivisions of land, which ultimately became insufficient to support the rank of knight. By the close of the eleventh century this was superseded either by primogeniture or by a system called *fraternitas* (brotherhood), in which the estate remained the property of all the heirs but was run by one who acted as head of the household. In either case, unless the family was really wealthy, only one son could afford to marry.

Marriage in the Middle Ages was another way of strengthening feudal and political ties, and of building the wealth of individual dynasties. Heiresses were sought after, since they brought additions to their husbands' estates; but knights might marry the sisters or daughters of their feudal overlords, or of anyone else with whom they wished to cement an alliance by a family tie. The Normans, who carved out new kingdoms for themselves in England, Ireland, southern Italy and Sicily, often married the women of families they had dispossessed, thus ensuring a kind of continuity.

Thus a future knight was born into a knightly family and lived in his father's house on the family estate. This probably meant a village where his father's serfs and free peasants, who rented land from him, did all the agricultural labour. His father might supervise the work of the peasants himself or, more likely, especially if he held more than one estate, he employed a steward to do it for him. A knight whose wife had brought property with her on their marriage, or had inherited land from a relative, might hold estates a considerable distance apart. If so, he might live in different houses at different times, travelling from manor to manor to ensure that his lordship was recognized and respected; or he might grant a manor in fief to a vassal knight if it was inconveniently distant from his main holdings.

The knight in these circumstances was typically a country gentleman, who spent most of his time at home on his estates. He and his neighbours in the same circumstances lived in the neighbourhood of a castle, and were the vassals of its lord or "castellan". The knight might own his own lands, without duty to an overlord if he lived in an area where such "allodial" tenure was common, or he might hold all his lands in fief from the castellan. The knight's feudal obligations to the castellan included loyalty and friendship, and specific services such as regular military service of forty days every year, with additional services, such as accompanying the castellan on journeys as part of a mounted escort, or taking part in a special, short expedition. He probably also had to spend periods as a guard in the castle garrison.

There were other kinds of duties the knight owed to his lord, which were civil rather than military. These included attending the lord's court and giving him advice, helping him to administer justice in his local courts, and in minor legal matters, such as witnessing documents, and occasionally deputizing for him.

The knights who owed service to the same castellan were probably all known to one another by name. They spent periods of their military service or their garrison duty in each other's company, and this meant that a lord's retinue or levy of knights going to war had a close relationship. They probably also had kin relationships because of the intermarriage of their families, and they would have lived together in the castle as boys while training and preparing for their future life as knights and vassals.

ABOVE *This carving from the edge of a backgammon board shows squires exercising with heavy two-handed swords. Presumably the edges have been blunted as neither appears to be wearing protective clothing. The acquisition of such skills formed an essential part of the training for knighthood.*

RIGHT *The month of July from the* Très Riches Heures *of Jean, duc de Berry. These beautiful paintings depict the agricultural tasks of the yearly round – in this case, reaping the corn and shearing sheep. The performance of such tasks by the peasant workforce on his estate formed the backbone of the knight's wealth.*

The son of a knight was under the charge of the women of the household for the first few years of his life. When he was about seven or eight, however, he was fostered out to the castellan to be brought up, together with the sons of other knights, in the castle. This was where he learned the business of knighthood. At first he would serve as a page, learning how to serve at table and performing other simple household tasks. At this stage, like the youngest boys at a public school, his status was menial and he could be ordered about by other members of the household – sent on errands, or given cleaning tasks.

Another, and potentially less pleasant, form of fostering for a knightly or noble child was to be given as a hostage to a lord in dispute with his father as a guarantee of good behaviour. Usually hostages were treated honourably and brought up with the lord's own sons and those of his knights, forming close bonds with them, but occasionally they were placed in grave danger. In 1152, when he was about eight, William Marshal was given up to King Stephen as a hostage during a truce in the siege of Newbury Castle, which was being held for Empress Matilda by William's father, John. John was supposed to use the truce to ask for help from Matilda, but instead he brought in new provisions and soldiers so as to withstand the siege. At this the King threatened to hang William if his father did not surrender the castle at once. William must have experienced a terrible moment when his father refused, saying that he had "the anvil and hammer on which to forge yet finer sons than that one". William was brought before the castle to be hanged, but King Stephen was moved by his youth and innocence and took him back to the camp. Later Stephen was advised by one of his knights to put William into a catapult and throw him over the castle walls, but fortunately the King was above such barbarism. He was evidently fond of the boy, for he was later observed by a servant William's mother had sent to spy, playing games with him in his tent. A glimpse of the young William's courage and charm can be seen when, catching sight of the servant peeping in, he shouted out "Welcome, Wilikin! How is my lady mother? How are my brothers and sisters?" William was a hostage for two months before being returned to his family.

In his early teens, a boy would graduate to the next stage in the knightly hierarchy in the castle and become a squire. A squire had certain specific duties to perform, which included taking turns to serve his lord at table, looking after his horses and harness, and, if he attended a tournament or went to war, taking charge of his lord's equipment and armour, and arming him before he went into action.

He would share sleeping quarters and take turns at these duties with a group of other squires like himself. During this period he would be trained to ride, and to fight with a variety of weapons on foot and on horseback. Physical fitness was essential for a knight, and squires had to develop the strength necessary to fight in chain mail which could weigh about 50 lbs (22.5 kg). Just to wear this for several hours at a stretch was tiring, because the whole weight of the suit hung from the shoulders. In addition, the squire would have to learn to wield with ease the heavy sword which dealt the devastating blows we hear about in romance and chronicle, the even heavier lance, and possibly also a battle axe or club.

From contemporary pictures of the exercises undertaken by young squires in castle yards, we can see that they learned to handle weapons first on foot and without armour, performing tests of skill such as hitting targets with a lance carried at a run, or thwacking each other with swords. This also taught them how to use their shields effectively. Then they would have to master the same skills while wearing armour, and finally while riding a horse. Squires trained together, and this helped to reinforce the knights' sense of brotherhood and professional solidarity.

The early career of a young knight named Arnold of Ardres, the son and heir of Count Baldwin of Guisnes, was recorded lovingly by the family chronicler, named Lambert. He tells us how Arnold was fostered in the court of Philip of Flanders, a great lover of tournaments and patron of the arts, to

BELOW *Squires on foot learning to handle the lance, from the border of the Romance of Alexander, dating from about 1340. The squire with the lance is tilting at the "Quintain" – a swivelling target on a post representing his opponent's shield. The other squire holds the quintain steady to prevent it swinging round and clouting the trainee as he charges past.*

RIGHT *A fresco in a Florentine palace, the Palazzo Davanzati, shows Italian knights at leisure indulging in the courtly pursuits of chess and love-dalliance. The refinements of social intercourse and polite manners formed an aspect of the knight's upbringing as important as his military training.*

whom Chrétien de Troyes dedicated his *Perceval*. Here he was to learn "good manners and be instructed in the office of knighthood". Many other young men of knightly and noble birth had also been placed under Philip's care to be brought up and trained but, according to Lambert, young Arnold outshone them all "by his handsome looks and prowess in every martial exercise". Arnold's later life is characterized by his great love of romances; he liked nothing better than to hear stories about the great heroes of the past – Roland, Arthur, and the famous leaders of the First Crusade.

This brings us to another important part of the chivalrous education a young squire received at a castle or court – his initiation into the finer aspects of courtly life: how to carve meat, how to serve his lord at table, how to dance, the exercise of courtly manners, the hunt, the banquet, and so on. He acquired a taste for courtly music and courtly literature, which included, as well as romances and books of instruction, treatises on hunting and warfare, the chronicles of his country and of the local noble family. He learned about stately ceremony, fine clothes, weapons and armour, as well as the rougher sports of knightly life. He may have learnt to read; he would certainly have learnt the rudiments of heraldry.

The squire was knighted, if he was in easy circumstances, on achieving a suitable age, usually the late teens or early twenties. If he did not have enough income to maintain the status of knight and its attendant expenses, he might remain a "bachelor" for several years, or even not be knighted at all. There was plenty of honourable employment for well-brought-up young men at courts and castles throughout Europe which did not require them to be knights; good squires were always valued, as were heralds and, for those of an intellectual bent, writers, whether they were historians or romancers. We have already noted how the ceremony of dubbing to knighthood developed in its several varieties, from the stately ritual of mass-knightings at formal peacetime occasions, to the hurried conferring of the essential elements either on or shortly before the field of battle.

THE ROLE OF THE HERALD

Heraldry played a vital role in the developing ethos of chivalry. In its origins it had been essentially practical; it was important at tournaments and essential in battles to be able to recognize who was, and who was not, on your side. When medieval armour had evolved to the stage where a knight was completely encased in mail from head to foot and wore a helmet which concealed his face the only way to recognize him was by particular signs and colours, regularly worn on his shield.

Shields were originally the only part of a knight's equipment to be decorated in this way; and in fact heraldry developed from the practice of decorating shields, which predated it. Later a knight's coat of arms would be repeated on his helmet, his surcoat, his banner, and his horse's caparison as well as on his shield; on state occasions his robe, and possibly also that of his wife, would carry the same design. By the fifteenth century heraldry had developed into a highly complex science, requiring years of training and extensive learning in its scientists, the heralds. At this point, an individual herald could reel off in answer to a query the arms of any noble family in his area, the origin and significance of the arms, the history of the family, and any particularly noteworthy deeds performed by any members of it.

In its early days heraldry was much more simple, and much more fluid. Jean of Marmoutier's account of the knighting of the young Geoffrey of Anjou, for example, relates that a blue shield with six small golden lions was put around his neck. This same shield appears on his tomb effigy, and the same beast in the same colours was also depicted on the shields of his son and grandson. This is early evidence of the association of particular devices with particular families, but at the same time other nobles were adopting devices more or less at random, and it appears that family exclusivity of emblems was not fixed until later.

During the twelfth century the practice of knights identifying themselves by special emblems on their shields became

ABOVE *A page from Matthew Paris's* Chronicle *showing shields with heraldic devices, together with the names of their owners. The manuscript dates from the second half of the thirteenth century, by which time the science of heraldry was already highly developed.*

widespread, and is referred to in chivalrous romances; by the time the earliest surviving "Rolls of Arms" were written (the French Bigot Roll, the English Glover's Roll, and the German *Clipearius Teutonicorum*, all written about the middle of the thirteenth century), the science of heraldry had already developed fixed rules. At the close of the thirteenth century an anonymous herald composed the first surviving treatise on the subject, *De heraudie*, which contains a detailed explanation of all the regulations and restrictions and practices of heraldry, already fully developed.

These early Rolls seem to indicate that only very important nobles and knights had their own coats of arms, but soon the lesser knightly families, including the German descendants of the "serf-knights", were all bearing arms, and finally squires and others associated with knighthood, who had not actually been knighted.

This is another way in which great lords and relatively humble gentry were brought closer together in their common participation in the ideology and rituals of knighthood. Just as access to the rank of knighthood was eventually legally restricted to those of knightly descent, so too the right to bear arms was subject to strict qualifications. Arms could be inherited, granted by a prince or lord, or captured; otherwise they were worn illegally, and it was part of a herald's business to know exactly when and how an "armigerous" family had come by its arms, and to prevent the assumption of arms by those who had no right to them.

The original function of a herald is splendidly demonstrated in Chrétien de Troyes' *Lancelot* (the Knight of the Cart), written between 1170 and 1190. At the great tournament which takes place towards the close of the poem, Lancelot, who has attended in borrowed armour in order not to be recognized, is resting in his lodgings and has left his plain vermilion shield outside the door, as the custom was. Along comes a herald-at-arms, looking at all the shields so that he will know who is taking part in the tournament later on. He does not recognize Lancelot's borrowed shield, so he steps into the house and instantly recognizes Lancelot himself. Lancelot forbids him to reveal his name to anyone, upon which the herald hastens away, shouting out, "Now there has come one who will take the measure!" This herald is clearly not a very grand or dignified person, because Chrétien mentions that he has left his robe and shoes behind in a tavern as a pledge, meaning he has no money and the tavern-keeper will hold on to the robe and shoes until he can find someone to pay his bill. So the herald looks for a patron among the knights – someone who will reward him with knightly *largesse* for the service of crying his fame (even if, as in this case, he mustn't mention the knight's name).

The same poem shows early heraldry in action, as the knights who have already been captured point out the notable con-

ABOVE *Two jousting knights, from an English manuscript of about 1445. Not only the shields but the knights' surcoats and their horses' caparisons are now decorated with their coats of arms. Knights at this time might also wear great helms crested with a device from their arms.*

testants to the Queen and her damsels:

> "Do you see that knight yonder with a golden band across the middle of his red shield? That is Governauz of Roberdic. And do you see that other one, who has an eagle and a dragon painted side by side upon his shield? That is the son of the King of Aragon, who has come to this land in search of glory and renown. And do you see that one beside him, who thrusts and jousts so well, bearing a shield with a leopard painted on a green ground on one part, and the other half is azure blue? That is Ignaurez the well-beloved, a lover himself and jovial."

Heralds were important at tournaments for recognizing the doers of deeds of prowess and promoting the fame of individuals; they performed the same function at battles, where they also acted as messengers between opposing armies and made tallies of the noble dead afterwards.

Heralds had a great deal to do with the development of tournaments from free-for-alls into colourful pageants; they were put in charge of organizing the participants, and created such ceremonies as the viewing of helms (where they set out the helms of all participating knights, before the tournament, for the judges and spectators to see), the calling of rolls of arms (where the heralds read out the names of the knights and their genealogies), and the presentation of prizes to the victors. Eventually, from its somewhat humble beginnings, the position of herald grew to be one of great distinction; heralds were highly valued members of society, who progressed through stages in their careers, from apprentice herald ("poursuivant") to herald, to King of Arms. The height of their great learning in their craft and in the world of chivalry generally was reached in the fifteenth century with beautifully illustrated records of contemporary arms, such as the *Blason des couleurs* of Sicily Herald, or the *Wappenboek* of Gelre Herald, Claes van Heynen. By this time heraldry had developed such sophistication that those well-versed in its intricacies could decipher a history of family honour from a device on its shield, such as the chains in the arms of the Zuniga's family of Navarre, which commemorated their ancestors' noble deeds at the great battle of Las Navas de Tolosa, when they cut through the human barrier of chained negro bodyguards which surrounded the tent of the Caliph.

Heralds and their encyclopedic knowledge provided for knights a way of codifying their honour and the honour of their families, and the development of heraldry coincided most happily with knights' desire to invest their peacetime activities with symbols and celebrations of honour, with colour and ornament, and with conscious evocations of the legendary past.

BELOW *A lady receives news of the death of her knight and his shield and helmet with crest are brought to her.*

Assuming that the new knight was not immediately able to settle on his estate and raise a family, he would be a "landless" knight, or one who would not inherit his patrimony for many years to come. Let us suppose that he gained employment at the court of a lord, and examine some of the peace-time activities which reinforced his sense of his knighthood and the honour of his calling.

The Hunt

Hunting and hawking were important knightly activities. Hunting provided valuable additions to the medieval diet, but for knights such considerations were secondary to its value as a sport. In northern and eastern Europe or Spain, where there were still huge areas of uncultivated land, including tracts of primeval forest, there was no need to restrict the access of peasants to the potential food source of wild animals, but in densely populated and highly agricultural areas, such as England, France and northern Italy, landowners, from kings to knights, valued their woods as game preserves and guarded them jealously against the depredations of poachers. The penalties for catching reserved animals, such as deer, were severe and included mutilation and flaying.

As land became scarce, hunting reserves could be enjoyed only by the richest and most powerful nobles and the knights in their household. Professional huntsmen were employed to look after the hounds and maintain the stocks of game. As a "noble" sport, hunting developed its own hierarchies and rituals over the years. A stag was the noblest quarry, followed by a boar; female deer, wolves, bears, foxes and hares were also hunted, but foxes and hares were considered inferior objects, while rabbits were left for the peasants to snare.

An excellent description of deer-hunting can be found in the Middle English romance, *Sir Gawain and the Green Knight*. While Sir Gawain rests in the castle, his host Sir Bertilak gets up early and with his other guests and his huntsmen takes to the forest:

> At the first sound of the baying of the hounds, the wild creatures trembled; the deer fled down the valley, driven mad with fear, and rushed for the high ground, but were quickly checked by the beaters, who shouted loudly at them. They let the harts with their high heads pass freely, the fierce bucks too with their broad antlers; for the noble lord had forbidden any man to interfere with the male deer during the close season. The hinds were kept in with cries of "hey!" and "ware"; the does are driven with great noise into the deep valleys. There one could see as they glanced past, the slanting flight of arrows; at each turn in the wood an arrow flew and strongly pierced the brown hide with its broad head. Oh! How they scream and bleed, dying by the banks, and always the hounds are rushing headlong after them...Any of the wild beasts that escaped the bowmen were pulled down and killed at the stations where men were posted with fresh hounds, after being harassed from the high ground and driven to the water. The men at the low-lying stations were so expert, and their greyhounds so big, that they quickly caught and pulled them down on the spot, as fast as the eye could see.

A gruesome description of the butchering of the dead animals ensues, which follows exactly the highly technical instructions for dismembering carcases

ABOVE *Knights and ladies ride out hawking, from the painting of August in the* Très Riches Heures *of Jean, duc de Berry. Hawking, and other forms of hunting, were useful sports which, by the time this painting was made in the mid-fifteenth century, had evolved into an aristocratic pastime attended by elaborate ceremonial.*

given in contemporary hunting manuals, such as the *Livre de la chasse* written in 1387 (about the same time as the poem) by Gaston, Count of Foix, for his friend Philip, Duke of Burgundy. This treatise is the product of one man's lifelong enthusiasm. It is a medieval encyclopedia of hunting, detailing the different hounds to be used for different quarry, the various methods of chase, the open and close seasons for all prey animals, different traps and baits, and incidental activities such as meals *al fresco* in the forest.

Deer could also be hunted with spears or swords instead of bows and arrows. It could thus be seen as another opportunity to exercise knightly qualities. Edward I was described by William Rishanger as a great lover of hunting, and he remarked how, as a young prince, Edward hunted "stags, which he used to chase on horseback. When he had one cornered, he would strike it down with his sword, rather than use a hunting spear." However bloodthirsty this practice may seem to the modern reader, it was considered a sign of great courage and spirit at the time. A later medieval commentator (Olivier de Serres, writing at the beginning of the sixteenth century), pointed out the healthiness and practical usefulness of hunting:

> The aim of hunting, which is a pleasant pastime, is connected to many
> benefits: it favours health, due to the fact that one has to get up early in the
> morning and exercise, and sobriety. Moreover, hunting tempers the spirit,
> making man patient, discreet, modest, magnanimous, bold, and
> industrious. We should not forget that hunting supplies the table with
> precious meats. Finally, it also allows us to check the land and hasten the work.

From the very earliest medieval times, hawking had also been popular, and it, too, had great potential for development into a high art, or rather a science. Many manuals and treatises on hawking were written by knights and nobles from all over Europe, such as the *Treatise of Falconry* by Emperor Frederick II of Germany, with its beautifully detailed illustrations on the care and training of the birds. A thirteenth-century treatise instructed the falconer to handle his bird as much as possible in order to tame it for training:

> You must keep him on your fist more than ever before, and take him into the

BELOW *The Count and his huntsmen take a break for their mid-day meal, eaten* al fresco *in the forest. Amidst the wineskins and the venison pasties, conversation is still fixed on the hunt – the chief huntsman is discussing the spoor brought to the table by two foresters to show the Count.*

RIGHT *An illustration from the* Livre de la Chasse *by Gaston, Count of Foix, showing a stag hunt in progress. The huntsmen are using a combination of deerhounds and a greyhound; a beater armed with a spear accompanies the dogs. The* Livre de la Chasse *is a detailed technical manual with precise illustrations.*

law-courts and into church, wherever people are assembled in crowds, and into the streets.

Hawks and falcons were very valuable and often given as prestigious gifts. Then, as now, the penalties for stealing their eggs were severe.

Churchmen (and women) who were of noble birth were reluctant to relinquish their hunting of animals and birds. A bishop visiting nunneries in the south of England in the mid fourteenth century found the nuns keeping greyhounds and indignantly wrote to them on the subject – not only was it against their rule to indulge in such pleasures as hunting, but the animals were eating up food which could have been given to the poor.

ABOVE *Another highly detailed technical manual written by a noble sports enthusiast – De Arte Venandi cum Avibus by Emperor Frederick II – contains much information on the care, training and working of falcons.*

THE TOURNAMENT

It is hardly possible to overestimate the importance of the tournament to the culture of medieval knights. It provided an arena for the display of all important knightly virtues: *prouesse* in the combat, *courtoisie* to the watching and judging ladies, *largesse* to the crowds of minstrels, heralds, armourers, squires and other assorted hangers on, and qualities such as the *franchise* and *debonnaireté* with which a knight should conduct himself in triumph and disaster (the qualities which later developed into the European gentleman's sense of fair play), and the *pité* which he should exercise to his defeated opponents.

It was regarded as a crucial training ground in which young knights could practise the handling of their horses and weapons, the tactics of attack and defence, and of co-ordinating their actions with a team of companions, who would in real battle form a military unit. It was an opportunity for knights to win praise and glory, and to find employment with great lords who attended the tournaments and frequently recruited talented knights there. To this end the activities of the heralds were of vital importance, as they recorded the names and arms of those who took part in tournaments and the deeds they achieved. It was also a splendid occasion for sexual display. It is clear from all sources that ladies played a variety of active roles in the tournament, from hosting them, to encouraging their individual knights, who competed wearing their "favour" (a sleeve or other token), judging the performances (before this role was completely taken over by heralds), giving the prizes and, on occasion, being the prizes themselves.

A knight could win considerable sums at tournaments, if he was successful; conversely, of course, he could also lose money. There can be no doubt that the prospect of winning valuable horses, armour and ransoms contributed to the extreme popularity of tournaments all over Europe and all through the period. We have already seen from the history of William Marshal that it was possible for a knight who was good at tourneying to travel from tournament to tournament, accumulating a considerable fortune as well as a formidable reputation. There were also knights for whom the sport was an addiction, who returned time after time to tournaments although their losses might reduce them to bankruptcy and ruin. Jacques de Baudricourt relates a story about a relative of his, the Seigneur de Baudricourt, whose consistent bad luck at tournaments often required him to mortgage his estate, and even his household valuables, in order to pay his

RIGHT *An illustration from the* Roman de Fauvel *showing the outcome of an encounter between two knights in the joust. The knight who falls from his horse is seriously wounded – a not uncommon result of jousting in real life.*

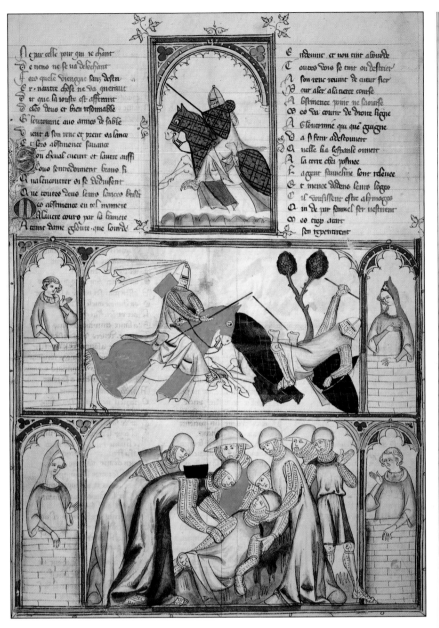

ABOVE *A tournament of the fifteenth century, presided over by King Richard II of England, who was a great devotee of the sport. Note how the jousting knights, encountering one another rather unusually without a tilt, have lost their splendid heraldic trappings.*

debts and losses. He wondered how it was that he always managed to pay off the mortgages and free his property for the next time, until he discovered that it was his wife whose financial prudence, caring for his estates and livestock, had saved him many times from ruin. When he returned home he confessed his wastefulness to his wife and she confessed her secret management and saving, and they forgave one another. She had never complained because, as she said, "all the honour that you win in the world I share with you".

The expenses of tourneying, though great, were much less serious than the physical dangers to which knights were inevitably exposed. In their early days, tournaments were fairly unregulated free-for-alls, and they were so violent that the only distinction between them and a real battle was the fact that they were acknowledged to be waged in sport. Two teams of knights, usually from two different areas or towns, would attack each other with real weapons, ranging over a designated area of countryside, aiming to take as many prisoners from the opposing faction as they could. Their only respite from the fighting was to go to the "neutral area", where they could disarm

THE TOURNAMENT AT CHAUVENCY

The thirteenth century was in many ways the golden age of tourneying; the sport had developed civilized rules and was already a glittering focal point of the knightly social life, but it had not yet become so theatrical and divorced from reality as it became in the later Middle Ages. One tournament, which took place at Chauvency in 1285, was recorded in great detail by the poet Jacques Bretel.

Heralds had proclaimed throughout the surrounding areas that a week of tourneying was being held by the Count of Chiny, Louis de Looz. The knights who wished to take part assembled at Chauvency on the Sunday, when they were entertained at the castle of Chauvency with a dance. During the dance one of the heralds pointed out to Jacques the most famous and distinguished knights. Among them were the Count of Luxembourg, and many knights from Flanders and Hainault as well as from France, where tournaments and jousts were currently banned.

On Monday morning the knights arose early and went to Mass. Jacques Bretel emphasizes the enthusiastic religious observance of the knights throughout the week, which was clearly well-served by the priests of Count Louis and his brother, even though at this time tournaments were still banned by the Church. After Mass, the event began with jousting, which took place outside the castle walls. Scaffolds had been put up containing seats for the watching ladies. The heralds began to call out the names of the contestants as they entered the lists, identifying each one effortlessly by his coat of arms. Six jousts took place during the course of the morning, with the usual tally of injury – at the first encounter both knights' horses were thrown to the ground by the impact, and one of the knights sustained a broken arm.

At noon a new group of knights arrived and the jousting continued all afternoon. At sunset the ladies came out of the stands, where they had been following the adventures of their favourites. Heralds,

ABOVE *A joust in 1342 before King Edward III of England, illustrated in Froissart's Chronicles. The joust was held by the king in honour of the Countess of Salisbury; the event was marred by the death of Sir John Beaumont.*

LEFT *A detail from the* Romance of Alexander, *showing squires sharpening swords on a huge whetstone.*

like the one in *Lancelot*, were often employed to shout the praises of one lord, who might be their employer. Jacques was delighted to hear one herald shout at the end of a joust: "Gerard of Looz burns with courage, prowess and boldness, and as soon as he has taken off his helmet steeps himself in courtesy, loyalty and

generosity. This he does both in the lists and at the castle." Everyone returned to the castle, singing songs and staging an impromptu musical contest. They then sat down to a banquet, followed by a dance.

On the following day this sequence was repeated, and in the evening the knights decided that on Thursday there would be a tournament *mêlée*, and instructed the heralds to proclaim it and invite all comers. On Wednesday there was no jousting, because a knight had been badly injured. The teams for the tournament were chosen; the knights of France were to fight the knights of Flanders and Hainault. Everyone was excited, and the knights outdid one another in boasting of the feats they would achieve to impress the ladies.

On Thursday, after attending Mass, the heralds escorted the knights onto the field. Jacques describes the colourful scene, with the sun glinting on brilliantly shining armour and beautiful banners; gleaming horses champ and whinny, eager to begin, and trumpeters and drummers perform blaring fanfares and rolls. The teams divided into four battles and commenced fighting, armed with swords and clubs. Jacques describes the fighting with relish, relating how the knights beat and thumped at one another, becoming hot and sweaty in the process. As they fought, pieces of armour and accoutrements flew off and littered the field, to be collected in sacks by the squires. Knights were injured, unhorsed, taken prisoner by their more fortunate colleagues. The field was large; the fighting ranged all over it and was still going on at sunset. Then the heralds called a halt and the knights returned to the castle for the final feast, discussing who had won the prizes, and grumbling if they had lost.

The next day after Mass, the knights and ladies departed to their homes. The impression left by the account is that of an opportunity to dress up in fine clothes and display courtly leisure and polished manners, together with masculine aggression and athletic skill in a savage contest.

BELOW *René of Anjou's beautifully illustrated manual,* Traité de la forme et devis comme on fait les tournois *showing a* mêlée *with swords in progress. Some knights in their enthusiasm have carried the fighting outside the lists, for which they will be disqualified.*

and rest for a time. This was the sort of contest in which William Marshal and his charge, Henry the Young King, took part with their teams of knights.

It was common for knights to be killed or suffer serious wounds in tournaments. At one tournament, held in 1241 at the German town of Neuss, eighty knights and squires were killed; one chronicler recorded that they had been suffocated by clouds of dust created by the combat, but another said that they had gone mad and killed each other in their frenzy. Suffocation inside the heavy and restricting armour was not uncommon; in 1279 Lantefrydus de Landesperach died of suffocation at a tournament in Strasburg, thirty years after his father had perished in the same way. In the same year Robert of Clermont, brother of the king of France, took part in his first tournament and received severe head injuries which permanently impaired his faculties; in 1216 Geoffrey de Mandeville, the Earl of Essex, was trampled to death in a tournament. Chroniclers often recorded those tournaments at which disasters happened, and then named only the most famous and nobly-born of the casualties. The list above is only a tiny fragment of the recorded deaths and injuries, which in turn represent only the tip of the iceberg in terms of the numbers of ordinary knights who met their deaths pursuing their favourite sport.

Even after the introduction of regulations which were intended to make the sport safer, such as the use of blunted weapons, or the erection of barriers in jousting which prevented the galloping horses of the jousting knights from crashing into each other, fatalities still occurred. As late as 1559, when tournaments had become stylized, ceremonious affairs, King Henry II of France was fatally injured jousting against his Constable, Montgomery, when a splinter from Montgomery's broken lance pierced his face through the visor of his helmet.

The peril of committing murder, even unintentionally, during a tournament was one of the reasons for the Church's ban on them. Other reasons were the encouragement they gave to such vices as pride, anger, and lustfulness, and their tendency to incite public disorder. Jacques de Vitry, the preacher, complained loudly about the harvests trampled down by charging knights, of the intolerable taxes they imposed on their poor peasants so that they could afford to participate, of the ferocity and cruelty of the knights to each other in the heat of the combat, the pride and indecent triumph of the winners, and the gluttony and debauchery exhibited at the feasts which usually accompanied tournaments.

The threat of public disorder was real and contributed to the bans which were imposed from time to time by secular as well as spiritual rulers. Tempers lost in a tournament could quickly change a sport into deadly earnest, and under cover of the general violence of a *mêlée* it was easy to pursue personal feuds and pay off grudges. In 1169, a tournament was held between the French knights of Gournay and the Flemish knights of Resson le Mals. Baldwin, the son of the Flemish Count of Hainault, chivalrously decided to fight on the side of the French, because they were outnumbered, at which his overlord Philip of Flanders was so furious that he attacked in earnest. In 1273, at a tournament taking place near Chalons, the Duke of Burgundy seized Edward I of England round the neck and tried to pull him from his horse. Edward considered this to be against the rules and lost his temper, galloping away with the Duke still hanging on to him. At this the

ABOVE *A carved ivory tabernacle with a strangely secular relief: ladies arm their knights for the joust. Note the lances, tipped with blunted "coronals" for combat* à la plaisance, *and the "favours" of the ladies displayed on the helms. One knight defends the castle; the other challenges from the greenwood.*

foot soldiers of both sides joined battle and even shot crossbow bolts at one another. A number of deaths occurred, among the spectators as well as the combatants, and the tournament became known as "the little battle of Chalons".

Tournaments were so popular that knights preferred to attend them than to undertake the real business of knighthood. Even Edward I of England, who was a great tourneyer himself, had to impose strict bans on tournaments during his campaigns against the Scots and the Welsh, because his knights kept sneaking off to tournaments every time there was a pause in hostilities. Ulrich of Lichtenstein mentions that in 1224 he and his brother Dietmar happened to be attending a diplomatic meeting at Friesach between the lords of Istria and Carinthia. The negotiations had to be interrupted because Ulrich and his brother had tempted the other knights to joust, and could not be resumed until they had held a spontaneous tournament.

In time, rule books were drawn up for tournaments, such as Edward I's, which insisted on the use of blunted or "bated" weapons, restricted the number of men who could accompany a knight, and ordained that foot soldiers and grooms should not be armed. The area in which the *mêlée* took place was more strictly defined as the "lists", for the convenience of the spectators and judges; the *mêlée* itself was generally preceded by "jousts" between individual knights, the sporting equivalent of single combat. Knights taking part in a tournament then had to register and, in some places, to pay a fee; only knights, or those who "bore arms", were allowed to take

ABOVE *An urban tournament, in this case taking place in the Piazza Santa Croce in Florence. Urban tournaments were particularly common in northern Italy, where many knights and nobles lived in the independent cities, and in Burgundy and Germany, where urban centres attracted tourneying societies.*

THE KNIGHT OF VENUS

Ulrich von Lichtenstein was an extra-ordinary character. As a young man he was a celebrated poet and jousting fanatic, who later earned a distinguished career as lord, knight and diplomat in his native Styria. He wrote his autobiography in about 1255, entitling it *Frauendienst* – Lady's Service. Written as a narrative verse poem, it strongly reflects the influence of romances and particularly the cult of service to a beloved woman. Historians are not sure how much of Ulrich's account of his activities to believe, though he obviously did make the journeys he mentions. Some of the events he describes, however, are bordering the realms of fantasy, and a strong vein of burlesque comedy runs through the whole.

In 1227, Ulrich tells us that he undertook, as a tribute to his lady and to prove his worth to her, a journey from Venice to Vienna, which took him through Italy, Bohemia and Austria. To honour love and ladies in general, he dressed in the costume of Venus, complete with two long blonde plaits – a disguise which, he insists, was never penetrated – and challenged all comers to joust with him. If they succeeded in breaking three lances on him, he would give them a gold ring. If he beat them, they had to bow to the four corners of the earth in honour of his lady. This "Venusfahrt" lasted a month, during which he claimed to have broken 307 lances on his challengers, and given away 271 rings.

His devotion to his lady was singular. He recorded that on one occasion, hearing that she was surprised to see that he still had all his fingers, because she thought one had been cut off in a tournament at which he had fought in her honour, he cut off the finger in question and sent it to her. On the other hand, it didn't interfere with his relationship with his wife, for he mentioned that during his journey he managed to spend three days with her, which gave him great joy. However, all his deeds of arms in his lady's honour did not succeed in impressing her enough to grant him her love, and when

he undertook his second jousting tour, the "Artusfahrt", in 1240, it was in the service of another lady.

On this journey, Ulrich went dressed as King Arthur, and was accompanied by six friends, who had assumed the costumes and characters of six of the Knights of the Round Table. This time any knight who succeeded in breaking lances on Ulrich was rewarded with membership of his "Round Table". The high spot of the tour came when Frederick, Duke of Austria, sent a herald to "King Arthur" with a message to thank him for leaving his seat in Paradise to visit Austria, and requesting the honour of attempting to gain admission to his order of the Round

ABOVE Ulrich von Lichtenstein, poet, statesman and famous jouster, in full armour with the figure of Venus displayed on the crest of his helm, from the Manessa Codex.

Table. A field near Neustadt was selected for the jousting. The Duke and his knights arrived and five days of individual jousting were followed by a general tournament (*mêlée*). Unfortunately, the Duke then cancelled the encounter, for reasons which are not entirely clear. Perhaps "King Arthur" and his knights were too successful, or perhaps the *mêlée*, as so often, was turning into a serious fight. Ulrich and his companions returned home.

part. Attacks were not permitted on, or by, knights who had surrendered themselves to captors.

The influence of romance literature on tournaments was at least as great as the influence of tournaments on romance. From a quite early date (1223) it was customary to hold tournaments in Arthurian dress. One of these, the tournament of Le Hem in Picardy in 1278, was recorded by the poet Sarasin. Lords Aubert de Longueval and Huart de Bazentin had organized the event, to which participating knights had to bring a damsel. De Longueval's sister, Jeanne, was dressed as Queen Guinevere; she and "Dame Courtoisie" opened the proceedings, which included the appearance of the "Chevalier au Lion" (Count Robert of Artois, who had recently been excommunicated for taking part in tournaments), who had supposedly returned from a quest in which he had conquered knights and freed imprisoned damsels. He even had a real lion on a chain. The knights who took part were supposed to defend the claim that Guinevere's knights were the best in the world, and jousted against each other for two days.

This, and many other tournaments like it, exemplified a tendency which grew more marked as time went by for tournaments to be richer, more ceremonious, more formal, more theatrical and ornate, more associated with grand state occasions and the wealth and status of individual lords or kings. In Germany, Burgundy and Italy the "urban tournament", held in the town square, enjoyed a more democratic popularity. In Italy, where the patriciates of the great lords tended to be centred on towns and cities, these urban tournaments shared many of the characteristics of the rich extravaganzas of northern France and Flanders, but there were some towns in Italy and many in Germany where tournaments were organized and run by genuine enthusiasts, who formed tourneying societies. Many towns competed jealously for the privilege of hosting tournaments; then, as now, the prestige associated with internationally popular sporting events went hand in hand with the opportunity to make a handsome profit from the crowds of knights, ladies, squires, grooms, armourers, heralds, minstrels, servants and spectators who attended every tournament. Urban tourneys could not compete with the great showcases of international chivalry for spectacle and the display of wealth, but they did continue to provide the kind of contest which was a useful military training as well as a chivalrous sport.

The Banquet

In common with other opportunities for ceremonial display and vivid pageantry, the banquet, either as a private celebration or as a great state occasion, became more and more stylized and elaborate as the period progressed. Banqueting had always played an important part in the social life of knights, and even in the early Middle Ages was used to mark occasions such as weddings, betrothals, comings-of-age, and, of course, tournaments. It quickly developed a formality and stateliness appropriate for the display of wealth and status.

By the fourteenth and fifteenth centuries even everyday dinner had become somewhat ritualized; the knight dined in the Hall of his manor house with all his household gathered together. Where you sat at the long trestle tables was a sign of your "worth"; to be seated below the salt meant that you

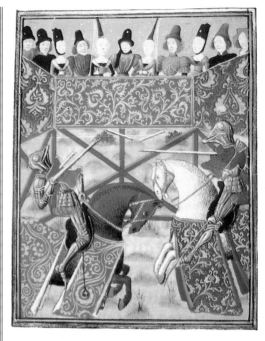

ABOVE *A real-life joust – Sir Piers de Courtenay and the Sire de Clary at Calais in 1389, described by Froissart in his chronicle of the Hundred Years War. Courtenay had been forbidden by the King of France to undertake this combat* à l'outrance *(with real weapons). The outcome was that he was badly wounded in the shoulder.*

were unimportant. The knight and his family, any guests and the most important household officers such as his steward would sit together at the high table, set apart from the rest at the top of the Hall. Before the meal the knight would hear petitions from the tenants on his estate and deal with any rewards or disciplines in his own household.

Medieval banquets were great occasions, when the chef would stretch his ingenuity to the utmost to decorate, and even to disguise, the dishes served. Often there would be some form of entertainment for the guests. At such a banquet, given by a great lord, the host and his most important guests would be seated along one side of the high table, facing the rest of the room. The table might be raised on a dais, and there might be a "minstrels' gallery" facing it, where musicians would play during the meal. The lord himself would be seated in the centre of the table, under a great canopy. The table nearest to the lord's right hand was where the most senior in rank of the other guests would sit; opposite it on his left would be the next most important people, and so on down in strict gradation.

The form which feasts took was quite different from modern state banquets. Each "course" – there were usually three at a banquet – would comprise a variety of dishes of roasted meats and poultry or fish (if it was a Friday or other fast-day), together with some sweet dishes served at the same time. Each person had a "trencher", a kind of plate made out of a slab of four-day-old brown bread slightly hollowed in the middle. After the banquet these would be gathered up and given to the poor. The trencher was renewed with each course. Meanwhile, guests would help themselves or, if on high

LEFT *A banquet in progress, from a late thirteenth-century manuscript. The noble guests, all seated at one side of the high table, can be seen to share goblets and dishes. Food was cut with knives and eaten with the fingers. Despite this, or perhaps because of it, contemporary treatises on table manners show a highly developed etiquette.*

table, be served with portions from the dishes, which were usually shared between two or four. Later in the period, or at great state banquets, silver or gold dishes were used as platters.

To be served from, or invited to share, the lord's platter was a mark of favour, but it was common for two guests seated next to one another to share a dish ("messe") or a cup. Medieval books of etiquette instructed guests to wash their hands properly, so as not to soil the tablecloth with finger-marks; not to drink from a shared cup if their mouth was full of food, not to slurp soup, pick their teeth with their knife, blow on their food or wipe their mouth with the tablecloth. If the guest was sharing a dish, he should not stick his fingers into it too deeply, or crumble bread into it in case he had sweaty fingers, or leave his dirty spoon in it. Belching and spitting were, not surprisingly, frowned upon, and so was scratching one's head at the table and gnawing or sucking on bones.

In the Middle Ages a much broader range of animals, and particularly birds, was eaten. Swans and peacocks were popular choices for banquets;

they could be elaborately dressed as a magnificent centre-piece, with a cured skin fitted over a wire frame on top of the roasted meat, so that they appeared sitting upright, particularly effective with the gorgeous tail of a peacock displayed. Other birds included crane, heron, bustard, gull, egret, curlew and, in smaller sizes, blackbird, lark, quail, plover, lapwing, thrush, snipe and bittern, besides the more familiar game birds, such as partridge and pheasant. Dishes full of tiny carcases would be served, and formed an important element of any state banquet at which clergymen, who were forbidden to eat the meat of quadrupeds, would be present. In the later Middle Ages, the bird which formed the central dish of a banquet was often used as a symbol for the swearing of elaborate oaths, as in the poem *The Vows of the Heron* and the famous real-life vows of the Pheasant and Swan.

Contact with more sophisticated cultures through the crusades and generally through trade led to widespread use of exotic imported foodstuffs, including spices, citrus fruits, dried fruits such as raisins and figs, almonds and (a rare luxury) cane sugar. At a really important feast a hand-carved sugar sculpture would be presented at the end of each course for the admiration of all present. The use of spices in cooking for the wealthy probably resulted in more highly flavoured food than modern palates would appreciate.

A banquet required elaborate service from the household officers in their formal roles: the steward and the marshal who orchestrated the activities of the lesser officials, the butler who served drinks, the cellarer who presided over the drink stores, the pantler who organized distribution from the "pantry", where dishes were brought from the kitchen and served into the Hall, the ewerer who was in charge of hand-basins and towels, the cook, the carver and the cup-bearer. Under these was a host of grooms and underlings to perform the menial tasks. Each knight at a tournament feast would have his meat carved for him personally by his own squire. Bringing dishes to the high table was done with style and to a musical accompaniment; clearing up the debris afterwards was a job for the less important waiters. At a great feast the chief offices of the household were performed by nobles or knights, who would receive handsome presents for their services afterwards.

In the presence of royalty or particularly exalted nobles, an elaborate tasting ritual took place, where a "taster" ate a small portion of each dish to make sure it was not poisoned. As time went by this was formalized with particular ceremonies involving special linen, a "tasting spoon" and special prayers.

The meal would be concluded with a sweet dish, perhaps dried fruit, and a sweet wine. At this point, and perhaps in between courses as well while the tables were cleared and re-laid, some form of entertainment would be laid on; jugglers, tumblers, minstrels, or troops of actors or mime artists were all known to provide additional spectacle at feasts. Often the entertainment would take the form of enactments of scenes from famous romances or from history. In some later medieval examples they became incredibly elaborate, as at the marriage-feast of Charles the Bold, Duke of Burgundy to Margaret of York in 1468. On that occasion there were six days of jousting, followed by feasts at which various tableaux were presented, including the twelve labours of Hercules, a model of the Duke's new castle at Gorcum filled with singers dressed up as wild animals, a collection of gardens containing golden trees with golden leaves and fruit, the whole event having been planned around a romance whose hero was Florimont, the Knight of the Golden Tree. To crown it all, on the final evening, guests were treated to the appearance of a large mechanical whale, which opened up to reveal sirens singing and was accompanied by giants who fought a mock-battle against 12 knights. This was the kind of lavish spectacle which would develop into the masques of the seventeenth century.

THE SECULAR ORDERS

The secular orders of knighthood which became so popular in the fourteenth and fifteenth centuries had little in common with their religious predecessors, the military religious orders. The latter were indeed religious, in the sense of committing their members to a way of life cut off from secular concerns, such as the pursuit of worldly honour and loyalty to individual secular lords, and governed by a monastic rule. The secular orders, on the contrary, were very much concerned with the rewards and celebrations of worldly honour and most of their statutes enforced specific loyalties, to their founding lord and his heirs, and, more commonly, to each other, so that a member had to do all he could to aid other members and their disputes were his disputes. In part this can be understood as an attempt to breathe new life into the ideology of knighthood; to recreate closer bonds of loyalty and brotherhood between knights who acknowledged specific objectives in a world in which the old-fashioned values of chivalry were becoming increasingly difficult to maintain. In part, the secular orders were formed for less idealistic reasons, such as the reinforcement of the privileges and the exclusive status of the knightly class, and the creation of useful alliances in the pursuit of diplomatic and political ends.

The orders were, of course, religious in the usual knightly sense; they sought to emphasize that piety and respectful religious observance were essential qualities of true chivalry. Many associated themselves with specific saints (St George was of course the most popular) or feast days, concerned themselves with the establishment of charitable foundations, endowed

ABOVE *A knight and lady exchange rings, in the presence of a chaperone. An illustration from a fifteenth-century manuscript of the poems of Guillaume de Machaut (c.1300-1377).*

chantry chapels and paid for masses; and all had ordinances for religious services before or after their meetings.

These orders were many and varied. Some were founded by kings or great lords, such as the Order of the Band, founded in about 1330 by King Alfonso XI of Castile, the Order of the Garter, founded in 1348 by King Edward III of England, the Order of the Star, founded in 1351 by King John of France, the Order of the Knot, founded in 1352 by King Louis of Naples, and the Order of the Golden Buckle, founded in 1355 by Emperor Charles IV, to name but a few. Some were temporary societies in which the members were bound together by particular oaths that they had sworn, such as the Order of the *Dame Blanche a l'Escu Vert* (the White Lady of the Green Shield) of Marshal Jean de Boucicaut. Others were basically associations of like-minded knights and these called themselves "Confraternities" or "Brotherhoods", as well as Orders. These were particularly popular in Germany, where many knightly brotherhoods were formed along the lines of tourneying societies, which had been in existence for some time.

Certain characteristics were shared by all orders and confraternities. All of them had constitutions and regulations laid down in statutes, which defined the objectives of the association and the rules governing eligibility for membership, and conduct of members. All held meetings or "chapters"

RIGHT *The institution of the Order of the Star by King John the Good of France in 1351, and a banquet of the Knights of the Star. The order was created in response to the Order of the Garter invented by King Edward III of England in 1348; a spate of orders and confraternities then followed.*

ABOVE *An example of a document proving knightly descent on both sides of the family, required for entry into most of the secular orders of knighthood (and some of the religious ones). This proof of the nobility of a Spanish knight, Don Pedro Manuel de Vilhena, was required for his entry into the Hospitallers.*

regularly, once a year or more frequently, to outline activities, celebrate achievements, initiate new members or discipline existing ones. All were exclusive about the social status of people who could be invited to join (the sole exception being the Order of the Ermine in Naples, which admitted men who had been knighted as a reward for their deeds, even if they were not of noble birth). All selected some members to act as officials, each of whom had specific duties to perform. All had special robes or special insignia, which could be worn only by members.

Noble birth, though in most cases an essential criterion for membership of a secular Order, was by no means the only one. Most Orders and confraternities would only admit members who had a good reputation and were "*sans reproche*". Robber knights, the impious who had been repeatedly excommunicated, and any knight who spoke ill of women were all excluded from membership by the constitutions of some German Orders, for example, and almost all had provisions for judging and punishing any members guilty of misconduct – which could range from showing cowardice in battle, to behaving discourteously toward ladies. The majority of Orders were exclusive to men, but some admitted ladies as well, such as the Order of the Dragon of the Count of Foix, the Order of St Anthony of the Counts of Hainault, and, at least in its early days, the Order of the Garter.

Whether they admitted ladies to membership or not, the service of ladies was an important element of most constitutions. The first Order, the Castilian Order of the Band, defined the two principal objectives of its members as the preservation of chivalric honour, and of loyalty, a value on which much store was set:

> Loyalty is one of the greatest virtues that there can be in any person, and especially in a knight, who ought to keep himself loyal in many ways. But the principal ways are two: first to keep loyalty to his lord, and secondly to love truly her in whom he has placed his heart.

Members of Marshal Boucicaut's Order of the White Lady of the Green Shield swore an oath to serve ladies for five years. This service included taking the part of widows or other women without menfolk of their own in legal disputes as well as the more obvious aspects of physical protection.

The honour and service of ladies was only one aspect of the avowed chivalric aims of secular orders which had been influenced by romance literature. The Round Table fellowship of King Arthur was said to have inspired King Edward III in his creation of the Order of the Garter:

> The King in the nobility of his heart resolved that he would rebuild the castle of Windsor, which Arthur first constructed and where the Round Table was first established, on account of the prowess of the knights who were there then, who had served him so well that he held them so worthy and noble that their peers could not be found in any kingdom: and it seemed to him that he could not honour them too much, so much did he love them.

Other orders too were influenced by romances, such as the *Roman de Troie* or the fourteenth-century French romance *Perceforest*.

The prestige which was associated with membership of an order such as these, in which membership was only open to those who had the most distinguished records of character and service, was a major factor in their success. The secular orders represent an important, new and vigorous growth of later medieval chivalry, in which practical aims were combined with a genuine respect for the values of chivalry and an attempt to revive those values in a valid contemporary context.

BELOW *The investiture of Richard Beauchamp, Earl of Warwick, as a Knight of the Garter by King Henry IV of England on the field of the Battle of Shrewsbury in 1403.*

CHAPTER FIVE

THE
KNIGHT AT WAR

The guiding principle behind the development of a knight's career in medieval warfare was schooling. There were no military colleges as such until the sixteenth century, and though his initial training and the tournament could teach basic skills, there was no substitute for experience in real battles, Young knights were encouraged to go abroad, individually or in small groups, to serve in foreign wars or crusades to gain experience in warfare, which would render them useful to their lords when they returned. This was the real-life equivalent of the knight-errantry of romance.

Wars of one sort or another were being waged all the time in medieval Europe. These ranged from local conflicts between competing lords or cities, to national conflicts within Europe, such as the Hundred Years War. Crusades might entail mass mobilizations to the Holy Land or smaller campaigns against individual cities or states, such as occurred during the Spanish *Reconquista* and the campaigns of the Teutonic Knights in Prussia and Lithuania. Knights from all over Europe, wishing to gain military experience and a reputation, travelled to take part in these conflicts as freelance soldiers, a policy that was actively encouraged from time to time, particularly by the Teutonic Knights who were often short of men and relied on outside help.

SWISS KNIGHT, 1476

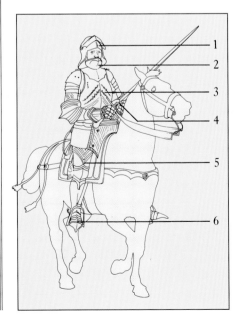

This knight is wearing German harness, in characteristically angular style. His helmet, known as a sallet (1) has a long tail behind to cover his neck; its hinged visor, now raised, protects only the upper part of his face. The chin and throat are protected by a separate piece of armour called a bevor (2). His breastplate (3) is in two parts, the lower overlapping the upper. His "hand-and-a-half" sword (4), so-called because the lengthened grip meant that it could be grasped with both hands, has a long blade with a sharp point for thrusting and stabbing as well as cutting. The surfaces of the armour, as here on the cuisses (5) have fan-like flutings. The feet are armoured in flexible pointed sabatons (6), with rowel spurs. He has no shield; full plate armour has made them obsolete.

In the course of these engagements, a young knight might find himself engaged in many different kinds of warfare. Pitched battles did occur and were usually critical in the course of a conflict, but were comparatively infrequent. Much more common were raids, in which parties of men entered enemy territory and destroyed as much as they could before any defence could be organized against them. Many of the military campaigns of the Middle Ages depended on control of a network of strategic fortifications, and this accounts for the large numbers of sieges throughout the period. Knights could gain experience, both as besieger and defender, sometimes in very quick succession, as at the Siege of Antioch in 1098. Casualties during sieges resulted more often from disease than from fighting. The single combats of romance were rare in real life, but there are one or two examples. Naval battles, too, were rare in the days before European nations developed standing navies, but again did occur.

ABOVE *Sea battles were extremely rare in the Middle Ages because it was not until the sixteenth century that states began to invest in permanent navies. Nevertheless they did occur – this fresco from the Palazzo Pubblico in Siena depicts a naval battle between Emperor Frederick I (Barbarossa) and the North Italian cities.*

WEAPONS OF WAR

The main weapons of the medieval knight were the sword and the lance. In a cavalry charge, the long, heavy lance would be the first weapon with which a knight would make contact with the enemy. After the charge, fighting would be hand-to-hand in a *mêlée*, rather similar to, but more deadly than, the tournament *mêlée*. Knights sometimes used a mace, a heavy club often reinforced with metal ribs at the head. This was a weapon favoured by military-minded clerics (who were not allowed to carry weapons with blades or to shed blood), such as the Bishop of Beauvais who captured the Earl of Salisbury at the Battle of Bouvines in 1214 by stunning him with a mace.

It was customary for knights to form about a quarter or a fifth of an army, the rest being composed of various kinds of infantry: men-at-arms, and archers or crossbowmen. Increasingly during the fourteenth century, knights dismounted and fought on foot during battles, though the cavalry charge was still an effective way of disrupting the enemy's ranks. The increased effectiveness of the longbow and the crossbow meant that even plate armour could be pierced, and the importance of cavalry in battle declined. Axes were another weapon favoured by knights and men-at-arms. A short-handled battle-axe, especially if wielded from horseback, could deliver fatal blows, like the one which killed the Duke of Alençon at the Battle of Agincourt.

The short bow, the weapon of the archers at the Battle of Hastings in 1066, was not as powerful or long-ranging as the crossbow, a weapon which had been known in classical times but was not widely revived until the late eleventh century. The Italian city of Genoa specialized in its manufacture. Trained mercenary Genoese crossbowmen featured in the armies of several medieval warlords. The crossbow was able to deliver its bolt at great speed over a long range, and was fired horizontally instead of into the air as with a bow. Its disadvantages were that it took a relatively long time to load the bolt, as the string had to be pulled back mechanically, using a lever or ratchet, and the steel bolts called "quarrels", were expensive.

The longbow, which had been popular in Wales in the twelfth century, became more widely known during the thirteenth and was made a crucial weapon by the English forces during their invasions of France during the

ABOVE *A medieval drinking horn from Sweden showing a fully armed and mounted knight.*

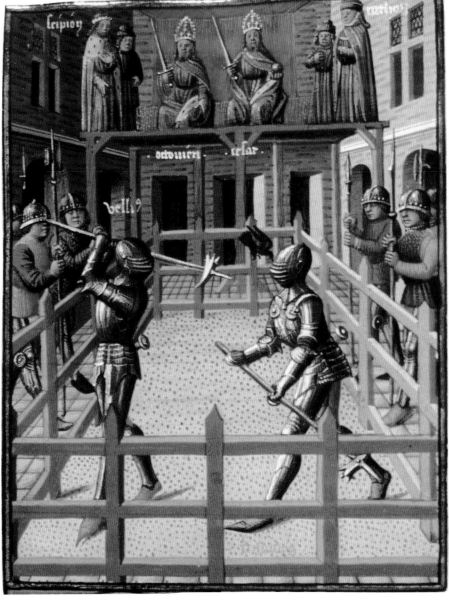

RIGHT *An illustration from a fifteenth-century manuscript showing single combat on foot with battle axes. Axes became an increasingly popular weapon both in jousts and in battle during the fourteenth and fifteenth centuries.*

127

fourteenth century. Properly used, it was deadly: a trained longbowman could fire up to twelve arrows a minute, and the bands of archers so effectively deployed by the English at the Battle of Crécy in 1346 could loose off tens of thousands of arrows per minute, producing a deadly rain. When used in a battle against a charging mass of enemy soldiers, it was not important to aim at a particular target, as it would be if the archer were acting as a sniper shooting from the walls of a besieged castle. Thousands of arrows falling onto a host of men and horses were bound to hit something. Horses were particularly vulnerable as they were not as heavily armoured as knights. Knights did not use bows of any kind, for their ability to destroy an enemy anonymously from a safe distance was at odds with the knightly ethos of individual combat and heroic achievement.

Slingshots were a popular weapon among peasant levies, as the ammunition was readily available and free. Stones of all sizes, and especially large stones, were valuable weapons in medieval warfare.

BATTLES

Knights played an important part in most battles throughout the Middle Ages, but the importance of the heavy cavalry charge as a battle-winning tactic, which had originally brought them to prominence, steadily declined as the period progressed. Knights had never fought without the support of infantry, and usually during the first half of the Middle Ages an army was composed of mixed cavalry and infantry, with proportions ranging from one knight to four foot soldiers, up to one knight to eight foot soldiers. But with time, the development of new weapons and new ways of fighting, the deployment of specially trained infantry emerged as the decisive factor in pitched battles.

The role of the knight in battle should be seen in parallel with developments in weapons technology, and the counter-developments in the knight's protective armour against the superior firepower of the infantry. During the tenth, eleventh, twelfth, and a large part of the thirteenth centuries, the knight reigned supreme. He was always supported by infantry in battle. The infantry was equipped with the despised bows, but they were intended to support the cavalry, to protect their horses from enemy missiles, and to fend off enemy frontal attacks, until the right moment came for the devastating cavalry charge that would decide the outcome of the battle. This was the outstanding battle strategy of the period: the cavalry charge, if delivered in a well-timed, well-organized way, broke the ranks of the enemy's soldiers, who would be overcome in the furious hand-to-hand fighting that followed. However, it was essential for the knights to act in unison for the charge to be effective. For every battle that was won by the cavalry sweeping the enemy from the field, another was lost by hot-headed, ill-disciplined knights charging under their own impulses rather than at the command of their leaders. Outstanding examples of battles won by mounted knights are those of Ascalon during the First Crusade (1098), Arsouf during the Third Crusade (1191), and Bouvines (1216).

At the Battle of Arsouf the crusading army was marching up the coast towards Jaffa, under the command of Richard Lionheart. They were

ABOVE *A mid-fifteenth century representation of the Battle of Agincourt, intended to show the success of the English archers (left of the picture) against the French cavalry on the right. It gives little idea, however, of the catastrophically crowded battlefield, where many knights died of suffocation and drowning.*

opposed by a larger Turkish force under Saladin. The Christian army was well-organized; its lines were drawn up as they had been for the march, with the infantry between the Turks and the horses of the armoured knights, protecting them from the arrows shot by the Turkish lightly armed cavalry. The less reliable knights of England, Brittany, Anjou, Poitou, Normandy and France were stationed centrally between the more experienced and highly trained Templars in the front, and Hospitallers in the rear. Richard was determined that his lines should stand firm, while allowing the Turks to exhaust themselves with repeated assaults, before unleashing his massed cavalry. Despite repeated requests to be allowed to lead a charge from the Master of the Hospitallers, who were bearing the brunt of the Turkish attack and were losing many horses to their archers, Richard refused to sound the trumpet signal for advance. At last the Hospitallers, desperately afraid that they would lose all their horses before they had a chance to strike at the enemy, began to charge without the signal, but Richard was prepared and gave them immediate support. He knew that to be effective the charge of the knights must be one, united, overwhelming wave, and at once gave the order for the signal to be sounded. The knights surged forward, broke the Turkish ranks, and within minutes the tide of the battle had turned, with the cavalry pursuing the fleeing enemy into a nearby woodland.

The Battle of Bouvines was also a closely fought contest, in which the steady, disciplined use of cavalry charges by the French knights of King Philip gained a victory over the much larger combined forces of Emperor Otto IV of Germany and King John of England. The Germans employed Flemish pikemen, who proved the most difficult of the enemy infantry to break, but a succession of well-timed attacks eventually smashed the lines of the allies' left, front and right divisions. The French gained control of the Angevin Empire in consequence.

These and other similar victories were achieved because infantrymen had not yet developed any weaponry or strategy that enabled them to withstand the onslaught of heavily-armed cavalry. Correspondingly, there was little real change in a knight's armour during this period; it consisted of a suit of chain mail, which began as a tunic and eventually stretched to cover the knight from head to toe and down to his finger ends, with a shield and a helmet. From the second half of the thirteenth century, the protection afforded by chain mail became inadequate and had to be supplemented by additional body armour. The "plate" armour of the later medieval knight began to make its appearance; greaves for the shins, vambraces for the arms, poleyns for the knees and cuisses for the thighs were strapped on over the chain mail, while the body was protected by a "coat of plates", a jerkin of padded cloth or leather on to which metal plates were sewn. The reason for these additional defences was the emergence of two weapons which could be used effectively against armoured, mounted knights: the pike and the longbow.

Although knights continued on the whole to prove a decisive element in battle until well into the fourteenth century, the future of warfare was shown by some grievous defeats suffered by cavalry forces, all inflicted by infantry. One of these was the Battle of Courtrai in 1302. The French army was opposed by a force composed largely of infantry, levied by the burghers of Flemish cities. These foot soldiers were armed with an early forerunner of

ARMS AND ARMOUR

A knight's armour was more than just protection against the more violent aspects of his lifestyle; it was intimately connected with his status as part of a military and social élite. Quality and craftsmanship in armour were valued by knights almost as much as efficiency; from the earliest days of the mail hauberk, armour was expensive and represented both a major capital investment and another opportunity to indulge the knightly love of finery. In the later Middle Ages particularly, armour became noticeably subject to the need to display wealth and keep up with the latest fashion. For this reason, many suits of armour, or "harness", which survive have been preserved as works of art.

Nevertheless armour's first purpose was to protect the knight against his enemies in battle, and developments in armour throughout the Middle Ages tended to be in response to new and better weapons. Chain mail, a crucial part of knights' armour for most of the period, was a good general protection but could not withstand a direct hit with a lance or arrow. This led first to the adoption of additional protective clothing, such as the metal-reinforced coat of plates, or the padded gambeson (though the latter was worn as much to keep mail from chafing the body as to stop weapons piercing it), and later to the development of armour constructed of solid metal plates, jointed for flexibility by smaller plates known as lames (hence the term laminated).

Plate armour weighed about the same as a complete chain mail suit (about 50 lbs/23 kg) but, if properly made to fit its wearer perfectly, was more comfortable because the weight was distributed evenly over the body instead of being suspended entirely from the shoulders. The only period in which knights were so burdened by their armour that they could not rise if they fell, was during the mid-fourteenth century, a period of transition from full mail to full plate armour when it was customary to wear both.

In the following examples the principal changes for each period are highlighted in the small line drawings.

NORMAN KNIGHT

C. 1066

NORMAN KNIGHT

C. 1180

For hundreds of years the basic form of body armour consisted of the chain-mail shirt, called the hauberk or byrnie. In one form or another, this was an essential piece of body defence until the late fifteenth century. We have ample evidence in the Bayeux tapestry of the equipment worn and carried by the Norman knights who rode to victory at Hastings; they had knee-length mail hauberks with elbow-length sleeves, split at front and rear for ease when riding, conical helmets with a nasal bar, and leather or padded cloth greaves. Only very high-ranking lords, such as Duke William or his brother, Bishop Odo of Bayeux, wore mail stockings to protect their legs and feet. Norman knights carried long, kite-shaped shields, often decorated with swirling shapes like this one, though there is no evidence that these decorations were associated with specific knights or families in the heraldic sense. Their main weapons were a sword and a long lance; the Saxons, by contrast, are often depicted wielding battle-axes and carrying smaller, round shields.

The knight's armour and equipment has not fundamentally changed for a hundred years, but it has undergone a process of improvement and refinement. The mail hauberk, worn over a tunic tightly padded with wool and called a gambeson, is just below knee-length and the arms have been extended to incorporate mittens. The knight slides his hands in and out of the mittens through a slit at the wrist, which is then laced up. His legs and feet are now also encased in mail. Over his hauberk he wears a long, sleeveless, loose fitting surcoat, which may bear his own distinctive device – the first beginnings of heraldry. His helmet is now round, the better to deflect blows and missiles, with a larger nasal bar. The neck of the hauberk extends into an aventail – which is laced to the helmet with thongs. His sword has the characteristic "fish-tail" pommel, and his lance a broader blade with lugs to prevent too deep penetration into opponents' bodies. His shield has become shorter and more triangular in shape.

KNIGHT
C. 1225-1250

The main development in the knight's equipment is the addition of the helm. This was originally a large, square-topped helmet which fitted on over the top of the chain mail coif (here resting on the knight's shoulders) and a padded arming cap, which was apparently worn either under or over the mail. For the first time the helm covers the whole face, with slits at eye-level for vision and perforations in front of nose and mouth for ventilation. The mail mittens about this time developed into gloves with separate fingers. The padded gambeson is now reinforced with leather – a cuirie (or cuir bouilli if the leather had been hardened by boiling) – and the legs are now protected by the addition of quilted cuisses on the thighs and the first sign of plate armour – poleyns on the knees.

TEUTONIC KNIGHT
C. 1270

This Teutonic knight is one of the remnants of the Schwertbroder – the Brethren of the Sword, a rather disreputable minor military Order who had been instrumental in the conversion of Livonia (modern-day Latvia and Estonia). Most of the members were killed in a massacre when they were surprised on an expedition into Lithuania, and the survivors were incorporated into the Teutonic Knights in 1237. By 1270 knights helms were once more domed over the crown of the head, since the curving surface deflected glancing blows. On top of the helm is a fitting where a crest can be attached. The hauberk is growing shorter and the gambeson is just visible beneath it. The shield is now much smaller and shaped like an iron. For this reason they are called heater-shields. The poleyns have been enlarged so that they completely cover the knee joint at front and sides. The sword has a new-style, wheel-shaped pommel.

SIR ROBERT SETVANS
C. 1306

Sir Robert is wearing a blue surcoat over his hauberk which displays his armorial bearings. These are also repeated on the ailettes – stiff leather plates attached to the shoulders which are presumed to have given protection against slashing blows at the neck. Through the slit in the surcoat the mid-thigh-length hauberk can be seen, and the padded gambeson just shows beneath it. Sir Robert has withdrawn his hands from the mail mittens which are now part of the sleeve of his hauberk, through the wrist hole, allowing the mittens to hang down. His knees are protected by ornamental poleyns and his lower legs and feet by mail chausses with prick spurs at the heels. Sir Robert would normally wear a padded arming cap prior to putting on his great helm, of the earlier, flat-topped shape, shown here at his feet without a crest.

SIR JOHN DE CREKE
C. 1325

SIR THOMAS CAWNE
C. 1360

ITALIAN KNIGHT
C. 1400

Plate armour is beginning to make its appearance, and Sir John's harness shows an early combination of mail and plate. His surcoat is shortened in front to show the three lines of defence underneath. First we see the knee-length aketon, a lighter version of the gambeson. Then the mail hauberk, which in its shorter form was called a habergeon. On top of the habergeon, we can see for the first time an additional protection – the coat of plates, a cloth garment on to which leather or metal plates were sewn. These were universally worn after about 1320, and were decorated, as here. The aventail is now a separate small cape of mail which is attached to the close-fitting bascinet by vervelles and hangs down to protect the neck. Sir John's arms and legs are protected by metal plates, strapped on over his mail; his feet also have plates, laminated for flexibility, and his spurs are the new rowel type which came in about this time.

Sir Thomas wears a typical fourteenth-century combination of mail and plate. His arms and legs are increasingly protected by plate armour – cuisses on the thighs, greaves on the shins, poleyns on the knees, upper and lower cannons of the vambrace on his arms, with winged couters at the elbow, and characteristically bell-shaped cuffs on his gauntlets. The surcoat has now become a short, tight-fitting tunic called a jupon, which still displays the knight's coat of arms. Under it he is almost certainly wearing a coat-of-plates, or possibly a solid breast-plate, though we cannot see it here. Underneath all his plate armour, however, he is still wearing a mail habergeon, which shows beneath the jupon and at the joints in his limbs. His bascinet is increasingly pointed in shape, with its mail aventail still in place. Sir Thomas also wears a typical belt of plates at his hips, to which are attached both his sword and his dagger.

The harness of this knight represents a late stage in the transition from mail to plate. His plate armour is more complete, but he still wears an aventail and a habergeon. His bascinet is fitted with the character-istic "pig-faced" visor, which, when lowered, pro-tected his face completely in battle. The breast-plate has been in use for some time, and now has developed such refinements as a protruding socket at the right arm-pit on which the knight can rest his lance as he charges. His gauntlets are becoming bell-shaped; the fingers are made of canvas. Plate armour now covers the legs front and rear (though as yet he does not wear a back-plate); greaves and cuisses are in two parts, hinged at the inner leg seam. The winged plates on poleyns and couters offer extra protection. The knight might still wear a jupon over his armour, but with this amount of plate defence the shield is becoming obsolete.

ITALIAN KNIGHT
C. 1425

GERMAN KNIGHT
C. 1470-80

JOHANN FRIEDRICH
1530

In the fifteenth century plate armour really came into its own and mail was worn only to supplement it at vulnerable joints or at areas which needed extra mobility such as hip and groin. This knight is obviously wealthy, because he is wearing a suit of Milanese armour of the finest quality. Northern Italy shared with Germany a reputation for producing the finest armour, and developed a characteristic smooth, rounded style. To go with the body harness he could choose one of two types of helmet; a close-fitting armet which covered his entire head, tapering in at the neck, or a sallet, as here, a more open style, which did not enclose the chin and throat, but had a curving neck guard behind. This one is a "Venetian" style sallet, with open face instead of a visor. His shoulders are protected by pauldrons, he wears both breast and back plates, and these are extended with overlapping plates to cover his hips. He wears mail chausses with fashionable long spurs.

This knight is wearing German or "Gothic" harness, which can be distinguished from Italian by its more angular, spiky appearance. It tends to be ornate and exaggerated; often the surfaces of the plates were rippled or fluted, and their edges were cusped. German armourers liked to decorate plates with points, and here we can see typically pointed sabatons on the knight's feet, poleyns on his knees, couters at his elbows and gauntlet cuffs. The breast-plate was often made in two parts, the lower overlapping the upper and rising to a point in the centre. The knight wears a Gothic-style sallet (helmet) with a closed face; his chin and throat are protected by a separate piece of plate armour called a bevor which was attached to the breast-plate. The knight's lower body is protected by a mail skirt, but on top of this he could also wear two plates called tassets to protect his upper thighs, which strapped on to his breast-plate. His sword is a "hand-and-a-half" sword, with longer blade and grip.

The style of armour which predominated during the first 30 years of the sixteenth century, is usually called "Maximilian", after the famous German emperor, especially when decorated with vertical fluting like this. It blended the Gothic with the Italian styles by having plates with burly, rounded shapes, decorated with bold fluting. The tassets have now been incorporated into the lower body armour, which is laminated for greater flexibility; the cunningly jointed gauntlets each have separate armour-plated laminated fingers. The pauldrons on the shoulders have raised ridges known as haute-pieces which gave extra protection to the neck. Close-helmets were universally worn at this time; following the contours of the head and face, they were hinged and fastened to an aventail of laminated plates at the top of the breast-plate. Close-helmets all had visors which could be raised for better air and visibility when the knight was not actually fighting. The knight wears new, square-toed sabatons, in imitation of civilian fashion.

the halberd, a weapon which combined a long bayonet-like blade at the top with a broad, axe-like blade at one side and a short hook or spike at the other, on top of a long pole. Knights could be hooked from their mounts with the spike, then stabbed with the bayonet or sliced or chopped with the axe. The long handle enabled the foot soldiers for the first time to inflict deep wounds on a charging horse or a knight before they were within range of his weapons. At the Battle of Courtrai, as often happened during the fourteenth century, the French knights underestimated their lower-class opponents and recklessly thrust aside their own infantry so as to charge, as they thought, to victory. Experience had taught them that the usual result was a disorganized, panicking rabble which could be cut down at will. This time it didn't work. The Flemings dug a deep ditch into which most of the knights in the front rank fell headlong, bringing the knights behind them down also. The vicious slicing blades of the Flemish *godendacs* made short work of the chivalry of France, flailing helplessly on the ground. The casualties at this battle were heavy – according to some estimates, up to 40 per cent of the French cavalry, which meant the cream of their knights, were killed.

At about the same time, the Scots pioneered a successful defensive technique using pikes, in which knots of infantry stood together with their pikes bristling outwards, presenting a wall of dense points towards the knights on horseback. Soldiers standing, kneeling and crouching presented three different levels and angles of spikes, and these *schiltrons* successfully repelled cavalry attacks at the Battles of Falkirk (1298) and Bannockburn (1314). The Swiss, in their struggles to be recognized as an emergent independent state, became adept in the use of pikes and halberds, and eventually enjoyed the reputation of being the finest, best-trained infantry in Europe, who could stand firm against any cavalry attack. They proved their superiority at the Battle of Morgarten in 1315 by cutting to pieces the knights of the duchy of Burgundy, who were famed for their chivalric prowess.

The potential of the longbow was first fully realized by the English. The long-range destructive power of bows and crossbows had long been recognized, and the famed Genoese crossbowmen were employed as auxiliaries by many medieval war-leaders, but not until the reign of Edward I were archers actually deployed as a major destructive force in themselves. The longbow, originally a traditional Welsh weapon, was adopted by the English army and a programme of intensive, compulsory training was set up in villages and towns throughout the country. Edward III, in his campaigns against the Scots during the 1330s, introduced the revolutionary tactic of having his knights dismount and provide armoured support for the longbowmen, while they fired thousands of deadly arrows into the advancing Scottish army.

During the Hundred Years War, the use of highly trained companies of English longbowmen enabled the English repeatedly to gain victory against the cavalry of French armies, many times their number. At Crécy in 1346 the superior rate of fire of longbows quickly told against the slower crossbows of the Genoese mercenaries in the French army. The retreating crossbowmen were actually ridden down by the French knights in their eagerness to come to grips with the English, but the knights charged only to be mown down by a storm of arrows.

ABOVE *A clash between two forces of mounted knights, from a fifteenth-century French account of the Hundred Years War between France (right) and England (left). This kind of cavalry encounter was the ideal battle scenario for most knights; without the levelling influence of archers, it was a contest of strength and skill between knights, an enjoyable extension of the tournament. Here the English knights, lances splintered and backs bent, are on the losing side.*

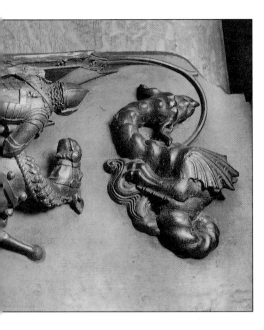

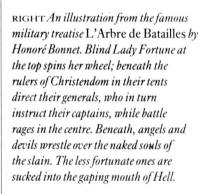

ABOVE *A mid-fifteenth-century knight, his armour pierced by a crossbow bolt, falls from his horse in a realistically detailed misericord in Lincoln Cathedral.*

RIGHT *An illustration from the famous military treatise* L'Arbre de Batailles *by Honoré Bonnet. Blind Lady Fortune at the top spins her wheel; beneath the rulers of Christendom in their tents direct their generals, who in turn instruct their captains, while battle rages in the centre. Beneath, angels and devils wrestle over the naked souls of the slain. The less fortunate ones are sucked into the gaping mouth of Hell.*

Similarly at the Battles of Najéra (1367) and Aljubarotta (1385) in Spain and Portugal, impetuous charges were swiftly terminated or turned into routs by carefully-positioned groups of archers. But the lessons of these experiences had still not been learned by the knights of France and Burgundy when, once again, an ill-timed cavalry charge was largely re-sponsible for their losing the day at the Battle of Nicopolis in 1396. This was nominally a "crusade" against the Ottoman Turks, and it had been called in response to a plea for help from King Sigismund of Hungary, whose kingdom was the one most threatened by the rapid extension of the Ottoman Empire. Knights from all over Europe responded to the call to arms, and a "crusader" force of about 6,000 eventually supplemented Sigismund's own army of about 20,000. After committing some massacres and atrocities against small Turkish civilian populations, the Christians decided to capture the important fortified city of Nicopolis on the Danube. They had no equipment to take it by storm, so they settled down in a leisurely fashion to blockade it, holding feasts and jousting before the walls to pass the time. The imminent approach of a large Turkish relieving force under the command of the Sultan Bajazet seems to have taken them by surprise. The Christian commanders argued as to how their forces should be deployed in the ensuing battle. King Sigismund was wisely in favour of holding back the cavalry until the Turks had tired themselves by engaging his infantry, and then using the shock cavalry charge to maximum effect. The French and Burgundian knights were insulted by this proposal; they had travelled far and were not to be robbed of the glory of victory over the infidel by foot soldiers. They insisted on being in the front line, and opening the battle with a charge.

The Turkish army was positioned on a hill, and had protected their position with rows of sharpened stakes. Having charged, the knights were obliged to hold back their horses, and some to dismount; though they fought bravely they were overwhelmed by successive waves of crack Turkish troops. More seriously, they were quickly cut off from the main body of the Hungarian army. Some of Sigismund's Wallachian and Transylvanian allies deserted when they saw what had happened to the cavalry, and the rest were quickly surrounded and subdued. Because of the atrocities they had committed on the way to Nicopolis, all but the most important knights captured during the battle were put to death. It was a shattering defeat for the Christian chivalry of Europe.

Knights were supposed to study treatises on war, which multiplied during the fourteenth century as the finest academic and legal minds in Europe joined the debate. The most famous, widely translated and popular of these was the *Tree of Battles* by Honoré Bonet. This book attempted to define in legal terms what constituted proper knightly behaviour in war. Much of Bonet's teaching concerned practical guidelines on knights' pay, the fixing and payment of ransoms (which should be set according to the captive's wealth), compensation for horses, armour or health lost while on campaign, and the division of booty, which technically all belonged to the prince who had financed the campaign and was supposed to be shared by him with his knights and soldiers. Bonet was not impressed by the kind of "chivalry" which brought disaster at Nicopolis. A knight's yearning for individual glory must be firmly subordinated to military discipline and the attainment of large-scale objectives. He recommended that any knight who disobeyed his commander's orders and challenged an enemy knight to single combat should be executed.

In the thirteenth century knights were protected by full plate armour, which consisted of a made-to-measure iron suit, cunningly jointed to allow its wearer freedom of movement. The smooth, polished, convex surfaces of the metal plates caused arrows or bolts striking it at any angle other than ninety degrees to glance off, and were strong enough to withstand most missiles unless delivered at point blank range. There can be no doubt that a fully armoured knight was well protected during battle; he was only vulnerable if he was knocked to the ground, when his restricted mobility and

RIGHT An illustration of some of the principal events leading up to the First Crusade, including the capture of Jerusalem by the Turks and their mistreatment of Christian pilgrims. Contact with the Muslim nations in the Middle East during the Crusades had a profound influence on western chivalry. The Crusaders' initial success was followed by a healthy respect for the abilities of their enemies.

BELOW An early manuscript of another military treatise by Peter of Eboli (c.1200) shows the aftermath of battle, with corpses being collected in a cart from the battlefield for mass burial.

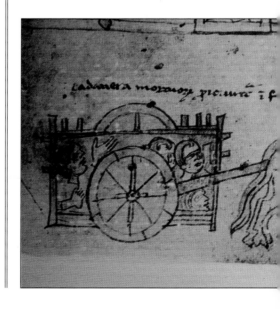

ABOVE: *An armourer engaged in the skilled and time-consuming task of making chain mail. Each link had to be individually connected and riveted in place. The armourer manipulates the wire with pliers, and will hammer in the rivet on his miniature anvil.*

the sheer weight of the harness might prevent his being able to rise again, and make him an easy target for the nimbler foot soldiers. Accounts of battles such as Agincourt record the horrible sight of infantrymen sitting astride fallen knights and driving daggers into the slits in their visors, or between the vulnerable joints of their harness. For this reason it was important for knights to fight together, and many accounts of real battles as well as romance battles relate the rescue of knights who had been cut off from their companions or been knocked down. Lives were saved by such actions, and the close comradeship between knights still flourished on the battlefields of Europe.

During the fifteenth century, plate armour became even more elaborate but the advance in firearms – handguns and cannon – made it largely obsolete. By the end of the fifteenth century the days of the cavalry charge (at least as a successful strategy in battle) were over. Though knights continued to take part in battles no new ideas emerged to revive the role of the knight in active warfare after they had been superseded by the infantry.

HERE COMES THE CAVALRY – ASCALON AND AGINCOURT

The eminence and prestige of early medieval knights owed much to the success in battle which they enjoyed, thanks to their mastery of the mounted charge with couched lance. The "irresistible first shock" of such a charge, if delivered in a disciplined, united manner, could shatter the ranks of enemy soldiers and have a decisive effect on the outcome of a battle, though much also depended on the hand to hand fighting following the charge. No battle of the Middle Ages demonstrates the success of the technique better than the Battle of Ascalon, in which a massive Muslim army was routed by a single cavalry charge.

The mounted knight was always vulnerable to the archer, however, and with improved weapons technology as the Middle Ages progressed, the cavalry declined in importance. The impotence of cavalry under adverse conditions and the power of the archers is very much the theme of the Battle of Agincourt.

The Battle of Ascalon:
29th July 1099

The Battle of Ascalon, the final battle of the First Crusade, was a decisive defeat of the crusaders' opponents, the Egyptian army under the command of Vizier al-Afdal. The army had been sent by the Fatimid Caliph of Egypt to recapture Jerusalem and to take revenge for the appalling massacre which the crusaders had perpetrated there.

Leaving a tiny garrison behind to defend the Holy City, the crusader princes marched their small army southwards to the plain north of the coastal city of Ascalon. Acting for once in perfect cooperation, the princes deployed their troops in nine "battles", three rows of three, which gave them equal strength should they be attacked from any direction during the march. Each "battle" consisted of a body of cavalry protected at the front by infantry, armed with spears and bows. When they reached the plain and saw the encampment of the Egyptian army, which outnumbered them by about 10 to one,

they drew up the entire army in a single line of battle.

The Egyptian army was also composed of cavalry divisions armed with lances, supported by archers on foot. They provided a solid target for the crusader knights to charge. Some eyewitness accounts attribute the beginning of the charge to Robert, Duke of Normandy, who caught sight of a golden ornament on the standard of al-Afdal and set off to capture it. But whatever its origin, the charge of the mounted knights proved devastating, sweeping the Egyptians before them into the sea. A letter to the Pope from Godfrey, Count Raymond and Daimbert, the Archbishop of Pisa, describes the battle:

> In our army there were not more than five thousand cavalry and fifteen thousand infantry, while the enemy could have had a hundred thousand horse and four hundred thousand foot. Then God's doing was marvellous in the eyes of His servants, since, before we entered the conflict, by our charge alone we drove this multitude to flight and tore away all their weapons, so that even if they had wanted to fight back they lacked the equipment...More than one hundred thousand Saracens fell there by the sword, but their fear was such that at the gate of the city of Ascalon around two thousand were suffocated in the crush. Countless more died in the sea; thorn bushes caught many. The world itself clearly fought for us, and had not the spoils of the camp detained many of our people, there would have been very few enemy left.

General al-Afdar himself escaped by ship, but he had been humiliatingly defeated by what he had thought was a tiny and disorganized rabble. The battle confirmed the reputation of the crusaders as unconquerable.

The Battle of Agincourt:
25th October 1415

Henry V of England invaded France in August 1415 after the French, not surprisingly, failed to accede to his demands, which included the crown of France and the hand in marriage of the Princess Catherine.

Henry had embarked on his campaign with a large, healthy and well-supplied army, but during the six-week siege of Harfleur it had been reduced by dysentery. About 2,000 men had died and about 5,000 had to return to England. This left Henry with fewer than half the soldiers he had brought with him. Against the advice of his remaining commanders, he decided to continue the campaign, and march through Normandy to Calais. He had about 1,000 knights and men-at-arms and about 5,000 archers, many of whom were already weakened by sickness, and they knew, as they prepared to set off on the 200-mile march, that the French had mustered an army and were waiting for them somewhere along the route.

The size of the French army is now rather difficult to estimate, as the reports of contemporary chroniclers vary wildly. Shakespeare's estimate that the English were outnumbered by about five to one is probably not far from the truth. The French were confident of victory, and had prepared a specially painted cart in which to parade the captured English king afterwards.

The French drew up in three divisions, in between the two villages of Tramecourt and Agincourt, blocking the path of the English to Calais. The villages were both surrounded by woods, which restricted the open field in which the armies could encounter each other. The French order of battle had the first two divisions composed of men-at-arms on foot, with squadrons of cavalry on each flank, but the French nobles were so anxious for the glory of conquest that large numbers of them insisted on being in the first two divisions, and they pushed the archers and crossbowmen, who should have protected them, to the rear.

The English army was drawn up with groups of knights and men-at-arms interspersed with archers in wedge-shaped formation. The line was slightly concave, allowing archers to fire on enemy troops engaging them from the side as well as from the front. Somehow Henry man-

ABOVE A fifteenth-century illustration of the Battle of Agincourt. It shows clearly how the French cavalry were caught in thick mud at the mercy of English bowmen.

aged to raise the morale of his troops with a speech, and gave the order to advance at a slow march towards the French lines. The chroniclers record that the English soldiers all knelt, made the sign of the cross, and kissed the soil, crumbling a little of it into their mouths. They then advanced about half a mile. The night had been rainy and the ground was wet and muddy. The archers set up ramparts of sharpened stakes, behind which they sheltered as they fired.

The French heavy cavalry was the first to attack, though they were unable to charge because of the heavy, clinging mud. The English archers kept up a continuous hail of arrows as the knights squelched slowly towards them. Because of their slow pace, the French were unable to gain sufficient momentum to break through the English line and were halted at the walls of stakes, where many of the horses at the front were impaled and their riders killed. The fighting was brief and the survivors returned to the French lines.

The cavalry had churned the soft ground into a horrible quagmire which hindered the advance of the French first division. As this massive formation reached its target, the English centre fell back a short distance, though the archers at the flanks held their ground. This packed the French soldiers into a narrow space between the two woods, and those who were at the front were surrounded on three sides by English archers. Some of the French men-at-arms were so jammed together that they could not lift their swords to strike, and the archers were firing at short range into the densely packed mass of struggling bodies. As the rear of the division piled forwards, those at the front were pushed over and trampled into the mud. Many deaths occurred from drowning or suffocation, as the living were crushed under mounds of the dead.

Many of the archers threw down their bows and executed the fallen Frenchmen with clubs or maces. Those who were continuing to fire often seized arrows from the bodies of the fallen. Where the men-at-arms of both sides did manage to engage each other the fighting was fierce; Henry himself was struck to his knees several times and lost part of the gilded crown, which decorated his bascinet, to a French axe blow. The French second division, whose ranks were thinned by desertion after the disaster that had befallen the first, engaged, but fared no better.

At this point, the French third division, which had been waiting in reserve, began to break up and leave the field, but they appeared to the English to be circling them so as to attack from the rear. Henry, fearing a new attack (the third division contained more men than the first two and still outnumbered the English), ordered the prisoners to be killed because he could not spare the troops to guard them. This is part of the reason why the casualties on the French side were so huge – probably about seven or eight thousand.

Although the Battle of Agincourt achieved little strategically, it was an important victory for the English because it utterly demoralized the French. They had lost so many of their best knights and commanders that they did not recover for some time. This paved the way for Henry's successes later in the campaign. If he had not died so young of dysentery in 1322, he might indeed have succeeded in gaining the crown of France.

RAIDS AND SKIRMISHES

Both in small local wars between contending lords, such as that between the Count of Hainault and the Duke of Brabant in the 1170s, and in larger national campaigns, much of the military action in which knights engaged consisted of raids on the territory of their opponents. The object of a raid was systematic, cold-blooded destruction of the enemy's wealth and resources, which meant killing his peasants and burning their villages. It is clear that this kind of activity was not viewed as in any way unchivalrous, but merely as part of the necessary strategy required to reduce the opposition. Known as "*chevauchées*", these campaigns were as valid and as important as battles and sieges. A detailed record of a *chevauchée* made by that paragon of chivalric virtue, Edward the Black Prince, son of Edward III of England, in the south of France in 1355 during the Hundred Years War has been left to us in a letter written by Sir John Wingfield to the Bishop of Winchester.

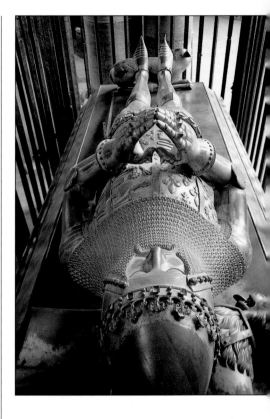

ABOVE. *The painted and gilded effigy of Edward the Black Prince in Canterbury Cathedral. Renowned as the Flower of Chivalry for such deeds as his courtesy towards the captured King of France after the Battle of Poitiers, Edward was feared and detested by the French victims of his* chevauchées, *destructive raids into enemy territory.*

> And, my lord, you will be glad to know that my lord has raided the county of Armagnac and taken several walled towns there, burning and destroying them, except for certain towns which he garrisoned. Then he went into the viscounty of Rivière, and took a good town called Plaisance, the chief town of the area, and burnt it and laid waste the surrounding countryside. Then he went into the county of Astarac, and took several towns and had them burnt and destroyed, and the countryside likewise, and took the chief town, called Samatin, which is as large as Norwich. (A long list of other towns and districts reduced to smoking rubble by the Prince's army follows.) It seems certain that since the war against the French king began, there has never been such destruction in a region as in this raid. For the countryside and towns which have been destroyed produced more revenue for the king of France in aid of his wars than half his kingdom...For Carcassonne and Limoux, which is as large as Carcassonne, and two other towns near there, produce for the king of France each year the wages of 1,000 men-at-arms and 100,000 old crowns towards the costs of the war...And by God's help, if my lord had money to continue this war and to profit the king and his honour, he could indeed enlarge the boundaries of his territory and take a number of places, because the enemy are in great disarray. In order to do this, my lord has ordered all the earls and bannerets to stay in different places along the border in order to raid and damage the enemy's lands.

This is interesting evidence of the economic calculations which inspired the policy of attrition. No merit is assigned to raiding as a means of reducing the numbers or the morale of the enemy; the numbers are unimportant, except that extra thousands of homeless, hungry people will be a further drain on the resources of the king.

Until the Battle of Tannenberg in 1410 put an effective stop to their activities, one way that a knight errant in search of military experience could be sure of getting some useful raiding practice was to join the Teutonic Knights of Prussia on their seasonal campaigns against Lithuania. Prior to the conversion of the Lithuanian leaders to Christianity, in 1386, this was also considered a crusade against the heathen. The Teutonic Knights promoted the Lithuanian campaigns as a proving ground and established their prestige among international knighthood by such means as the "Table of Honour" in their headquarters at the magnificent Marienburg castle, at which the most successful crusaders were honoured.

ABOVE *Marienburg castle, the Prussian headquarters of the Teutonic Knights in (formerly) East Prussia – now Poland. Originally built as a functioning fortress, as the Knights extended their territories it became a magnificent hotel for visiting European nobles and their knights, who wished to participate in the Order's campaigns against the pagan Lithuanians.*

Campaigning in Lithuania was, however, far from easy. The territory of the enemy was separated from that of the Teutonic knights in Prussia by a broad belt of trackless forest, relieved only by normally impassable bogland, and the severe climate of the area meant that there were usually only two "windows" in the year during which raiding could take place: about two months during the winter, when it was cold enough for the surface of the bogs to freeze over, but not so cold as to kill the common soldiers while they marched (which happened in the winter of 1322/3); or a period of about one month in the "summer", when a combination of sunshine and winds dried out the surface of the bogs. It was essential for the forces of both sides to be able to strike and withdraw quickly, and a summer rain storm or an unexpected thaw could mean disaster, as it did for the Lithuanian forces fleeing from the renowned Teutonic Master, Winrich von Kniprode, and his knights when they were trapped by the thawing of the frozen river Strawen in the winter of 1348.

Raids in winter would be conducted by a party of knights and soldiers hacking their way through the forest, or sometimes travelling in boats on the river Niemen. They bivouacked when they had penetrated within striking range of the enemy, and then rode out, burning, looting, destroying and killing in the surrounding countryside. Before the enemy could mobilize against them, they retired with as much plunder as they could carry. In the summer, longer campaigns were mounted which aimed at the permanent gain of enemy territory rather than the impoverishment and depopulation of the area.

Both sides in this war of attrition had about equal success, maintaining the status quo during a period of more than 100 years of almost continuous warfare, without inflicting permanent damage or defeat on the other side. Princes and knights from all over Europe came to this theatre of war, especially from northern Europe, (southern European knights were more likely to get involved in the intermittent attempts to reconquer Spain). King John of Bohemia was one of the first of the great princes to make the expedition in 1328. After his death at the Battle of Crécy (where he had asked to be placed in the thick of the fighting even though he had gone blind), King John was portrayed by the chronicler Froissart as a paragon of chivalry. He saw the Teutonic Knights as noble idealists:

> Their praiseworthy state and their memorable holiness of life attract us; they suffer heavy and unbearable labours and expenses for the extension of the orthodox faith, and have made themselves into an unbreakable wall to defend the faith against the Lithuanians and their partisans, whoever they may be – pestilential enemies of Christ! – as we have seen ourselves; every day they expose themselves fearlessly to danger and death, hemmed in, divided, hopelessly slaughtered and afflicted!

King John and his Bohemians were followed throughout the fourteenth century by Germans, Englishmen, Flemings, Austrians, Frenchmen, Bavarians, Dutchmen, Hungarians, Burgundians, Scots, Provençals, and Italians. Some of these, like the Duke of Austria in 1378, had taken crusading vows which needed to be fulfilled at the scene of the only current crusade; the Grand Master had to mount a special short raid in December so that the Duke could fulfill his vow before Christmas. Others were gaining experience in as many wars as they could in the traditional manner, such as Henry, Earl of Derby, later King Henry IV of England, who came twice on campaign to Prussia and once to Granada in Spain. When Henry arrived for the winter season in 1390 he brought with him, in his personal service, thirteen knights, eighteen squires, three heralds, ten miners and engineers, six minstrels as well as over 100 ordinary soldiers and assorted volunteers. Other magnates brought even larger retinues, such as the Duke of Lorraine who brought 70 knights in 1378, or the Margrave of Meissen who arrived with a staggering 500 knights in 1391.

SIEGES

With the development of strategic fortification, the capture of castles by siege became an increasingly common military objective. A whole system of tactics and technology grew up around the needs of the besiegers and the besieged. The techniques of the besiegers fell into four main categories: to starve the inhabitants into submission by blockade; to attempt to enter the castle or town by assault, climbing the walls or storming or battering them; to

ABOVE *A late fourteenth-century representation of the Battle of Crécy. Painted forty-two years after the event, the picture shows hand-to-hand fighting between the mounted knights of France and England, rather than the carnage which really took place.*

ABOVE *Simone Martini's fresco of Guidoriccio da Fogliano at the Siege of Monte Massi in 1328, showing the encampment of his besieging army. The knights leave their lances and shields outside their tents for recognition, just as they would outside their lodgings at a tournament.*

undermine the walls or towers at a critical point and make them collapse; or to gain entrance by guile or treachery.

Blockading a castle or a fortified town was often an effective means of reducing it to submission, but it involved special risks to the besieging force. It was likely to take a long time, particularly if the inhabitants had had sufficient notice to build up their stores. An efficiently provisioned garrison or town could hold out for months, or even years. During this time the attacking force would be much less comfortably stationed than the besieged. Encamped around the castle or town for any length of time, they would probably run short of food themselves, and conditions would certainly become insanitary. Outbreaks of disease connected with poor sanitation and unhealthy food were common among besieging armies, and often devastating. Kings and lords, likely to be in better health to begin with than the common soldiers, were not protected from the ravages of disease, though it might take them longer to succumb. The Black Prince and King Henry V, great fighting leaders and strong, healthy men, were both cut down in their prime by dysentery and fever contracted on gruelling campaigns. A long siege also brought the risk of a relieving force arriving to help the besieged. Moreover, it was difficult to sustain the morale of the troops, who frequently deserted in large numbers during long periods of inaction. The practice of holding tournaments during sieges was an attempt to prevent boredom and loss of morale among knights.

So a successful assault was often preferable from the besiegers' point of view. But assaulting a strongly fortified medieval castle, with its highly developed defensive features, was hazardous; the attackers were in a disadvantageous position again. They could be fired at from the battlements, and from the loopholes in the walls, while the archers were protected behind shutters or masonry. If they reached the walls they could have heavy objects dropped on their heads from a projecting platform with holes in its floor (a

ABOVE *Besieging a well-fortified and provisioned town or castle could be a long and wearisome business. It was important to keep up the morale of the soldiers by holding games and tournaments, or they might desert. Here knights encamped at a siege are playing chess to amuse themselves.*

brattice if wooden, a *machicolation* if stone). To enter the castle, they had either to climb up the walls with scaling ladders or cross over from siege towers, both of which left them vulnerable, particularly to attacks by fire. Alternatively, they could try to batter through the gates or the walls with a battering ram, or with huge missile-throwing siege engines.

The siege engines were mainly of three types. Ballistas, which were effectively giant crossbows, had an arm which was forced back by tension and then released, catapulting a missile into the castle. Mangonels were like giant catapults, but worked on the principle of twisting and releasing a tensile material, such as horsehair. These, too, could be used to project large, heavy missiles. The third kind was the trebuchet, in which the missile was thrown by the effect of counterpoise, supplied either by a heavy weight or by a group of men pulling on ropes. This was the most powerful of the three. These weapons were not usually employed as anti-personnel but as artillery to bombard and weaken the castle walls. In this case the missiles were huge stones. They could also be used to frighten or demoralise the inhabitants; it was not unknown to lob stinking carcases of horses or sheep over the walls in the hope of spreading disease among the people, and it appears that the crusaders on the First Crusade used to catapult the severed heads of dead Muslim soldiers into besieged towns.

Siege towers were a sophisticated version of a scaling ladder. They had to be the same height as the castle wall, and could be several storeys high. They permitted men to climb across onto the battlements of a castle simultaneously, and they provided some measure of protection while they were climbing. Constructed of wooden frames and ladders, they were covered in soaking wet hides to prevent the besiegers from setting fire to

RIGHT *A charming illustration from the thirteenth-century* Histoires d'Outremer, *showing crusaders catapulting the severed heads of their captives over the walls of a besieged town.*

ABOVE: *A scene from the Romance of Godfrey of Bouillon, showing Count Godfrey directing his men in an assault on a walled town using scaling ladders, during the First Crusade.*

them. While the men in the upper storeys were trying to lay bridges from the top of the siege tower to the wall, men at the bottom would batter at a gateway with a ram.

When the crusaders of the First Crusade were besieging Jerusalem, they knew that they had to take the city quickly, because it had been well provisioned against their arrival and the surrounding countryside emptied of food, water and fuel, so that their own supplies were very scarce. The crusaders were lucky to be provisioned by some Italian and English supply vessels, which provided them with ropes, timber and building materials. They could therefore construct siege towers. These were huge, and were rolled with great difficulty into position for the attack to commence. (Rolling the towers meant that any irregularities in the land had to be levelled, and any moat filled in before they could be brought up to the wall.) It was then discovered that the Saracens defending the city had concentrated their forces on the section of the wall opposite the biggest siege tower, so during the night before the planned attack it was wheeled to another position half a mile away.

During the assault, the Saracens managed to ignite many of the siege engines and some of the towers. They hung big wads of padding down the front of the walls to deaden the blows of battering rams, and prevented the towers from getting close enough to the walls to lay their bridges down and cross over by pushing them away with long timbers. The siege tower commanded by Godfrey of Bouillon managed to set fire to the cotton padding suspended from the wall, and by good luck the thick black smoke was blown back into the city, blinding the soldiers on the battlements. In the confusion, the crusaders seized the timbers which had been used to fend them off and secured them to the tower, laying their bridges over the top and crossing to the wall. The knights who entered managed to open the gates and let in the army, and the city was taken.

Undermining the walls of a castle was a skilled technique which required specialists. Besieging forces eventually came to employ a special unit of experienced miners and engineers who could select the best spot to weaken. The miners tunnelled underneath a wall or tower and hollowed out

CASTLES

Castle-building developed rapidly during the twelfth century and by its close most of the features which we associate with the military functions of castles had been fully realized. After that, the period of innovation and evolution was succeeded by one of consolidation, and variations on the same themes. At the close of the Middle Ages, greater social stability, combined with the advent of artillery, reduced the necessity for massive fortifications and the castle developed more of the features of a residence.

Motte and bailey castles

These were the earliest structures which should be called castles. They comprised a combination of defensive earthworks with a permanent building, which could serve as a springboard for attack and as a strong centre from which to administer as well as defend the locality. Lambert of Ardres gives a good description of the motte and bailey castle built by Arnold of Ardres (the grandfather of the Arnold we have already met) in 1117:

> Arnold, lord of Ardres, built on the motte of Ardres a wooden house, excelling all the houses of Flanders of that period both in material and in carpenter's work. The first storey was on the surface of the ground, where there were cellars and granaries, and great boxes, tuns, casks, and other domestic utensils. In the storey above were the dwelling and common living rooms of the residents, in which were the larders, the rooms of the bakers and butlers, and the great chamber in which the lord and his wife slept. Adjoining this was a private room, the dormitory of the waiting maids and children. In the inner part of the great chamber was a certain private room, where at early dawn or in the evening or during sickness or at a time of blood-letting, or for warming the maids and children, they used to have a fire. In the upper storey of the house were garret rooms, in which on the one side the sons (when they wished it) on the other side the daughters (because they were obliged) of the lord of the house used to sleep. In this storey also the watchmen and the servants took their sleep. High up on the east side of the house was the chapel...there were stairs and passages from storey to storey, from the house into the kitchen, from room to room, and again from the house into the loggia, where they used to sit in conversation for recreation, and again from the loggia into the oratory.

The square keep

In time, the wooden tower-house on the motte and the wooden palisades and fences were replaced by stone structures. The square stone keep was itself defensible if the moat, rampart, ditch and outer curtain wall were breached. Classically, the keep was a single, solid, rectangular building, with towers at each corner and rooms in the centre. Later the keep expanded outwards and enclosed a courtyard, while principal buildings adjoined the inside of its walls. A good example of the square keep is Rochester Castle,

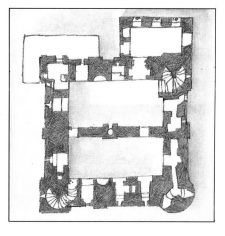

ABOVE *A plan of Rochester castle showing the central dividing wall. Even after the outer wall had been breached in 1216, the defenders managed to hold out for a while by retreating behind this barrier.*

TOP *Rochester castle, showing the round tower built by Henry III after his father King John's engineers had undermined its square predecessor to capture the castle.*

LEFT *A motte and bailey castle – the earliest medieval fortified building.*

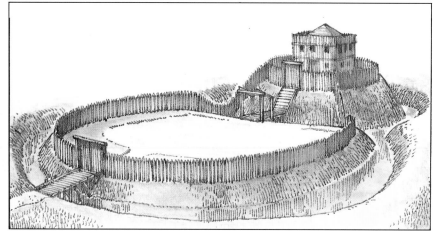

which was begun in 1127 and was improved continuously throughout the twelfth century. It was successfully besieged by King John in 1216; his sappers undermined one of the corner towers, which was later replaced under Henry III by a round tower. The strong central dividing wall inside the keep enabled the castle's defenders to continue holding it for a time even after John's forces had breached one side.

"My fair daughter" – Château Gaillard

The Crusaders learnt a great deal about the construction of castles in the east, imitating and improving on the buildings of the Byzantines and the Muslims. Château Gaillard, built by Richard I of England to protect his duchy of Normandy from the French king, Philip Augustus, represented the height of twelfth-century castle building and incorporated all the latest defensive features. These

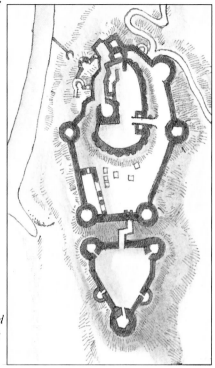

RIGHT *A plan of Château Gaillard, showing the successive areas which could be defended from a besieging force. This is known as "concentric fortification".*

BELOW *Built on a rocky promontory with unclimbable walls, Château Gaillard represented the best defensive technology available at the time of its construction and was thought to be impregnable.*

included shuttered crenellations, enabling archers to fire from cover, machicolations, projecting structures with holes in the floor, which enabled the defenders to drop material onto the heads of the attackers, battered plinths, which both reinforced the strength of the wall bases and provided a convex surface off which missiles dropped from above would ricochet up amid the attackers, and concentric fortifications, which gave the defenders several lines of defence and enabled them to retain the advantage of height over their attackers when they had retreated behind the next curtain wall.

After Richard's death, Château Gaillard was successfully besieged by Philip, who took it in 1203, though with great difficulty, from Roger de Lacy, the Earl of Pembroke, and his garrison, who were holding it for King John. The inner ward might not have been taken if John had not built a chapel next to the curtain wall; a handful of French soldiers got in through a window of the crypt and lowered the drawbridge to their fellows.

The thirteenth century: Conway and Beaumaris

These two castles were important links in a great chain of castles built by King Edward I of England after his conquest of Wales in 1283. Conway, a coastal fortress, incorporated the whole medieval town within the vast enclosure of its curtain wall. The castle itself is positioned at the apex of a roughly triangular shape. Its defences are linear rather than concentric; it has no keep, no single tower stronger than the rest, but eight equally formidable towers interspersed around the wall. Beaumaris is perhaps the most perfect concentric castle; attackers who breached its octagonal outer wall would be exposed to withering fire from the square central castle, which had two massive gatehouse towers and six smaller towers projecting outwards so as to give maximum range over the inner ward. The space between inner and outer walls is narrow, so as to prevent attackers grouping in large numbers at one area.

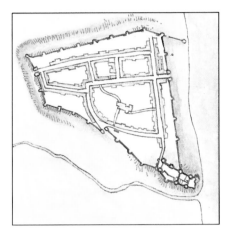

ABOVE *Conway castle was part of a chain of coastal fortresses. Its curtain wall encloses the whole town.*

BELOW *A deep, wide moat, strong walls defended by projecting round towers, and a lethal trapping area for besiegers between the outer and inner concentric fortifications made Beaumaris Castle supreme.*

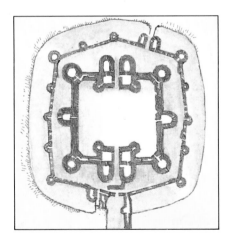

ABOVE *Beaumaris, perhaps the most perfect concentric castle. Once past the outer wall attackers were trapped in a narrow space and exposed to fire from the central castle.*

The fortified town: Rhodes

The massive fortifications enclosing the principal town of Rhodes were built and manned by the Knights Hospitaller in the fourteenth century. Again, concentric fortifications exploit the technique of trapping attacking forces in a "killing area" between the outer and inner walls. This fortress withstood one great siege only to fall to another, in 1522, by which time the increased destructive power of artillery bombardment was making all fortification vulnerable.

ABOVE *A view of the palace of the Grand Master of the Order of St John and part of the massive crenellated defensive walls of Rhodes town.*

RIGHT *A fine example of a castle on its way to becoming a château – this fairy tale fifteenth-century palace, the castle of Saumur, from the* Très Riches Heures *still has a moat, drawbridge and defensible gatehouse, but the main buildings speak more of comfort and status than practical fortification.*

The Fortified House

In the later Middle Ages, lords were more concerned to display wealth and provide comfortable living accommodation than strong fortifications. The grim and practical narrow-windowed, squat towers of previous centuries were superseded by more elegant establishments, but where some of the defensive features of castles were retained, such as crenellated battlements, machicolations and arrow loops, their purpose was belied by the presence of thinner walls and larger windows and they became more decorative than practical.

a large space, propping up the roof with timbers. Then they filled the space with combustible material – cotton, straw or brushwood, packed with pig fat or petroleum. Then they retired and fired the excavation, and the combination of the heat with the weakness of the foundation usually brought down the tower or wall.

The corners of square towers were particularly vulnerable to this kind of attack, which was one reason why castles were increasingly designed with round towers, which were structurally stronger. A classic example of the technique is displayed in the siege of Rochester Castle in Kent in 1215 by King John. The castle was held by about a hundred knights, with numbers of archers and crossbowmen, for the rebellious barons of England. Bombardment by siege engines had had no effect, so the king sent for his miners to undermine the massive wall of the keep and bring down one of the corner towers. The king's men entered through the breach. The knights continued to resist for a while, protected by a central dividing wall, but when the promised relief force did not appear, they eventually surrendered.

Mining, though often successful, was a slow operation. It was impossible where a castle was built on marshy or wet ground or on solid rock, and sometimes breaches in the curtain walls created by mining operations were filled up again overnight by the desperate defenders.

Castles were frequently captured by guile or treachery. When Philip Augustus of France was besieging Château Gaillard in 1203, six of his soldiers climbed through a drain to reach a window in the chapel crypt, and succeeded in lowering the drawbridge of the middle ward to admit the rest of the besieging force. The defenders retreated to the inner ward but a combination of bombardment and mining created the final breach and the siege was over. The Siege of Antioch, during the First Crusade, which lasted for seven months, was only terminated by treachery. Bohemond of Otranto, that colourful character, had spies in the city among the Armenian Christians. A man named Firouz, who was in command of three towers along the curtain wall, had been forced to become a Muslim but wanted to return to Christianity. He offered to surrender his towers to Bohemond's men, and came to terms. During the night of 3rd June 1098, 60 men climbed unopposed up a scaling ladder, took possession of the towers, and then opened two of the city gates to the crusading army.

Besiegers did not always succeed. Though many towns and castles were forced to surrender to besieging armies, many others managed to repulse them. Sometimes this could be done by a surprise sortie, like that led by Bohemond against Kerbogha's relieving army shortly after the fall of Antioch. A good account of one of these surprise attacks can be found in Froissart's chronicle of the siege of Hennebont in 1342. Hennebont was being held by the Countess of Montfort for Edward III against a French besieging force. A famous English knight, Sir Walter Manny, arrived with a force of soldiers to help defend the castle:

> After the entertainment, Sir Walter Manny, who was captain of the English,
> enquired of the Countess the state of the town and of the enemy's army.
> Upon looking out of the window, he said he had a great inclination to
> destroy that large machine which was placed so near, and much annoyed
> them, if any would second him. Sir Yves de Tresiquidi replied that he would
> not fail him in this his first expedition; as did also the lord of Landreman.

ABOVE *King Louis IX of France and his knights capture the fortified town of Damietta in Egypt, taking it by storm in 1249 during the Seventh Crusade.*

They went to arm themselves, and then sallied quietly out of one of the gates, taking with them three hundred archers; who shot so well, that those who guarded the machine fled; and the men-at-arms who followed the archers falling upon them, slew the greater part, and broke down and cut in pieces this large machine. They then dashed in among the tents and huts, set fire to them, and killed and wounded many of their enemies before the army was in motion. After this they made a handsome retreat. When the enemy were mounted and armed, they galloped after them like madmen. Sir Walter Manny, seeing this, exclaimed, "May I never be embraced by my mistress and dear friend, if I enter castle or fortress before I have unhorsed one of these gallopers." He then turned round, and pointed his spear towards the enemy, as did the two brothers of Lande-Halle, le Haze de Brabant, Sir Yves de Tresiquidi, Sir Galeran de Landreman, and many others who spitted the first coursers. Many legs were made to kick in the air. Some of their own party were also unhorsed. The conflict became very serious, for reinforcements were perpetually coming from the camp; and the English were obliged to retreat towards the castle, which they did in good order until they came to the castle ditch: there the knights made a stand, until all their men were safely returned...The Countess of Montfort came down from the castle to meet them, and with a most cheerful countenance, kissed Sir Walter Manny, and all his companions, one after the other, like a noble and valiant dame.

Defenders had their own techniques to counteract the efforts of besiegers. It was a great advantage to be able to hurl missiles down from the height of the

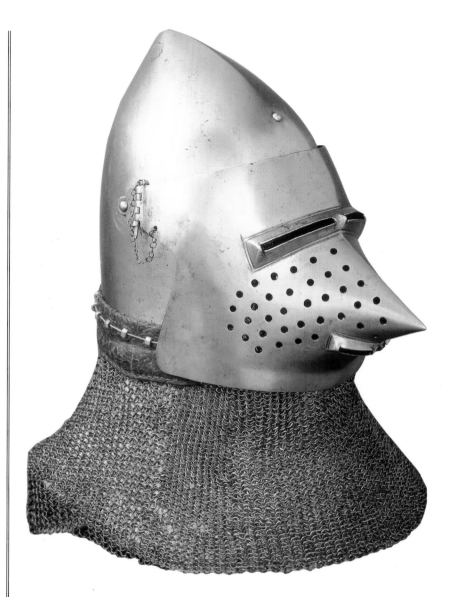

RIGHT *The kind of helmet which was universally popular with knights from the mid-fourteenth century onwards – the "bascinet". It provided complete protection in battle for the knight's face, but allowed him to breathe, while the hinged visor with its pointed snout gave him a sinister appearance.*

walls onto the heads of the attackers, and there are many accounts of injuries and deaths as a result of being hit by stones and arrows, as well as Greek fire and other burning material. At the Siege of Caen in 1346, for example, the defenders dropped burning straw on top of an English knight, Sir Edmund Springhouse, who had fallen from a scaling ladder into the ditch, and burnt him alive. The ingredients of "Greek fire" are not certainly known, but probably included sulphur, naphtha and quicklime. It burnt on water, was very difficult to put out, had an intense heat and stuck to whatever it touched. Other things that could be dropped over battlements or through machicolations (openings in parapets between supporting corbels) included boiling oil, red-hot sand and quicklime, which could inflict serious burns through joints in armour or through the hinged visors in the type of helmet called a bascinet.

The blows of battering rams could be deadened by lowering wads of padding from the walls on ropes, and defenders could also grip the head of a ram with long pincers to make it difficult to manoeuvre. Mines could be detected by placing pans of water on the ground and watching for any disturbances on the surface. Then the defenders could cut a counter-mine, either catching the attacking miners or cutting them off from their objective.

PHYSICIANS AND SURGEONS: MEDIEVAL MEDICINE

Medieval medicine could be appallingly primitive and must have killed at least as often as it cured. Contact with the Arab world during the crusader period brought some improvements, since Arab medical science was more advanced than the crude methods of the Franks. Herbal recipes of considerable sophistication but doubtful efficacy existed for a variety of ailments, but could do nothing against the epidemics of "flux" which tended to erupt in the unhealthy conditions of besieging armies, encamped before towns or castles for several months.

With no understanding of the need for cleanliness, minor wounds would often fester and prove fatal, like the arrow-wound which killed Richard Lionheart in 1199. Drastic remedies were required to save a limb threatened by gangrene. The biographer of the famous Castilian knight, Don Pero Niño, recorded how a leg wound which he had received during an expedition against the Moors of North Africa in 1403 festered from lack of proper attention. On his return to Spain, his doctors advised amputation as the only way of saving his life. But Pero Niño insisted that they should cauterize the wound with hot irons and try to save the leg:

> They heated an iron, big as a quarrel, white hot. The surgeon was afraid to apply it, having pity for the pain it would cause. But Pero Niño, who was used to such work, took the glowing iron and himself moved it over his leg, from one end of his wound to the other.

By good fortune this treatment proved successful; the leg healed and Don Pero Niño made a full recovery.

A German knight named Jorg von Ehingen was crippled by a similar injury, received in 1457 while fighting in the Spanish *Reconquista* against the Moors of Granada. He survived to be an old man, but recorded:

> I was badly wounded in the shin by an arrow, and, although the wound healed, subsequently it broke out again when I returned to Swabia, and I retained into my old age a hole in the shin and a flux.

During the crusades many soldiers, from the humblest to the highest, perished through disease, which killed more than did the enemy. The intense heat and the often unsuitable food that the soldiers scavenged to supplement their meagre rations, contributed to the swift spread of dysentery and typhoid, known in the Middle Ages as "plague" or "flux", and severely depleted their numbers. In 1250, the French army of the Seventh Crusade was in retreat after their terrible defeat at the Battle of Mansourah. Encamped outside the walls of the city of Mansourah, they were seized by a pestilence that raged through the camp. King Louis IX of France was struck down, along with thousands of others. Having ordered a retreat to Damietta, the army was attacked by the Egyptians, and in its weakened state fell easy prey. So many knights had died that grooms wore their armour to mount guard; the Egyptians claimed that they had killed or captured 50,000. Twenty years later during the Eighth (and last) Crusade the same thing happened outside the walls of Carthage, and this time Louis himself died of dysentery and was canonized a short time later.

CHAPTER SIX

DECLINE AND SURVIVAL

Throughout the Middle Ages, the strains imposed by the exigencies of real life on the ideal knight were sometimes intolerable. Many medieval commentators – not all of them clerics – were critical of wicked knights and their activities, but they never ceased to esteem the great knights of the glorious past as the standard pattern for all knights. Nevertheless, history all through these centuries provides us with many examples of unspeakable brutalities committed even by knights with a reputation for chivalry, such as the campaigns of the Black Prince in the South of France which are remembered even today with horror. This brings us to the unacceptable face of knighthood.

The truth is that the very conditions which had engendered knights and their code contained the seeds of their destruction. The feudal loyalty and the ideal of service, which lay at the very core of knighthood, was impossible to sustain through the changing economic and political conditions of the later Middle Ages. No medieval ruler before the mid-fifteenth century employed a standing army which was on a regular payroll. Because knights were responsible for providing their own equipment and retinues when they were summoned to war, booty taken on campaigns was looked on as the legitimate reward for their economic and personal risk; as the business of fighting as a knight became more and more expensive, fewer of the traditional stock of

KNIGHT OF EMPEROR MAXIMILIAN ON TRIUMPH PARADE, 1518

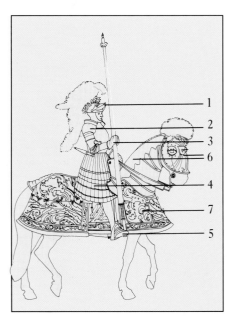

The knight wears a magnificently decorated harness with a close-helmet (1), crested with coloured plumes. His shoulders are now protected by heavy pauldrons (2) with a raised collar to ward off blows at the neck. His gauntlets (3) are of a mitten form. For the purposes of the parade, the knight has put on a velvet, fluted skirt (4) typical of this period. His sabatons (5) are now square-shaped at the toe rather than pointed. His horse too is armoured; he wears a decorated chanfron (6) to protect his face, and a mail crinet over his neck. The caparison (7) is now shorter, and beautifully worked with gold wire brocade. Under it the horse might also be carrying further armour plates – a peytral for his breast, flanchards for his flanks and a crupper for his hindquarters.

155

landed gentry, who had always made up the backbone of the knightly class, had either the funds or the inclination to take it up. The results were twofold. On the one hand, the sons of knights who showed a disinclination to assume the expensive burden of knighthood had to be persuaded or bribed to do so by their rulers with honours and rewards, such as membership of the exclusive secular knightly orders. On the other hand, "knights" who had no other means of support than the spoils of war became professional soldiers who depended on a constant state of hostilities for their livelihood and lived off the land in a ceaseless round of rapacious depredation. The later history of medieval knights therefore presents a paradoxical elevation of the traditional, idealized knighthood, while at the same time a disgraceful debasement of the practical embodiment of it.

THE DECLINE OF KNIGHTHOOD

A curious phenomenon may be observed in some parts of medieval Europe in the fourteenth and fifteenth centuries: the refusal or reluctance of men who were by birth and fortune eligible for knighthood to take it up. In part this can be accounted for by the sheer expense involved in maintaining the equipment a knight needed if he were called to perform his military obligations. The highly developed plate armour of these centuries, ever more refined and heavy and strong, had to be manufactured by specialists – northern Italy, Austria and Germany were the homes of the most skilled (and expensive) armourers. A suit of plate armour had to be fitted to the contours of its owner. It had to be strong enough to protect its wearer from the weapons he was likely to encounter in battle or tournament, and was often tested for strength by having crossbows fired at it. War-horses, too, were expensive. With the increased weight of body and horse armour, a war-horse had to be specially bred for the power and stamina necessary to carry such heavy burdens for hours at a time. They also needed extensive training to perform under the stress of combat. Such beasts were worth perhaps fifteen or twenty ordinary horses, and a knight, who had to have several horses in case – as often happened – they were killed under him in battle, might have to invest the equivalent of several years' income in his horses alone, and perhaps half as much again for his armour.

For knights who were not particularly prominent or wealthy, to risk such valuable articles, not to mention their own persons, in military service was a severe financial burden. Not surprisingly, many knights, who were simply country gentlemen, preferred to stay at home and manage their estates. Their value in the musters of their overlords was overshadowed by the prospect of their own ruin. Laws were made enforcing gentlemen who owned property yielding an income of a certain fixed amount or more to become knights (in England from 1292 onwards this was £40 per year); failure to do so made them liable to pay a fine, which was equally valuable to the king because he could buy the services of mercenaries with it. North Anglian gentleman John Paston I paid his fine to avoid being knighted in 1457, though his son John was knighted at the age of twenty one.

At the same time as the traditional source of knights was declining the privilege, knights were being made in greater numbers from less illustrious parts of society. Knighthoods began to be given as rewards to successful burghers whose services had been financial rather than military and, at the other end of the scale, to professional soldiers of lowly birth, who could be dubbed on the battlefield. There was in practice no monopoly on who could dub knights, though numerous medieval rulers attempted to confine it exclusively to royalty; tradition in this case was more attended to, and traditionally knighthood could be conferred by anyone who was already a knight. Nobles, lords, and lesser knights all indulged in the practice of knighting their own squires and other members of their retinues.

The strict ideas of previous centuries about the duties, obligations and moral fitness of candidates for knighthood were not attended to. There was no longer a universal assumption that any nobly born young man would serve his apprenticeship in arms and then be knighted. Many nobles no longer troubled to have themselves knighted; some even conferred knighthood on their children while they were still far too young to have much idea of what it meant, or able to discharge its more practical obligations.

In addition, the knights who did serve on campaigns began to be less distinguished from other, lower ranks of soldiers. Squires, sergeants and men-at-arms all wore armour, though not as much as a knight; some monarchs even provided horses for their archers so that they could achieve the necessary speed and mobility while conducting raids in enemy territory. Knights themselves, as mounted warriors, were of less value than formerly in the military formation of an army, and were increasingly deployed to fight on foot, side by side with the common soldiers.

BELOW *A superb sixteenth-century suit of armour of German manufacture. This is a tournament suit. Surfaces which were once smooth and polished to deflect missiles are here decoratively fluted.*

157

All these factors combined to make knighthood less desirable than in previous centuries, and its decline was regarded with dismay by rulers and commentators alike. Medieval kings and princes still regarded knights as necessary in their armies as well as in their civil administrations but, apart from the view of knights as a valuable source of military manpower, there were other equally important social and cultural factors to consider. The later Middle Ages were moving rapidly towards the economic conditions prevailing in modern times. The world turned increasingly by means of commerce rather than by older ethics of feudal loyalty and personal ties. This was so in the spheres of trade, law, medicine, the arts, and equally so in the military sphere. Yet here in particular, loyalty was an essential element in what was increasingly a professional relationship. Kings and princes and lesser lords sought to maintain and reinforce the loyalty of their own retainers by stressing the honour of their service and rewarding it with displays of *largesse*, intended not as financial recompense so much as to boost their knights' sense of worth and self-esteem. In the fourteenth and fifteenth centuries this often took fanciful and theatrical forms; the burgeoning of secular orders was merely one sign of a conscious cultural revival of the ancient forms and values of chivalry. Even though extravagant and flamboyant feasts and tourneys and vowing ceremonies derived their inspiration largely from romance and legend, they were still quite clearly related to the sturdy tradition of a lord rewarding his followers with gifts and praise, a practice which had been central to the evolution of knighthood from the days of the early Middle Ages and was still vital in its late flowering.

ABOVE *The magnificent tomb of Philippe Pot, seneschal of the Court of Burgundy at the height of its fame for producing the bravest knights and the most lavish spectacles and tournaments in Europe.*

158

CHIVALRIC SPECTACLES AND CEREMONIES

There were still many knights who valued their status, and wished to preserve its exclusivity to those bred and reared in the tradition of knightly privilege. For these men, knighthood still represented a special, exclusive caste whose members were brothers, no matter what their nationality. International tournaments, participation in military campaigns, membership of exclusive secular orders, the swearing and performance of extravagant vows, the continued healthy flourishing of chivalric literature – all these helped the later medieval knights to preserve their belief in the prestige and worth of their order. The traditional values of chivalry represented by tales of

RIGHT *One of the many aspects of late medieval knighthood which provoked censure from churchmen was the delight which many young knights took in extravagant and silly fashions. This knight exactly fits the description of one commentator, that he would wear no shoes unless they were not fit to walk on. Hats and coats were so slashed and tasselled that they resembled rags rather than clothes.*

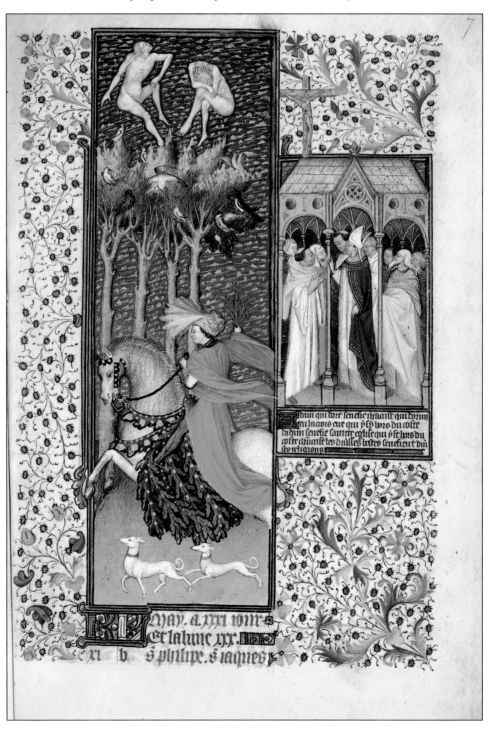

BERTRAND DU GUESCLIN – THE MIRROR OF CHIVALRY

If William Marshal is the most famous of the early knights, his counterpart for the later period must be Bertrand du Guesclin. The two men had much in common, but the fourteenth-century conditions of knighthood are well illustrated by the differences between their two lives. Like the Marshal, Du Guesclin was so famous that his life story was preserved by one Jean Cuvelier in a long narrative poem.

Bertrand was born in about 1320, the eldest son of a Breton knight of modest circumstances. His early years were characterized by a defiance of his father's ban on playing rough games with peasant boys, but eventually he graduated to tournaments, in which he excelled. Unusually for a knightly hero, Bertrand was short and stocky, with broad shoulders and long arms, and all records of him agree in noting his remarkable ugliness.

In the 1340s Brittany was engulfed by civil war. Succession to the duchy was disputed between the last duke's niece and half-brother. The niece, Jeanne de Penthièvre, married Charles of Blois, nephew of King Philip of France, and appealed to her husband's powerful relatives to intervene on her behalf; the half-brother, claiming the inheritance under Salic law (which stated that succession could not go through the female line or to a woman), appealed to the King of England, Edward III. Bertrand du Guesclin, according to Cuvelier, became a freelance guerrilla leader (supporting Jeanne but not on her pay-roll), and retreated to the Breton forest of Broceliande – scene of many a magical adventure in the romances – and equipped his own band of armed followers, using his mother's jewels as capital. By a cunning trick he captured the castle of Fougeray in 1350 and, in 1354, during a spectacular ambush, seized the famous English captain, Hugh of Calveley, and a hundred men. For these exploits he was knighted at the somewhat advanced age of 34.

Retained as a waged knight of Charles de Blois, Bertrand and his band of Bre-

ABOVE: *The lifelike tomb effigy of Bertrand du Guesclin at St Denis in Paris. Du Guesclin's heart was buried in his native Dinan in Brittany, but the king insisted that his body be interred in Paris with all the honours due to one who was widely regarded as the saviour of France.*

tons came to the relief of Rennes in 1356, which was being besieged by the Duke of Lancaster. During a truce, his younger brother Olivier was illegally taken prisoner by an English knight, Sir Thomas of Canterbury. Bertrand was so enraged by this unknightly conduct that he rode into the English camp and burst into the Duke's tent, where a game of chess with Sir John Chandos was in progress. A judicial single combat – the idea being that the winner was in the right – followed with Sir Thomas. Bertrand won this fight, gaining the respect of Lancaster and all the English knights. His subsequent career was full of encounters with the same names – Hugh of Calveley, Robert

Knowles – sometimes fighting in the same cause, more often fighting as enemies and taking one another prisoner.

The Cuvelier biography gives a good flavour of what the life of an active knight at war could be in the late fourteenth century. Rules for conduct in warfare, particularly in the matter of paying ransoms, were laid down and largely observed by knights.

Du Guesclin also fought in foreign wars, but not as a knight-errant. A blunt professional soldier with no use for romance, he had always got on well with the common soldiers, because he was punctilious in ensuring that they were paid on time. His practical attitude and wide experience gained him enormous respect among knights and mercenaries alike, and in 1365 his king made use of Du Guesclin's reputation to assemble some of the "free companies" who were still at large in France, terrorizing whole areas of countryside, and persuade them to pillage elsewhere. The country he selected was Castile, where the unpopular King Pedro (the Cruel) was being challenged for the throne by his illegitimate half-brother, Enrique of Trastamara. Du Guesclin led his mercenary army to the assistance of Enrique – free companies, English, French, Norman, Breton, Picard, Gascon and others flocked to his command. Among them was Hugh of Calveley, fighting under his old enemy, offering his services with the words, "Fair brother and comrade Bertrand, mirror of chivalry, because of your loyalty and your courage, I am yours, and all these my men are yours" (according to Cuvelier).

The "crusaders" met with easy success: Pedro the Cruel fled and Enrique was crowned King. Though Du Guesclin had not actually engaged any Moors, he was granted the title of "King of Granada" (still entirely under Moorish occupation at the time) as well as a more concrete prize – some less substantial properties in Spain. Unfortunately, in 1367 Pedro invited Edward the Black Prince to help regain his inheritance. Against Du

Guesclin's advice, Enrique decided on a pitched battle against the English army – the Battle of Najéra – and lost. Du Guesclin fought bravely to cover his master's retreat but was captured. Asked to name his own ransom, he suggested 100,000 crowns, a fabulous sum which had never been paid for anyone not of royal blood. Du Guesclin paid for this piece of bravado by selling much of his property, and he received large contributions from King Charles and from his old friend, Jeanne of Brittany. On his release, Du Guesclin again raised his mercenary army and wrested Castile from Pedro, who had lost the support of the Black Prince by failing to pay him what he had promised.

In 1370 a renewed outbreak of the war with England caused Charles V to need his "mastiff of Brittany" badly. Du Guesclin returned to France and was made Constable, an extraordinary and confident move by Charles. The Constable of France was effectively the commander-in-chief of the whole French armed forces, and traditionally such an important role could not go to anyone but the highest ranking nobles. But Charles wanted to wage a war of attrition; he did not want a hot-headed duke committing his armies to pitched battles against the English, a policy which had already cost France too dearly at Crécy and Poitiers. Du Guesclin expressed some trepidation at the prospect of giving orders to members of the King's own family, the royal dukes of France, but they promised faithfully to obey him, and he accepted the post.

Fighting once more against his old comrades in arms, Hugh of Calveley and Robert Knowles, Du Guesclin put into action a plan of gradual erosion of English territories; while they conducted their traditional raiding parties, he retaliated by achieving more substantial gains of castles and towns. Gradually the English were pushed back towards the west coast. Du Guesclin seemed unstoppable.

His relationship with the king was close, until Charles decided in 1378 to invade Brittany, whose duke, Jean de Montfort, was still siding with the English. This was an unpopular move, and Du Guesclin repeatedly begged the king to

ABOVE *Jean Fouquet's beautiful miniature of the investiture of Bertrand with the Sword of the Constable of France by King Charles V. It was a controversial decision, because Bertrand was of comparatively humble origins; he refused to accept it until he was assured that the princes and dukes of France would obey his orders.*

make peace and withdraw. The king responded in 1380 by sending him to besiege Chaliers and Chateau-neuf-de-Randon. At the latter he fell victim to one of the diseases which often raged among the encampments of besiegers and, fearing that he was mortally ill, made preparations for his end. He requested to be buried beside his dearly loved first wife, Tiphaine, at Dinan, and instructed his constable's sword to be taken to the king, with the words "others might have made better use of it. Tell the king I am grieved not to have served him longer, but I could not have served him more faithfully". As he lay dying, the English commander of the town came to surrender and placed

the keys in Du Guesclin's hands. Almost his last words were to instruct his knights to spare the unarmed civilians: "The churchmen, the poor, the women and children are not your enemies."

After his death, his grateful king allowed his heart to be buried in Dinan, according to his last wishes, but the rest of his body was buried with fullest honours in the church of St Denis in Paris. Du Guesclin was a hero to the people as well as to his paymasters; an outstanding military leader, he took the duties of knighthood seriously. Besides loyal service and fidelity to his word, he did his best in violent times to protect the helpless poor from the depredations of soldiers. But Du Guesclin was very much a new kind of knight, who was essentially pragmatic in his attitude to soldiering. He foreshadowed the professional soldier of later centuries, agreeing with Bonet that war should be conducted in a disciplined, responsible manner, without knightly heroics or unnecessary brutality.

knight errantry, in which deeds of arms were performed with equal measures of courage and courtesy, were still respected by such men.

Modern writers often accuse the knights of the later Middle Ages of being escapists who sought to glamourize knighthood by dressing it up in the borrowed finery of romance, while their tourneys, feasts and *pas d'armes* became ever more distant from the grisly realities of late medieval warfare. The astonishing extravagance of many late medieval chivalric spectacles is taken by these commentators to be a sign of decadence; in their view, the knights expended their energies in creating ever more elaborate rituals whose sole purpose was self-congratulation, while devising feats of arms which brought them no risk and fighting in battles where, well protected in their armour casings, they spared one another's lives while showing no mercy to their social inferiors.

The offensive part of late chivalric activity seems to be the knights' willingness to accord the same value to deeds performed at spectacular tourneys or *pas d'armes* as to real battles and sieges, or rather, only to praise and celebrate such militarily useless achievements as single combats or the use of exaggerated courtesy towards the enemy knights, instead of applying chivalric values to the less glamorous aspects of medieval warfare – the constant round of brutality, atrocity, death and destruction visited by armies on the helpless civilian populations of Europe. Knights, it is supposed, closed their eyes to the horrors of war, and lived in a fantasy world.

It is true that much chivalric literature tends to be the record of glorious achievements by individual knights, rather than a balanced, historical account of medieval society as a whole. But the cult of individual glory, like the provision of worldly rewards by rulers, had a practical purpose. To suppose that so much energy, effort and money were spent by knights and lords simply in an endless game of self-aggrandizement in an attempt to ignore the unpalatable truths about the decline of their military importance is absurd. Just as the devastation and depopulation of an enemy's territory had a clear military purpose, so, in the absence of standing armies and formal military training, did the pursuit of reputation in tournaments, jousts and wars by individual knights. As it had for hundreds of years, it gave them experience and made them more valuable as soldiers. To contemporaries, there was no distinction between the activities and objectives of fourteenth-century knights and those of their predecessors. Like William Marshal or Guy of Warwick before them, they were following the prescribed curriculum of the only school of arms available to them, that of successful performance at jousts, tournaments and then real warfare. The only differences were of style and sophistication, and of these they were largely unaware; but these are probably responsible for the opprobrium of twentieth-century critics. For certainly the jousts and tourneys, feasts and ceremonies of the later Middle Ages were often vivid and startling creations.

TOURNAMENTS

The grand tournaments of the later Middle Ages were less likely to provide the combat experience useful to knights in real battle than the encounters of the earlier period. As they developed, they became more theatrical, more expensive, more exclusive, and less relevant to actual warfare. Rules defining

ABOVE *The tournament became a theatrical extravaganza: on this occasion, the "Tournament of the Kings of Great Britain and Ireland" at Bayonne in 1565, the knights participating in the* mêlée *are dressed in the sixteenth-century idea of classical armour. This is one of the "Valois" tapestries, made to commemorate festivals held by Queen Catherine de' Medici, the mother of Henry II of France.*

RIGHT *A splendid overhead view of a large tournament held in the Piazza Navona in Rome, late in the seventeenth century, which gives a good idea of the arrangement of the lists, the tilt, and the spectators' stands.*

the eligibility of participants on the grounds of their lineage and the soaring expense of tourneying armour and equipment effectively barred young knights of limited means from launching their careers by attending international tournaments in the way that William Marshal had done. The introduction of safety precautions, such as blunted weapons and barriers, had reduced the likelihood of injury to the knights, but had also reduced the resemblance of the lists to a battle-ground. The joust, an encounter of skill between single knights, increased in importance until it was the main feature, with the *mêlée*, the only part of the tournament which provided effective combat training, relegated to the last day.

The tendency for tournaments to become contests of athletic skill did not completely remove their usefulness. They became *less* like real battles, but they did not become *un*like real battles until well into the sixteenth century. In common with all other aspects of late medieval life, they became more complicated and better regulated. A splendid medieval treatise on how to hold the perfect tournament was written and gorgeously illustrated by the remarkable René of Anjou, who was a devotee of the sport, besides being King of Jerusalem (in name only), King of Sicily and Duke of Anjou, and an extraordinarily accomplished artist. His book, the *Traité de la Forme et Devis d'un Tournoy*, explains how heralds should draw up and deliver challenges to joust, how they should establish the probity and precedence of the knights participating, how the helms, crests and banners of the knights should be displayed beforehand for the benefit of the spectators, ladies and judges, how the performances should be judged and prizes awarded. It also expounds such practical matters as how to set up the lists, barriers, retreats and the spectators' stands, and suggests ways to decorate the town or castle where the tournament is to take place.

Competitors were permitted a fixed number of "courses" at one another down the tilt or, if the combat was on foot, a fixed number of blows with a specified weapon across the barrier. Scoring in jousts was done by the heralds according to whether a knight's lance had struck his opponent on the helmet, or on the body armour, or best of all (but increasingly rare) had thrust him out of his saddle. Tournaments survived even into the seventeenth century as a court spectacle intended to impress visiting foreign dignitaries with the wealth, power and status of the host monarchs.

LEFT *Another ritual associated with the tournament: the winning knight is presented with his prize by his hostess – a jewel decorated with ostrich feathers. Illustration from the* Traité de la Forme et Devis d'un Tournoy *by* René of Anjou.

PAS D'ARMES

One way for a knight to make his reputation in the fifteenth century (if he could afford it) was to hold a *pas d'armes*, a special kind of joust in which a knight or a team of knights would defend a road or a bridge against all challengers. This became increasingly popular as a sport and spectacle and provided opportunities for knights to gain international reputations, and also to redeem tourneying vows that they had taken.

For instance, in 1434 a young Castilian knight, Suero de Quiñones, requested permission from King Juan II to hold a *pas d'armes*. He had pledged to wear an iron collar and chain around his neck every Thursday – a symbol of his enslavement to the love of his lady – until he had taken part in a feat of arms. The event came to be known as the *Passo Honroso*: it was to take place in July and last for thirty days, with the aim of breaking 300 lances. In the traditional way, the Leon King of Arms was sent to proclaim the tournament and elaborate preparations were begun at once. Rules were declared, judges selected (one of them being the famous knight Don Pero Niño, an undefeated jousting champion) and the defending team of nine knights made up.

The place selected for Suero and his companions to defend was a bridge at Orbigo, which was soon transformed by the erection of lists, stands, a dining hall where defenders, challengers and visiting spectators could eat, and twenty-two tents to house the crowd which usually assembled at such spectacles. Knights from all over Spain and even one from Germany arrived to take up the challenge. The usual method of scoring, the count of broken lances, was anxiously watched, since the successful achievement of the *pas* depended on reaching a total of 300. The result was disappointing, for after four weeks of continual encounters between defending and challenging knights, the total number of lances broken was only 180. The occasion was also marred by the death of an Aragonese knight, Asbert de Claramunt, who was killed instantly when his opponent's lance broke his visor and penetrated his left eye. The prohibition on giving knights killed at tournaments a Christian burial was still in force in Spain and the local bishop refused permission to bury the knight in holy ground, so a makeshift grave had to be dug outside a hermitage which stood near the bridge. The jousts continued, however, and were recorded as a glorious chivalric deed by a knight who was present, Pero Rodrigues de Leña.

Many similar events were held in France, Flanders and Burgundy, where they had originated, and the Burgundian court in particular was famed for the elaborate settings and sumptuous decor of their *pas* and tourneys. Perhaps the most famous of all was the *Pas de la Fontaine de Pleurs*, in which one of the chivalric paragons of the age, Jacques de Lalaing, the chamberlain of Duke Philip the Good of Burgundy, vowed to defend a "Fountain" near Chalon sur Saône for a year against all comers (though "all comers" were not to exceed four knights per month). A pavilion was erected on the island of St Laurent in the Saône, and outside the pavilion stood life-size models of a unicorn bearing three shields, and a lady whose eyes ran with tears, so arranged as to trickle down onto the shields, thus giving the *pas* its name. The shields were painted white, violet and black; a knight who wished to take up the challenge was to touch the shields. If he touched the white

BELOW *Henry, Prince of Wales, the eldest son of King James of England, was an enthusiastic jouster and was anxious to revive the chivalric virtues and customs of the knights of old before his tragically early death in 1612.*

THE SIEGE OF MALTA

The Knights Hospitaller were besieged for the second time by the army of Suleiman the Magnificent in 1565. Their naval raids along the coast of North Africa and throughout the Mediterranean caused such damage and annoyance to the Ottoman Empire that it was decided to dislodge them from their great fortress on the island of Malta. The knights had established their headquarters on Malta in 1529, after Suleiman had succeeded in driving them from the island of Rhodes. A huge investment had been made in fortifying their stronghold, which was built principally on the two headlands commanding the larger of Malta's natural harbours. When news reached the Grand Master of the Order, Jean de la Valette, that the old enemy of the Order was preparing to attack once more, he recalled all the knights to the citadel and began to make preparations to withstand a massive siege.

Stores of provisions were laid in, sufficient to feed the garrison for a year. This numbered about eight hundred knights and two thousand men-at-arms, sergeants and servants, but they did not have to provide for the population of an entire city, as they had on Rhodes. Besides collecting all available food and weapons into the fortress, La Valette had conducted a scorched-earth policy in the surrounding countryside, poisoning the wells and burning anything that could be useful to the Turks.

Control of the island depended on the two fortresses of the Order; first the castle of St Elmo, an outpost which overlooked the harbour mouth on its north side, and then the main fortress of Sant' Angelo on the south. La Valette had decided to concentrate his resources on the larger fortress. St Elmo's was not expected to do more than delay the enemy forces for a couple of weeks, and the handful of knights who manned it knew that they had no hope of surviving.

The Turks landed their forces in May and commenced the siege by setting up a barrage of massive cannons opposite St

ABOVE *Jean de la Valette, Grand Master of the Knights Hospitaller at the time of the siege of Malta, in a commemorative medal struck shortly after the successful conclusion of the siege. A more permanent memorial was the renaming of the main harbour of Malta after him – Valletta.*

Elmo. Both the forts were built on solid rock, so the walls could not be undermined, but this was no longer necessary to besieging forces equipped with the latest artillery. For several days the guns maintained a constant bombardment, which was followed in early June by an assault by Turkish soldiers. The knights, however, were well-prepared to fend off this attack, having provisioned themselves with the traditional anti-personnel weapons of besieged forces, such as Greek fire. The Turkish soldiers wore long flowing robes and were particularly vulnerable to this kind of weapon; the knights were able to inflict many casualties, and during one of the several attacks which took place during the next two weeks they killed some of the Turks' most senior commanders, including one of their three generals, Dragut. But the defenders of St Elmo themselves suffered casualties, which

were much more serious than those suffered by the Turks because they could not be replaced. Wounded knights manned the ramparts of the castle sitting in chairs, until on 23 June, after holding out for more than a month, sheer weight of numbers overwhelmed their resistance and the Turks overran the castle, killing all the survivors.

The Turks then attempted to reposition their artillery to fire on the fortress of Sant' Angelo from the north, but they couldn't and instead had to move their men and machines inland to attack the fortress from the south. In early July they attacked in force, but the knights managed to repel them, wiping out a large number of the crack Turkish Janissaries, who were sailing into the harbour, by firing a broadside into their boats from a concealed gun-emplacement. The Turks went back to concentrated cannon-fire for a fortnight, under which even the recently reinforced massive stone defences began to crumble. On 2 August the knights repulsed a direct assault, and on 7 August had to face another and larger one. The Turks split their troops so as to attack at two key points at once. One of these pincer movements was stopped by the ingenious design of the fortifications, which trapped thousands of the besieging force between the inner and outer walls, where they were massacred by the knights. The other attacking force was called off when they were at the point of breaking through into the citadel, because their commander had been told of a counter-attack on the Turkish encampment and hurried to meet what he thought was a new Christian army sent from nearby Sicily to relieve the knights. When he reached the camp he found that it had indeed been burned and plundered, but the perpetrators were a handful of the Hospitallers, who were stationed at the old fortified city of M'dina across the island.

The Turkish miners, with great difficulty, next succeeded in undermining the bastion of Castile (sections of the de-

ABOVE *A fresco depicting the vast encampment of the Turks in Malta, with, in the background, the massed artillery bombardment of the tiny fortress of St Elmo.*

fences were still manned by knights of each nationality, as they had been on Rhodes), and exploded a mine on 18 August, causing a large breach in the wall. At the same time, the Turks moved a siege tower up to another wall, whereupon La Valette ordered his men to demolish the wall with cannon. The Turks attempted to breach another wall with an early time-bomb, which had a slow-burning fuse; luckily for the knights, it was found in time and thrown back over the wall into the enemy, where it exploded and killed many soldiers.

This was a critical period in the process of the siege, where small incidents could swing the advantage either way. The knights were well-provisioned and their morale was high, but they were still massively outnumbered and their outer defences had been badly breached in two places. The Turks, on the other hand, were short of provisions. They had not expected the knights to hold out for so long; also they were supplied by sea and, as they were within easy reach of the Christian end of the Mediterranean, their ships were being captured and plundered before reaching them. Their two remaining generals were quarreling about what should be done next, and like many besieging forces they had fallen prey to sickness and fever in the camp. An attempt was made to capture the little city-fort of M'dina, but this was abandoned when the governor made all the citizens dress as men-at-arms and walk about on the ramparts to make it look much more strongly defended than it really was.

One more attack was launched on 1 September, but the Turks were so demoralized by now that this was easily repulsed. On 7 September the relief force from Sicily arrived, and the Turks were ordered to embark at once, especially as the commander of the fleet was anxious to set off on the long journey home before the autumn gales set in. The other commander, learning how tiny the relieving army was, ordered his men to disembark again and engage them, but this resulted in another defeat for the Turks and they left for good.

The Knights Hospitaller had succeeded in defeating an army of about thirty thousand of the best Turkish troops, and their achievement was honoured throughout Europe. New recruits and funds poured in, and the damaged fortresses were rebuilt (and renamed Valetta after their great general and Grand Master), where they remain as monuments to late medieval military architecture.

shield, it meant that he had chosen to give and receive twenty-five blows with axes; the violet shield meant the same number of blows with swords, while the black shield meant twenty-five encounters with lances at the tilt. Beside these images stood a herald, who was to record the names of challengers, verifying their correct noble lineage, and which type of combat they had chosen. If the challengers succeeded in defeating Jacques, they would win a golden model of their chosen weapon; however if he defeated them, they had to wear a golden bracelet on their arm until they could find a lady who could unlock it for them.

Jacques was defending the Fountain of Tears alone, and in total he received (and accepted) twenty-two challenges during his year in occupation. They were unevenly spread however, with several months in which the shields remained undisturbed, but with a sudden flurry of activity in the final month. Some of his opponents were little-known squires (who were now entitled to take part in jousts together with fully-fledged knights), but one was the famous Sicilian knight, John de Boniface, who had already fought against Jacques at a tournament in Ghent four years previously. He broke the rules by touching two of the shields, requesting both the lance and axe combats; but Jacques was eager to oblige his illustrious opponent. The jousts on horseback were abandoned after Boniface lost a vital piece of armour, and he was dashed to the ground in the exchange of axe blows, after which he set off, his golden bracelet locked around his arm, apparently hoping that his mistress would have the key. The *pas* was rounded off with a magnificent banquet for all the contestants, at which prizes were awarded and a painted sugar sculpture of the island, pavilion, unicorn and lady was brought out between courses.

Many other similar events are recorded, based either on a romance or around some "legend" made-up for the purpose. They required months of elaborate preparation and considerable expense, but the rewards were rich in terms of knightly renown, particularly if they were recorded in detail. It was typical for the challengers to have to declare their intentions formally by striking shields hung on a tree or on a *perron* (pillar), or sometimes by sounding a horn. This practice seems to have derived directly from romances such as Chretien's *Yvain*, in which a knight defends a fountain in the magical forest of Broceliande, and the challenger provokes him to combat by casting water from the fountain onto a *perron*.

Another form of encounter between individual knights which became popular during the fifteenth century was the single or group combat *à l'outrance*, meaning with real weapons of war, as opposed to most sporting jousts and *pas d'armes* which were fought with blunted weapons, *à plaisance*. This appears to have originated in the tradition of enemy knights challenging each other to combat in real wars, and especially during sieges, but as time went by it became formalized by the issue of standard letters of challenge. These, too, were often associated with vows, such as the vow sworn by an Aragonese squire, named Michel d'Oris, that he would never take off a certain piece of his armour until he had fought against an English knight. One Sir John Prendergast accepted this challenge, and a correspondence ensued in which the contest was specified in exact detail – a certain number of courses with particular weapons – but it seems never to have taken place, though many others are known to have.

ABOVE *The biographer of the famous Burgundian knight Jacques de Lalaing, hero of the* Pas de la fontaine des pleurs, *sits down to begin his own contribution to the growing body of literature celebrating the cult of outstanding individual knights.*

ABOVE *Another of the Valois tapestries, this time showing knights fighting on foot across barriers. With improvements in armour and better regulated contests, jousts had become much safer for knights, though accidents did still occur. Note the broken weapons and armour littering the ground; the squires will collect these later.*

VOWING CEREMONIES

The connection between late medieval tournaments and the performance of vows is interesting. In the fourteenth and fifteenth centuries it was common for knights to make vows, which usually involved them in some kind of handicap until they had performed a specified feat of arms. This might be a personal objective for a single knight, such as the vow made by Suero de Quiñones, or the English knight, Sir John Weberton, who swore to defend the border castle of Lanark for one year to show himself worthy of his beloved lady (he died in the attempt), but often vows were taken by groups of knights. For example, the chronicler Froissart records meeting a group of young English gentlemen at Valenciennes, who each wore a patch over one eye. When asked the reason for this, they explained that they had all vowed only to see with one eye until they had achieved some deed of arms in France.

Froissart does not mention the circumstances in which they had taken the vow, but it might well have been in a vowing ceremony, a tradition inspired by a romance, the *Romance of Alexander* by Jean de Longuyon, in which the most famous champions of Alexander's army, at a feast one night during the siege of Ephesus, made vows on the principal dish at the banquet – a peacock – to achieve specific feats during battle on the following day. The idea of vowing on a bird was seized upon and imitated eagerly by medieval knights. We have already mentioned the Vows of the Swan in 1306 on the occasion of Edward I of England's eldest son being dubbed to knighthood (see Introduction); these are echoed in a literary treatment of the subject, the poem *The Vows of the Heron* which describes a similar scene. On the eve of their invasion of France, Edward III and his knights vow on the heron to do famous deeds of arms on French soil. The Earl of Salisbury requests his wife, Joan of Kent, to close one of his eyes, then makes his vow:

> "I swear by Almighty God...that this eye will never be opened, for storm or for wind, for evil or for fortune, or for any let or hindrance, until I shall be in France and have lit the fires of war there."

The most famous vowing ceremony of all, and that which has attracted most criticism from modern writers, was the Vows of the Pheasant, which took place in 1454 at Lille. Constantinople had finally fallen to the Turks the previous year, and Philip the Good, Duke of Burgundy, was attempting to raise men, money and enthusiasm for a crusade to liberate it from the infidel. Duke Philip was passionately devoted to reviving the ancient standards of chivalry, and in 1430 had founded his own noble Order, the Order of the Golden Fleece (*Toison d'Or*). At this spectacular feast, which had been in preparation for months, the guests comprised a glittering collection of princes and nobles from other parts of France, and for their entertainment a stupendous spectacle was staged. A joust preceded the feast, at which Adolf of Clèves in the guise of the Swan Knight (legendary ancestor of Godfrey of Bouillon) challenged all comers, but the tableaux at the banquet itself were even more striking. A fountain had been set up which featured the statue of a child, pissing rose water, and a variety of ingenious models were displayed for the delight of the company. At the climax of the proceedings, a giant dressed as a Moor led an elephant into the hall. On top of the elephant was a "castle", and inside that a lady dressed as Holy Church in white satin with a black cape, who addressed the assembled nobles with an account of her sufferings over the years at the hands of the Turks, and pleaded for their help to deliver her from oppression. At this point the Toison d'Or King of Arms entered, accompanied by two Knights of the Golden Fleece and two of Duke Philip's illegitimate daughters. The King of Arms was carrying a live pheasant, with a gem-encrusted gold collar round its neck, and presented it to the Duke. The Duke then rose and made a solemn vow to mount a crusade against the Turk, either in the company of the King of France, or alone, and to meet the Turkish Sultan in single combat if he wished. The other great nobles present followed him in swearing extraordinary oaths, that they would not sleep in a bed, or would stand up to eat, or wear no armour, until they should have achieved feats of arms against the Turks.

According to Olivier de la Marche, who recorded the proceedings, this was done "in accordance with the ancient custom of presenting a peacock or other noble bird at a great feast before illustrious princes, lords and nobles, to the end that they might swear expedient and binding oaths". The Vows of

ABOVE *Portrait of Philip the Good, Duke of Burgundy, founder of the Order of the Golden Fleece (whose insignia he is wearing round his neck) and instigator of the famous Vows of the Pheasant in 1454.*

RIGHT *The Knights Hospitaller prepare to defend their fortified town of Rhodes from the besieging Turkish army.*

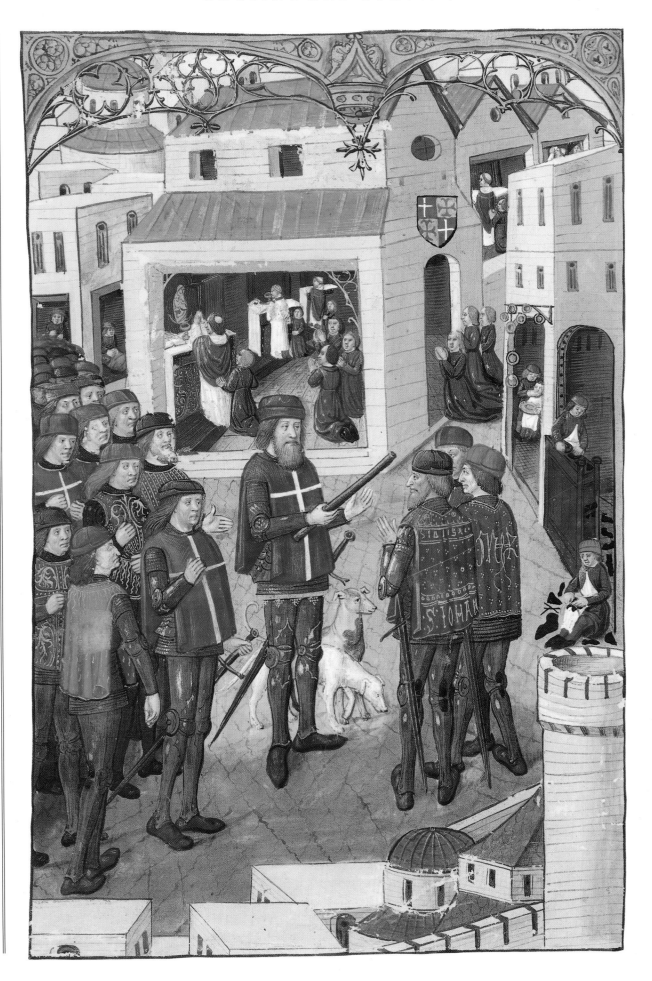

the Pheasant are sometimes cited as a perfect example of the decadence of late medieval knighthood, because the crusade against the Ottoman Turks, which was the occasion for this theatrical extravaganza, never took place. But the vows were not made merely for the sake of vanity. Duke Philip really intended to launch his crusade, and for the next two years made serious preparations for it, which included further meetings with his nobles and knights to encourage their commitment to the enterprise and the levying of taxes to raise the necessary funds. Detailed plans were made to solve the practical problems of shipping the army to Constantinople and ensure its supplies in the hostile Eastern Mediterranean. But Philip's troubles at home forced him to abandon the idea in 1456. In the context of fifteenth-century chivalry, this was a characteristically flamboyant expression of noble intention; given the size of the venture he was planning, Duke Philip could not have launched it in any other way.

MERCENARIES

There had always been mercenaries in the employment of medieval kings and lords who waged war. Duke William of Normandy shipped mercenaries across the Channel to England in 1066, and the great Spanish adventurer, El Cid, had once fought on behalf of the Moors. No king was so proud of the army he had raised by feudal levy that he was unwilling to augment it with trained specialists, such as Genoese crossbowmen or Swiss or Flemish pikemen. There was a difference, however, between a mercenary, who would fight for anyone who paid him enough, and a knight, who fought for his traditional lord or for a worthy cause which would enhance his reputation, and accepted the spoils of war as the legitimate reward for the risks he was taking. But by the fourteenth century it was no longer possible for kings to levy armies, or nobles to keep their retinues of knights, by calling on feudal duties alone. The service given by a knight to his lord was frequently rewarded with pay, according to the terms of a contract.

This was not universally true all over Europe. In Italy, where city states were in a state of almost continual war with one another, the agreements drawn up between mercenary captains and the great lords or city councils who employed them were simply contracts of employment, covering specific military services, valid for a defined period of time, and regulated by *ordinamenti*, conditions of employment. In parts of France and Spain, the idea of defining wages by contract was frowned upon, but the practice of giving wages certainly was not. Honoré Bonet, the author of the famous military treatise, *The Tree of Battles*, explained the distinction between a paid soldier and a retainer to whom pay was given:

> Sometimes wages are given to a man for his labour and for his subsistence as, for instance, to a man-at-arms, or a sergeant, or a crossbowman, who must live and clothe and equip himself with what he takes from his wages...There are others who take wages rather for their trouble than for their subsistence, for they eat and drink of the subsistence of their lord, and take robes from his livery.

A sort of compromise between a contract of employment and a gentlemen's understanding was reached in England in what became known as the

ABOVE *A superb nineteenth-century rendering of a professional soldier –* A Condottiere *by the English painter Frederic, Lord Leighton. This man's expensive armour cannot hide his insecurity – he is not an insensitive thug, but he certainly is not a knight.*

indenture system. An indenture was a contract agreed between a king and a lord, or a lord and a knight, defining terms of service and the payment for it. It differed from the mercenary's contract because it attempted to define the employment of the knight in terms of loyalty and lifelong service (in peace and in war) to one lord. The contract, when drawn up and signed, was cut in two, with a jagged edge (hence the name), to prevent forgery. In 1386 John of Gaunt drew up the following indenture with Sir Thomas Beek:

> This indenture, made between John, King of Castile and Leon, Duke of Lancaster on the one part, and Sir Thomas Beek, on the other part, bears witness that the said Sir Thomas is retained and kept by the said King and Duke to serve him in times of peace as in times of war for the term of his life, and to work with him in whatever place should please the said King and Duke, well and suitably equipped for war.
>
> And the said Sir Thomas in times of peace will have wages and food and fuel wherever he may be sent by the letters of the said King and Duke at his command.
>
> And the said Sir Thomas will take for his fee, as well in times of peace as in times of war, twenty pounds a year, for the term of his life.
>
> In time of war, the said Sir Thomas will take wages and board at court, as other bachelors of his condition will receive, from the hands of the treasurer of the said King and Duke for the war for the stated time.
>
> With regard to prisoners and other profits of war taken or won by the said Sir Thomas or any of his men, from the commencement of his year of war and the equipping of himself, his men, horses and equipment, the said King and Duke will treat him as he treats other bachelors of his state and condition...

The distinction preserved by this kind of hybrid between properly rewarded loyal service and professional contract was increasingly difficult to observe. In practice, it was only a short step from a knight who took out an indenture with a lord to the disagreeable figure of the fourteenth-century mercenary knight. Mercenaries were of course not all of knightly origin, but a surprisingly large number were – younger sons and landless knights, who had put all their resources into their equipment and needed constant employment in war. As Philippe de Mézières put it, mercenaries were often:

> ...the second and third born sons and others, who have little or no portion in the inheritance of their fathers, and who by poverty are often constrained to follow wars that are unjust and tyrannical, so as to sustain their estate of nobility, since they know no other calling but arms: and therein they commit so much ill that it would be frightening to tell of all the pillaging and crimes with which they oppress poor people.

When there was war, the people suffered from looting and pillaging, but equally, when there was no war, there was nothing for these men to do and no way for them to maintain themselves except by preying on the civilian communities. This is aptly illustrated by the story told by Sacchetti of Sir John Hawkwood, the famous English mercenary captain, who was met on his way by two friars, who wished him peace. "May the lord take away your alms," was his truculent reply, adding by way of explanation that since he made his living by war, peace was the last thing he wanted.

The large bands of mercenary soldiers, usually led by mercenary knights, who roamed at large in the countryside, fully armed, every time a

ABOVE *A posthumous portrait of John of Gaunt, Duke of Lancaster (through his first wife Blanche) and King of Castile and Leon (through his second wife Costanza). The fourth son of King Edward III, John's thwarted dynastic ambitions were eventually fulfilled in his son Henry, who became King Henry IV of England.*

THE FIELD OF THE CLOTH OF GOLD

King Henry VIII of England and King Francis I of France shared many characteristics, both in character and position, and both monarchs were enthusiastic devotees of the tournament. In his youth, Henry had designed his own tourneying armour, later importing specialist German armourers with the permission of another royal tourneying enthusiast, Emperor Maximilian I of Germany, and establishing his own armoury at Greenwich. He maintained permanent tiltyards at Greenwich, Westminster and Hampton Court, and loved to celebrate great occasions, such as his accession to the throne, with lavish tournaments. Francis I was also an eager practitioner, anxious for a great chivalric reputation. He had requested to be dubbed to knighthood by the Chevalier Bayard, the most famous knight of the age, *sans peur et sans reproche*.

When they met outside Calais in the June of 1520, the occasion was primarily a diplomatic one, intended to forge peaceful and amicable relations between their two countries (they were at war within two

BELOW As a young man, King Henry VIII of England was a great athlete who could vault fully armed into the saddle, and loved tournaments. Here he is depicted jousting in the lists before his first wife, Catherine of Aragon.

RIGHT *Panorama of the Field of the Cloth of Gold (now at Hampton Court Palace). The artist has used some licence; the field was actually further inland from Calais than it appears here, and you could not really see London in the distance. Note the tree hung with shields in the traditional way – jousters chose their combat weapon by striking the appropriate shield.*

years, however). The political aspects of the meeting were kept very low-key, however, and the splendid tournaments, jousts and feasts which accompanied it appeared in the eyes of contemporary observers to take precedence over everything else. The arrangements for this great display of chivalric arts had taken months to prepare; the tents pitched in the field sparkled and shone with gold thread and embroidered gems, giving the occasion its popular name of the "Field of the Cloth of Gold".

The dimensions and construction of the tiltyard were the subject of lengthy correspondence between the household officers of each court. These have survived, together with a "panoramic view" of the scene at Hampton Court which, however, employs a certain degree of artistic licence. In the traditional style of the great fifteenth-century *pas d'armes*, a

tree was erected from which the three shields signifying combat with sword, axe or lance were hung. Challengers touched the shields to indicate their preferred type of joust.

Each of the two kings led his own team of seven knights in the contests that followed, and bands of knights who had come as "challengers" in response to the proclamations which had been made in France, England and the Low Countries, joined their chosen team. This was not difficult, as all the challengers were either English or French. The kings were of course vying to outdo one another in their splendour and magnificence; Francis's horse wore purple satin trimmed with gold and embroidered with black plumes, Henry's wore cloth of gold fringed with damask. The liveries of the two teams reflected this theme – French knights wore cloth of silver trimmed with purple velvet, English knights cloth of gold and

russet velvet. The kings themselves appeared in a succession of sumptuous costumes, bearing chivalrous or patriotic mottoes. The kings jousted against each other and each other's knights (Henry rode one of his horses so hard in the jousting that it died later that night). Knights within teams jousted against each other as well as against their opponents. More than 300 spears were broken in these jousts and, unhappily, a French knight was fatally wounded after jousting against his own brother.

The jousts were followed by tourneying, but this consisted of knights fighting one another, two against two, instead of the traditional *mêlée*. Games of skill on horseback took place between the bouts, and other, less traditional sporting contests, were added, such as archery, in which Henry excelled. He also attempted to introduce an impromptu wrestling match, as one chronicler records:

The king of England and the king of France retired together to a pavilion and drank together, and then the king of England took the king of France by the collar and said to him "My brother, I want to wrestle with you," and gave him one or two falls. And the king of France, who is strong and a good wrestler, gave him a "Breton turn" and threw him on the ground...and the king of England wanted to go on wrestling, but it was broken off and they had to go to supper.

Largesse was used almost as a weapon; if one king admired the other's horse, he was obliged to make a present of it, and several gifts exchanged hands in this way during the post-tournament drinking and feasting which concluded most days. At the end of the week's festivities, prizes were awarded – with both the kings heading the list of prizewinners.

IOANNES·ACVTVS·EQVES·BRITANNICVS·DVX·AETATIS·S
VAE·CAVTISSIMVS·ET·REI·MILITARIS·PERITISSIMVS·HABITVS·EST

ABOVE *The lavish funeral monument to the great mercenary captain Sir John Hawkwood (known to the Italians as Giovanni Acuto) commissioned from Paolo Uccello by the grateful citizens of Florence.*

treaty or a truce enforced a cessation of hostilities, were a terrifying social menace. They would ravage the countryside independently of any official army as "free companies". Because they were all experienced soldiers, it was almost impossible for any native levies to defeat them. For example, after the Treaty of Bretigny in 1360 had created a temporary lull in the Hundred Years War between England and France, a vast international band of mercenaries were suddenly laid off. They had nowhere to go, so they banded together and called themselves the "Great Company". This notorious band was composed pincipally of Germans and Hungarians, led by a freebooting Provençal, Montréal d'Albarno, who was one of the first leaders to realise the advantages of professional reliability, and enforced strict discipline on his men. Much of northern and eastern France had already been so devastated by the war that there was nothing much left for them to steal, so they moved southwards, looting and killing as they went. A French army was raised, under the command of Jacques de Bourbon, to crush the Great Company, and met them in battle at Brignais in 1362. But the Great Company had now grown so strong, so numerous, so warlike and powerful, that the French army was cut to pieces. The Company moved on towards Avignon, a rich and powerful city, home of Pope Innocent VI, where they laid siege to the town. The contemporary French chronicler, Jean de Venette, recorded how:

> They came to Pont-Saint-Esprit, a city near Avignon, and took it by force of arms. There they passed some time wasting the adjacent countryside horribly. They planned in some fashion or other to subjugate ultimately the whole city of Avignon...Finally, however, after receiving large sums of money from the Pope and with his absolution, it is said, they left the country round Avignon and scattered in various directions through the world, doing harm wherever they went.

But the Great Company did not all scatter – many of them simply passed through southern France into northern Italy, where they reformed as the "White Company", under the leadership of Sir John Hawkwood (known in

BELOW *A court spectacle which went horribly wrong: the* Bals des Ardants *in 1392. King Charles VI of France was one of the dancers disguised as wild men when his brother Louis, Duke of Orleans, set fire to their costumes. The other dancers burned to death, but the king was saved by the presence of mind of the Duchess of Berry, who smothered the flaming monarch in her skirts.*

Italy as Giovanni Acuto). Here they became part of a tradition of mercenary companies in the employment of factious Italian cities. These soldiers were named *Condottieri* after the *condotta*, or contracts according to which the legal-minded Italians defined the obligations of each party. The earliest band of Condottieri were Catalans from northern Spain, who had originally been employed in a territorial dispute between Aragon and Naples about sovereignty over Sicily. When this war was over and they could find no further employment in Italy, their condottiere, Roger de Flor, led them eastwards and they conquered Frankish Greece.

The *condotte* were drawn up between the leaders of the mercenaries and their employers, and stipulated in great detail the exact number of men who would be contracted to fight, how they would be equipped and armed, where they would fight and how long for. The employers pledged themselves to pay for services rendered, and in some cases to compensate soldiers for horses lost on campaign (the majority of condottieri were heavily armed cavalry). Though the condottieri were generally notorious for changing sides if someone made them a better offer, Hawkwood at least was concerned for his professional reputation and enjoyed much respect for his fidelity to his word.

However satisfactory (or otherwise) the condottieri were to their employers, they were a plague to the ordinary people in the war-ravaged Italian countryside. The lawyer, Bartholomeo de Saliceto, was explicit:

> What shall I say of those companies of men at arms who overrun the territories of our cities? I reply that there is no doubt about their position, for they are robbers...and as robbers they should be punished for all the crimes that they have committed.

Many chroniclers record the devastation that was left behind in a countryside, either during war or "peace", after an army of such men had passed through, describing it as a desert, uninhabited, uncultivated, with towns and villages burned and left to rot, and fields which had been full of crops or pasture rank with weeds and young trees.

The activities of the condottieri would seem to be incompatible with those of knights; but surprisingly, some contemporaries did not feel this to be true. Young knights were advised to travel to Italy to seek experience in the wars there; one German writer, Konrad of Megenberg, specifically recommended it to poor knights as a sure source of employment and fortune. In the *Chevalier Errant*, written in 1394 by Thomaso, Marquis of Saluzzo, a young condottiere called Galeas of Mantua is held up as a model of chivalric virtue. Galeas' career, as described by the Marquis, is extraordinarily similar to that of the ideal knight described by Geoffrey de Chargny and given literary form in *Guy of Warwick*. Galeas had undertaken his career as a knight errant, in search of adventure, for the sake of his lady's love. His adventures included jousts and tournaments as well as sieges and battles; he had fought for the French against the English during the Hundred Years War, and was knighted for unhorsing a famous English knight in single combat; he had even been on a pilgrimage to the Holy Land, and taken part in wars against the infidel Turk in the service of Peter of Cyprus and Sigismund of Hungary. Here is the perfect example of the international knight-adventurer, whose knightly deeds embrace the courtly world of jousting and love as well as the sterner scenes of battle.

INVS PHLIPPVS HISPANVS DESCOLARIS   RELATOR VICTORIE T

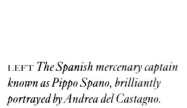

LEFT *The Spanish mercenary captain known as Pippo Spano, brilliantly portrayed by Andrea del Castagno.*

Nor was Galeas of Mantua alone. The paragons of late medieval chivalry, like their predecessors, followed an apprenticeship in arms at tourneys and at international battles with service in the armies of their lords. The Spanish hero, Don Pero Niño, the Burgundian, Jacques de Lalaing, and the Frenchman Pierre de Terraile (Chevalier Bayard), were internationally famous jousters and sought deeds of arms, but also saw repeated military action. Jacques was actually killed by a cannonball during the siege of Pouques in 1453. The concept of the "Flower of Chivalry", the perfect gentle knight, *sans peur et sans reproche*, was still valid in the late sixteenth century, when it was applied to those who combined outstanding achievement with knightly virtues, such as England's Sir Philip Sidney.

ROMANCE AND KNIGHTLY LITERATURE

It has been said that if a single event can be seen as heralding the end of the Middle Ages it was the invention of printing. In the case of romance literature, however, printing inspired and made possible a last creative flowering. The medieval literary fascination with knights and chivalry enjoyed a long and brilliant Indian summer. The fifteenth century saw the genre of romance revitalized with long, tortuously constructed verse and prose romances, highly stylized and self-consciously nostalgic in their tone. Their examination of the infinite variety of knightly conduct became increasingly complex and frequently fell into self-parody, as with the brilliant *Orlando Furioso* of the Italian poet Ariosto, and, of course, Miguel Cervantes' *Don Quixote*. Both these works intended to satirize the worst excesses of romance literature, and particularly the striving for individual glory through ever more extravagant feats of arms. In *Orlando Furioso* (first edition 1516), the hero Orlando, barely recognizable as the epic hero of the *Chanson de Roland*, has been driven mad because his beloved Angelica has rejected him in favour of a Saracen foot soldier. Intertwined with this main story are many other episodes, focussing

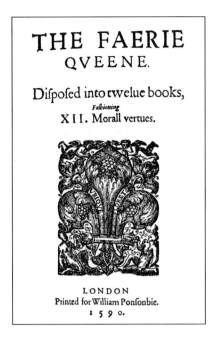

THE FAERIE
QVEENE.

Difpofed into twelue books,
Fafhioning
XII. Morall vertues.

LONDON
Printed for William Ponfonbie.
1 5 9 0.

ABOVE *The title page of the 1590 edition of
Edmund Spenser's* The Faerie Queene,
*originally planned to be an allegorical
exposition of knightly virtues in twelve
books, with twelve personified virtues as the
heroes of each book.*

ABOVE RIGHT *A fine nineteenth-century
engraving by Walter Crane (1845-1915)
of Book I Canto viii, of* The Faerie
Queene, *in which the heroine Una enlists
the aid of Prince Arthur to fight the giant
who has imprisoned the hero of the book, the
Red Cross Knight (Faith).*

on the wars between Christians and pagans near Paris, and the rather more
successful love affair between Ruggiero and Bradamante (legendary foun-
ders of the d'Este family). Cervantes' epic, *El ingenioso hidalgo Don Quixote de
la Mancha,* tells of an elderly hero who, besotted by reading too many chivalrous romances, rode off on his wheezy old horse, Rosinante, on a quest of
knight-errantry to achieve glory for the sake of his "lady", accompanied by
his prosaic servant, Sancho Panza. His attempts to find adventure, including
his famous charge at the windmill, eventually disillusioned him and on his
death-bed he dictated a will specifying that his niece may only marry a man
who can be proved never to have read a book of knight-errantry. Cervantes
concluded his work by declaring that:

> My sole aim has been to arouse men's scorn for the false and absurd stories
> of knight-errantry, whose prestige has been shaken by this tale of my true
> Don Quixote, and which will, without any doubt, soon crumble in ruin.

By 1615, when *Don Quixote* was completed, these prophetic words had
already largely come true. But in the preceding 150 years there was still room
for straightforward re-tellings of the old subjects of romance, like the
Arthurian cycle which was given new depth and power in Sir Thomas
Malory's masterpiece, *Morte Darthur,* and the splendidly fanciful version of
the First Crusade, *Gerusalemme Liberata* by Torquato Tasso. The latter,
written in 1575, was an immediate success, translated into all major
European languages. The English translation of the poem by Edward
Fairfax influenced the poet Edmund Spenser in his own astonishing journey
through the magical forests of romance in *The Faerie Queene.*

One of the interesting features of the later romances is the appearance
of a new treatment of heroines. Ladies in romances had by no means all been
passive figures, waiting for their knights to decide their destinies (though

some had); but never before had they so actively taken matters into their own hands that they donned armour and set out on quests as lady knights, like the pagan warrior Clorinda in *Gerusalemme Liberata*. An inspired creation, she secretly loves her enemy, Tancredo, and accepts baptism from him as she dies in his arms, after he had inflicted a fatal wound in single combat. Spenser's Britomart, another armed Amazonian, embodies Chastity in his allegorical scheme, in which the hero of each book was to be the exemplar of a particular knightly virtue. Britomart, armed with an invincible sword and magic armour, is a wonderfully charming character who breathes new life into the knightly ideal by blending a knight's courage and desire for justice with her own spirited femininity.

THE NEW AGE

By the late fifteenth century the role knights had played in their heyday, in the twelfth and thirteenth centuries, was obsolete. Their belief in themselves as a military élite was undermined by the advances in artillery, their search for individual prowess in arms as an international brotherhood eroded by the growing nationalism of a Europe which was rapidly fragmenting through irreconcilable religious and political differences. But their belief in themselves as the ruling class continued to provide them with a valid role in the new world emerging from the cataclysms of the Renaissance; the knight as the brave and courteous warrior, with his obligations to protect the weak, evolved into the knight as representative of a class fitted by birth and education to govern and lead. The knight lost the sharp outlines of his shining armour and softened into the more peaceful outline of the European gentleman. He retained the knight's sense of responsibility as a leader of the community, whose privileged position was justified by his protection of the status quo, but other features of the knights' chivalric code passed into the cultural consciousness of western Europe, to be revived from time to time in the succeeding centuries and adapted to suit the changing times.

RIGHT *A scene from the fourteenth-century prose* Lancelot, *in which the Lady of the Lake presents the young Lancelot to Arthur and Guinevere. The traditional Arthurian romances enjoyed a revival as soon as printing ensured their wide availability.*

CONCLUSION

Although the subject of knights, their historical deeds, their fictional deeds, and their code of chivalry, continued to inspire the scholars and creative writers of Europe after the fifteenth century, it became more and more difficult for anyone to understand what it had been like to be a medieval knight. Since the Middle Ages no other group in any European society has attained such a position of military, social and cultural dominance, let alone the kind of international dominance which we have seen in our study. Gradually the countries of Europe developed their own standing armies of professional soldiers in which, with the advent of efficient gunpowder artillery, knights' cavalry played a smaller and smaller part. With the loss of their military superiority the knights subsided into "gentry" – a much more broadly based section of society – and civil and political duties took the place of the calling of arms, which had been the essence of knighthood. An equally serious cultural and imaginative change took place after the Renaissance, when the cold clear light of classical learning and reason, particularly in countries where Protestantism predominated, led people to condemn the Middle Ages as a time of barbarism, superstition and ignorance. In this spirit comes the condemnation, by Elizabethan theorist Roger Ascham, of Sir Thomas Malory's *Morte Darthur*:

> ...the whole pleasure of which booke standeth in two speciall poynts, in open mans slaughter and bold bawdrye: In which booke these be counted the noblest Knightes, that do kill most men without any quarell, and commit foulest adulteries by sutlest shiftes.

In the succeeding centuries the knights' most lasting and powerful legacy was their literature, in particular the best of the medieval romances and chivalrous treatises, and the histories and chronicles of writers such as Froissart and theorists such as Geoffrey de Chargny and Ramon Lull.

In 1759, at the height of the "Age of Reason", the great scholar, J.B. de la Curne de Sainte Palaye, published his *Memoires sur l'ancienne chevalerie*. It contained extracts from many medieval French romances (in which De la Curne de Sainte Palaye was widely read) and, together with his subsequent book, *Histoire littéraire des troubadours*, stimulated a revival of interest in the art and, more especially, the literature of the Middle Ages. So for centuries knights were perceived by antiquarian scholars only through the romantically tinted medium of chivalrous literature, which enabled them to reconstruct the ethos of "Chivalry" in great detail, but not to gain much insight into the reality of their lives.

In late eighteenth- and early nineteenth-century England, "Gothic" became a popular and fashionable style in architecture and novels and

ABOVE *The heroes of the Middle Ages continued to inspire great art and literature. Here is Tiepolo's imagined version of the mid-twelfth-century marriage of Emperor Frederick I (Barbarossa) decorating the palace of the prince-bishops of Würzburg.*

contributed to the development of Romantic poetry. Keats and Coleridge, and later Browning and Tennyson were all fascinated by the idea of the Middle Ages; their poems inspired British painters of the Pre-Raphaelite school to turn to the art of the later Middle Ages and the Renaissance for its rich, brilliant, gem-like colours, emphasis on pattern, decoration and minute detail, and also for its narrative and symbolic subjects.

The revival of interest in "Chivalry" in nineteenth-century industrial society was an important cultural phenomenon, which began in Britain and spread to other countries. The supposed code of honour of medieval knights seemed to answer a need felt by many people at a time when the pressures of an increasingly industrial, mechanical, commercial and urban society

LEFT *A carved wooden panel showing the scene from the* Morte Darthur *in which the mortally wounded king is transported by barge to the Isle of Avalon, accompanied by mourning queens. This panel decorates the King's Robing Room in the House of Lords, London.*

ABOVE: *An excessively idealized vision of a young knight's dedicatory watch and prayer before his dubbing to knighthood the following day:* The Vigil *by John Pettie R.A. (1839-1893).*

seemed to threaten traditional values and beliefs. In 1790 the statesman and political historian, Edmund Burke, said of the fate of Marie Antoinette:

> Little did I dream that I should have lived to see disasters fallen upon her in a nation of gallant men, a nation of men of honour, and of cavaliers. I thought ten thousand swords must have leapt from their scabbards to avenge even a look that threatened her with insult. But the age of chivalry is gone. That of sophisters, economists, and calculators, has succeeded; and the glory of Europe is extinguished for ever.

In the early nineteenth century the enthusiasm for tales of medieval knights was fuelled by the astoundingly successful novels of Sir Walter Scott, who also obligingly expounded his theories on chivalry in an essay in the 1818 edition of the *Encyclopaedia Britannica*. In common with the other great nineteenth-century apologists of chivalry, he made of it something much more moral and ideal than it had ever been in the Middle Ages. There was a genuine belief that the code of chivalry had force and relevance for nineteenth-century Britain, but the key concepts for the Victorians were purity, nobility, high moral seriousness and that excessive gallantry and tenderness towards women which is rather nauseating to twentieth-century tastes. The favourite hero of the Victorian medievalists was the pure, and somewhat characterless, Sir Galahad, rather than Sir Lancelot, whose knightly character had been corrupted by his guilty love for Guinevere. Tennyson's *Idylls of the King* probably expressed this consciousness of moral chivalry best. Tennyson developed a theme which was already strongly expressed in Malory's *Morte Darthur*. In *Morte Darthur* the tensions generated by Lancelot's adulterous love affair with the queen become unbearable and are obviously going to destroy the Round Table fellowship. At this point King Arthur says:

> "...my heart was never so heavy as it is now, and much more I am sorrier for my good knights' loss than for the loss of my fair queen; for queens I might have enough, but such a fellowship of good knights shall never be together in no company."

Similarly for Tennyson, the noble ideals of the Round Table are brought down by the corruption and evil generated by the guilty love affair, and his King Arthur explains this to Guinevere when the destruction of the Round Table appears inevitable. His summing up of his aims in forming the Fellowship are perhaps the clearest expression of the Victorian understanding of chivalry:

> "I made them lay their hands in mine and swear
> To reverence the King, as if he were
> Their conscience, and their conscience as their King,
> To break the heathen and uphold the Christ,
> To ride abroad addressing human wrongs,
> To speak no slander, no, nor listen to it,
> To honour his own word as if his God's,
> To lead sweet lives in purest chastity,
> To love one maiden only, cleave to her
> And worship her by years of noble deeds,
> Until they won her; for indeed I knew
> Of no more subtle master under heaven
> Than is the maiden passion for a maid,
> Not only to keep down the base in man,
> But teach high thought, and amiable words
> And courtliness, and the desire of fame,
> And love of truth, and all that makes a man."

This is both more and less than the ideals of real medieval knights, who certainly admitted the power of love to inspire them to noble deeds and the desire for fame, but would probably have been less impressed with the idea of purest chastity; and who consistently maintained a sturdy independence of spirit and the subordination of moral purpose to secular goals such as the attainment of wealth and the enjoyment of power. King Arthur continues to Guinevere:

> "And all this throve before I wedded thee,
> Believing, 'Lo mine helpmate, one to feel
> My purpose and rejoicing in my joy.'
> Then came thy shameful sin with Lancelot;
> Then came the sin of Tristram and Isolt;
> Then others, following these my mightiest knights,
> And drawing foul ensample from fair names,
> Sinn'd also, till the loathsome opposite
> Of all my heart had destined did obtain,
> And all thro' thee!"

Enthusiasm for this new and lofty version of knightly ideals took hold in aristocratic as well as artistic circles, the most famous result being the Eglinton tournament. This took place in 1839, the year after Queen

Victoria's coronation, which, originally, it was intended to celebrate. Its host was the young and extremely wealthy Earl of Eglinton, and it was held at his castle in Ayrshire. Initially over a hundred and fifty young bloods came forward, inspired by the prospect of entering the lists, wearing shining armour and riding on spirited steeds, but the practical difficulties and the horrifying expense of the enterprise left a mere thirteen knights to defend the honour of modern times on the first day of the tournament. Armour had been procured from a recently opened, specialist shop in London, and a special tiltyard had been set up near Regent's Park, where the eager young knights attempted to acquire some of the necessary skills. Alas, on the day itself the tournament was flooded by a torrential downpour and the enormous crowd – perhaps up to a hundred thousand spectators had turned up – were treated to the unedifying sight of knights sloshing and slithering in the mud, missing one another altogether in their "courses" down the sodden lists.

Advances in historical research into the Middle Ages have prompted a certain cynicism about the very lofty and pure standards of behaviour supposed to have been held by medieval knights. The grim and brutish reality of medieval life for the majority seemed to sort ill with the high civilization of the ideal and the almost vulgar displays of wealth which often accompanied it in later medieval chivalry. The romantic glamour cast by Scott and Tennyson over the figures of real or fictional medieval knights has inescapably coloured everyone's perceptions of the subject and was transmitted directly, in a characteristically less subtle form, into the great Hollywood epic films of medieval heroes. Much mud has been slung by historians, convinced that knights gradually lost touch with their original purpose and forgot the ideals, founded on loyal service and the upholding of justice, in pursuit of rich, vain self-glorification. This is the view classically expressed by the great historian, Huizinga, in his book *The Waning of the Middle Ages*, and repeated many times since; that "chivalry" was a moral code only applied by the lucky few in their behaviour towards each other, in a huge, extravagant, fantastical game which took the knights, particularly of the later period, ever further and further from the "harsh realities" of the period. This view is intimately connected with the modern obsession with fact. In the Middle Ages, as any study of medieval historians will show, fact was not nearly so important as meaning. It was an age of symbols, and the deeds of arms achieved at some richly decorated tournament could and did stand for the same values as those achieved in a battle or siege. No doubt that, from the twelfth century on, knights were in love with their own image; but some facets of that image have proved to be of genuine and lasting worth, and have certainly made a major contribution to the ethos and culture of western Europe. As Jane Austen said, "Respect for right conduct is felt by everyone".

In today's world, dominated by business and finance as much as by politics, perhaps the best analogy for the knights of the past and their social importance is the company, where the chairman is castellan, the directors his knights, the workforce his people. Though the ethics of the business world are not of course so idealistic or so clearly defined as the ethics of chivalry, nevertheless they do exist and have formed the subject of manuals and treatises on conduct, and also of a genre of popular romance. Like knights, businessmen form an international community with great political and economic power; and in terms of influence over the lives of their employees, their power and responsibilities are as great, and probably as often respected or abused, as those of medieval knights.

BELOW *The mystical beauty of this painting of the death of King Arthur by James Archer is somewhat marred when one follows the fixed gaze of the dying king to a half-materialized ectoplasmic angel at the top left bearing the Holy Grail.*

FURTHER READING

KNIGHTS AND CHIVALRY

RICHARD BARBER *The Knight and Chivalry* (London 1970)
Tournaments (London 1989)
FRANCES GIES *The Knight in History* (New York 1984)
MAURICE KEEN *Chivalry* (London and New Haven 1984)
RAYMOND RUDORFF *Knights and their World* (London 1974)
J. VALE *Edward III and Chivalry* (Woodbridge 1982)

MEDIEVAL HISTORY

MARC BLOCH *Feudal Society*, trans. L.A. Manyon (London 1961)
GEORGES DUBY *The Chivalrous Society*, trans. Cynthia Poston
(Berkeley 1977)
ERIC CHRISTIANSEN *The Northern Crusades* (London 1980)
J. HUIZINGA *The Waning of the Middle Ages* (London 1924)
MAURICE KEEN *The Pelican History of Medieval Europe*
(London 1968)
DONALD MATTHEW *Atlas of Medieval Europe* (London 1983)
STEVEN RUNCIMAN *A History of the Crusades*, 3 vols
(Cambridge 1951-4)
R.W. SOUTHERN *The Making of the Middle Ages* (London 1953)

MEDIEVAL ROMANCE

W.R.J. BARRON *English Medieval Romance*
(London and New York 1987)
CHRÉTIEN DE TROYES *Arthurian Romances*, trans. W.W. Comfort
(London 1975)
W.P. KER *Epic and Romance* (London 1908)
RAMON LULL *The Book of the Order of Chivalry*,
ed. Alfred T. P. Byles (London 1926)
JOHN STEVENS *Medieval Romance: Themes and Approaches*
(London 1973)

INDEX

ACKNOWLEDGEMENTS

Key: a = above; b = below; l = left; r = right.

Abbreviations: BL = The British Library; BN = Bibliothèque Nationale, Paris; EP = Edimedia, Paris; PG = Photographie Giraudon, Paris; MC = The Mansell Collection; VAL = Visual Arts Library, London.

Quarto would like to thank the following for providing photographs, and for permission to reproduce copyright material. While every effort has been made to trace and acknowledge all copyright holders, we would like to apologise should any omissions have been made.

Page 7 a © The Hulton-Deutsch Collection/The Hulton Picture Company b VAL; p.8 © Marianne Majerus; p.9 © The Hulton-Deutsch Collection/The Hulton Picture Company; p.11 MC; p.12 MC; p.13 Walker Art Gallery, Liverpool/Bridgeman Art Library, London; p.18 l Archivo Mas r ET Archive; p.19 Scala; p.20 © The Hulton-Deutsch Collection/The Hulton Picture Company; p.21 a ET Archive/Biblioteca Marciana, Venice b Scala; p.23 Musée Condé Chantilly; p.28 MC; p.29 l EP/Biblioteca Apostolica, Vatican; r Scala/Biblioteca Marciana, Venice; p.31 VAL; p.33 MC; p.34 a Musée de L'Eveche, Bayeux/Bridgeman Art Library, London b Musée de la Reine Mathilde, Bayeux/Bridgeman Art Library; p.35 Bernisches Historisches Museum, Bern; p.36 VAL/Corpus Christi College, Cambridge; p.37 © Marianne Majerus; p.38 MC; p.39 Winchelsea Settled Estates/Northamptonshire Record Office; p.40 BL; p.41 The Bridgeman Art Library; p.42 VAL/Musée, Le Mans; p.43 BL; p.46 Archivo Mas/Escorial; p.47 BL; p.48 Scala/Castello, Malpaga; p.49 l Archivo Mas/Escorial r Private collection/The Bridgeman Art Library; p.50 EP/BN; p.51 ET Archive/BL.; p.53 Louvre; p.54 Reproduced by Courtesy of the Trustees of the British Museum; p.55 Lauros-Giraudon/Musée Condé Chantilly; p.56 VAL; p.57 a EP/BN b BL; p.58 Reproduced by Courtesy of the Trustees of the British Museum; p.59 EP/BN; p.60 VAL/The Pierpont Morgan Library; p.61 a The Bridgeman Art Library/BN b EP/BN; p.62 PG/BN; p.63 ET Archive/BN; p.64 BL; p.65 Bayerisches Staatsbibliothek, Munich; p.66-67 EP/BN; p.69 MC; p.70-71 VAL; p.74 VAL; p.75 l Woodmansterne r VAL/Bibliothèque Municipale, Dijon; p.77 MC; p.78 The Master and Fellows of Trinity College, Cambridge; p.82 EP/BN; p.83 MS; p.84 EP/BN; p.86-87 EP/BN; p.88 VAL/BL; p.89 l Museum and Library The Order of St. John r VAL; p.90 ET Archive/Templar's Chapel, Cressac; p.91 BL; p.92 Archivo Mas; p.94-95 MC; p.96 a Scala/Palazzo Pubblico, Siena b ET Archive/BL; p.97 Angelo Hornak Library; p.100-101 Phaidon Press; p.101 Private Collection/The Bridgeman Art Library; p.102 VAL; p.103 Scala/Palazzo Davanzati, Florence; p.104 BL; p.105 a VAL/BL b ET Archive/Biblioteca Marciana, Venice; p.106 Private Collection/The Bridgeman Art Library; p.107 EP/BN; p.108 EP/BN; p.109 l EP r EP/BN; p.110 a The Bodelian Library, Oxford b VAL; p.111 EP/BN; p.112 MC; p.113 Scala/Palazzo Vecchio, Florence; p.114 Universitäts Bibliothek Heidelberg; p.115 VAL/BN; p.116 EP/BN; p.117 EP/BN; 118 VAL; p.119 Phaidon Press/BN; p.120 EP/BN; p.121 ET Archive/BN; p.122 Museum and Library The Order of St. John; p.123 BL; p.126 Scala/Palazzo Pubblico, Siena; p.127 l VAL/Historiska Museum, Stockholm r VAL/BL; p.128-129 Archbishop of Canterbury and Trustees of the Lambeth Palace Library; p.134 a A.F. Kersting b ET Archive/BN; p.135 PG/Musée Condé, Chantilly; p.136 VAL; p.137 l EP r Walters Art Gallery, Baltimore; p.139 ET Archive; p.140 Angelo Hornak Library; p.141 MC; p.142-143 a Scala/Palazzo Pubblico, Siena b VAL/BL; p.144 a BL b Weidenfeld & Nicolson/BN; p.145 EP/BN; p.146-147 J. Allan Cash Photolibrary; p.148 J Allan Cash Photolibrary; p.149 l J. Allan Cash Photolibrary r PG/Musée Condé, Chantilly; p.151 l VAL/BL r VAL/BN; p.152 Reproduced by permission of the Trustees of the Wallace Collection, London; p.156 Kunsthistorisches Museum, Vienna; p.157 The Board of Trustees of the Royal Armouries; p.158 Lauros-Giraudon/Louvre; p.159 EP/BN; p.160 VAL/Basilica, St. Denis; p.161 EP/BN; p.162-163 Scala/Uffizi, Florence r Scala/Museo di Roma; p.164 EP/BN; p.165 Reproduced by Courtesy of the Trustees of the British Musuem; p.166 Museum and Library The Order of St. John; p.167 National Maritime Museum, Greenwich; p.168 EP/BN; p.169 l MC r Scala/Uffizi, Florence; p.170 BL; p.171 EP/BN; p.172 Birmingham Museum and Art Gallery; p.173 Beaufort Collection/photo Peter A. Harding; p.174 Reproduced by courtesy of The College of Arms; p.175 Reproduced by gracious permission of Her Majesty the Queen; p.176 Scala/Duomo, Florence; p.177 EP/BN; p.178 Scala/Uffizi, Florence; p.179 © Marianne Majerus; p.180 MC; p.181 EP/BN; p.183 a Lauros-Giraudon/Wurzburg, Résidence des Princes-Eveques b © The Hulton-Deutsch Collection/The Hulton Picture Company; p.184 MC; p.186 The Bridgeman Art Library/Manchester City Art Gallery; p.187 Cambridge University Library/ *Tournaments, Jousts, Chivalry and Pageantry in the Middle Ages*, Richard Barber and Juliet Barker, 1989.